Studies in Women and Religion /
Études sur les femmes et la religion : 7

STUDIES IN WOMEN AND RELIGION / ÉTUDES SUR LES FEMMES ET LA RELIGION

Studies in Women and Religion is a series designed to serve the needs of established scholars in this new area, whose scholarship may not conform to the parameters of more traditional series with respect to content, perspective, and/or methodology. The series will also endeavour to promote scholarship on women and religion by assisting new scholars in developing publishable manuscripts. Studies published in this series will reflect the wide range of disciplines in which the subject of women and religion is currently being studied, as well as the diversity of theoretical and methodological approaches that characterize contemporary women's studies. Books in English are published by Wilfrid Laurier University Press.

Inquiries should be directed to the series coordinators, Eleanor J. Stebner (Faculty of Theology, University of Winnipeg, Winnipeg) or Tracy J. Trothen (Queen's Theological College, Queen's University, Kingston).

STUDIES IN WOMEN AND RELIGION /
ÉTUDES SUR LES FEMMES ET LA RELIGION

VOLUME 7

Women in God's Army

Gender and Equality in the Early Salvation Army

Andrew Mark Eason

Published for the Canadian Corporation for Studies in Religion /
Corporation Canadienne des Sciences Religieuses
by Wilfrid Laurier University Press

2003

This book has been published with the help of a grant from the Canadian Federation for the Humanities and Social Sciences, using funds provided by the Social Sciences and Humanities Research Council of Canada. We acknowledge the financial support of the Government of Canada through the Book Publishing Industry Development Program for our publishing activities.

National Library of Canada Cataloguing in Publication

Eason, Andrew M. (Andrew Mark), 1966-
    Women in God's army: gender and equality in the early Salvation Army / Andrew M. Eason.

(Studies in Women and Religion ; 7)
Co-published by the Canadian Corporation for Studies in Religion.
Includes bibliographical references and index.
ISBN 0-88920-418-7

    1. Women in the Salvation Army—Great Britain. 2. Sexism in religion—Great Britain. I. Canadian Corporation for Studies in Religion. II. Title. III. Series: Studies in women and religion (Waterloo, Ont.) ; 7.

BX9721.3.E28 2003   287.9'6'0820941   C2002-905579-2

Cover design by PJ Woodland, using a photograph entitled
Female Salvationists at a Training Depot in Tring, Hertfordshire, c. 1890.
Courtesy of The Salvation Army International Heritage Centre, London, England

Order from:
Wilfrid Laurier University Press
Waterloo, Ontario, Canada N2L 3C5
www.wlupress.wlu.ca

Contents

Acknowledgements

I OWE A DEBT OF GRATITUDE to the numerous people who assisted me in the completion of this book, which began as a thesis a number of years ago while I was a student at the University of Windsor in Ontario, Canada. At each stage of my work I benefited immensely from the constructive criticism that I received from the members of my thesis committee: Professors Maureen Muldoon, Dorothy Sly and Jacqueline Murray. Each of these scholars guided my intellectual development and encouraged me to explore my chosen topic in much greater detail than I had anticipated. Even when the size and scope of this project became quite ambitious, they continued to offer enthusiastic support as each chapter slowly unfolded. Mention should also be made of Professor Pamela Milne, who also teaches at the University of Windsor. I have been the fortunate recipient of Pam's encouragement, friendship and assistance over the last few years, and for this I have been truly blessed. My gratitude must be extended as well to Professor Elizabeth A. Johnson, whose work as a Catholic feminist theologian provided me with the initial stimulus I needed to pursue my work on women and equality in the Salvation Army. I was privileged to take a course from Professor Johnson at the University of Notre Dame in the summer of 1995, and through her engaging lectures and ideas I quickly discovered the possibilities of scholarship from a feminist perspective.

My profound appreciation is also extended to those who helped me to locate the primary and secondary sources found within this book. First and foremost, I must acknowledge the kind assistance of the Salvation Army, which was always willing to honour my incessant requests for material over the last few years. A number of Salvationists deserve special thanks. Much time and energy was expended on my behalf by the staff of the George Scott Railton Heritage Centre and the Salvation Army Training College Library in

Toronto, especially Major Ira Barrow, Major David Pitcher, Major Florence Curzon, Karl Larson and Bill Porter. The George Scott Railton Heritage Centre is truly a world-class facility for anyone interested in studying the early history of the Salvation Army. Additional research assistance was provided by Gordon Taylor, the Archivist and resident expert at the Salvation Army's International Heritage Centre in London, England; and Envoy Dr. George Hazell, Coordinator of the Salvation Army's Heritage Centre in Sydney, Australia. Both of these skilled archivists helped me to locate some of the information that went into the statistical tables in chapter 6 of this book. Rebecca Hine, a researcher at the International Heritage Centre, was also gracious in her assistance during the final stages of my work. I would also like to thank the interlibrary loan departments at the University of Windsor and the University of Calgary. Given the rarity of many early Salvation Army books and periodicals, the services and expertise of these departments were called upon countless times. Finally, I must not forget the warm and expert assistance I received from the staff at the British Library in London, especially from those associated with the Manuscripts and Humanities Reading Rooms.

Thanks are also extended to Professor Marilyn Legge, the past coordinator of the Studies in Women and Religion series of the Canadian Corporation for Studies in Religion. It has been a pleasure to work with her on the lengthy journey from thesis to book, and I have appreciated her encouragement and patience throughout the writing and funding process. This book has been published with the help of a grant from the Humanities and Social Sciences Federation of Canada, using funds provided by the Social Sciences and Humanities Research Council of Canada. I also owe a word of thanks to the gracious and competent team at Wilfrid Laurier University Press: Brian Henderson, Carroll Klein, Jenny Wilson and Leslie Macredie. Their collective expertise skilfully guided the book through the various stages of the editing and publishing process.

The visuals found throughout this book were generously provided by the Salvation Army's archival facilities in London, Toronto and Alexandria, Virginia. Special thanks are extended to the staff at these centres for this privilege, especially Gordon Taylor, John Hughes, Major Ira Barrow, Major David Pitcher, Susan Mitchem and Scott Bedio.

Most importantly, this book is dedicated to my parents, Ruth and Lloyd Eason, who from birth have showered me with love and support, not to mention a passion for the history of the Salvation Army. As a child growing up in a Salvationist family, I fondly recall the numerous times I accompanied my father when he made audiovisual presentations on the beginnings of the organization in Britain. With such a stimulating and nurturing environment, it is not surprising that I turned to the Salvation Army as a subject for study. While not afraid to be critical of this organization, I continue to have a profound respect for both the work that it does and the history that it has bequeathed to present and future generations.

Preface

THIS BOOK PROVIDES a much needed re-examination of female experience and opportunity within the Salvation Army in Britain from its
Victorian origins to 1930. It makes the case for a revised understanding of
women's roles in this evangelical body by looking critically at its long-stand-
ing claim to provide its trained female personnel or officers with an equitable place alongside their male counterparts. From its earliest days the
Army's official documents included statements on women's right to preach,
hold any office and participate fully in the public life of the denomination.
In order to leave no room for misunderstanding, these same pronouncements went on to assert that the organization "refuses to make any difference
between men and women as to rank, authority and duties, but opens the
highest positions to women as well as men."[1] Given women's exclusion from
positions of authority in the established churches of nineteenth- and early
twentieth-century Britain, this principle of sexual equality was quite remarkable, and it continued to be reiterated in Army circles well beyond 1930.[2]
Nevertheless, historians have done little to chart how successfully this axiom
was implemented in the lives of first- and second-generation female
Salvationists.

   Failing to engage in this type of critical evaluation, the majority of popular and academic works on female officers have simply assumed that this
egalitarian principle was realized in most, if not all, aspects of Salvationist life
in Britain and overseas.[3] Focusing largely on the dramatic expressions of
female preaching in the organization, especially during its earliest days, they
have presented this religious body as an egalitarian challenge to the gender-
defined hierarchy of the Victorian age. A much different story emerges, however, when one consults the broad range of primary sources having a bearing
on the equality issue, including the relevant statistics on Salvation Army

leadership. Such evidence suggests that any liberating opportunities for female preaching and authority were ultimately overshadowed by the presence of culturally confining attitudes and practices. Notwithstanding their claim to be set apart from the world, Salvationists reflected and reinforced many of the surrounding society's assumptions about gender. This was strikingly apparent in their adherence to the Victorian notion of sexual difference, which associated each sex with distinctive traits and responsibilities. Under this arrangement, reason and authority were associated with men, while emotion and self-sacrifice were identified with women. Furthermore, with the exception of preaching, where feminine passion was seen to complement masculine reason, this type of gender complementarity fostered a profound culture of separate spheres within the denomination. Male officers dominated the leadership positions within the Army, while most female officers assumed subordinate and sacrificial roles in corps (church) ministry, social work and the home.

This kind of gender segregation found ample ideological support in the Salvation Army's evangelical theology, which often did more to legitimize than to challenge sex-based distinctions and divisions. The doctrines of sin and holiness were cases in point, because they typically discouraged women from fighting for a more visible and equitable position within this religious body. Even though holiness teaching, in particular, could occasionally justify the public work of female Salvationists, it was invariably tied to a patriarchal hierarchy that demanded submission and unquestioning obedience. This authoritarian environment did little to encourage dissent or address sexual discrimination. Meanwhile, sin was identified with self-assertion and self-interest, an association that effectively denied women the very qualities they needed in order to maintain their right to a public life. The equation of sin with self served to cultivate a morality based upon self-sacrifice and self-denial, simply adding to the pressures that women felt to put the needs of others ahead of their own. Added to these problematic theological tenets was the organization's adherence to male headship and masculine God-language, both of which sanctioned women's subordination to men. Under this arrangement a married female officer usually became an appendage of her husband, and in practice she derived her status from his rank and appointment. Taken together, these factors worked against any substantial realization of sexual equality in the organization.

To make clear the theoretical assumptions that undergird this study and provide the foundations for my arguments, the first two chapters of this book deal with methodological and historical background. Chapter 1 highlights the sociological and theological tools to be used in the body of this work, while chapter 2 draws specific attention to the evangelical and Victorian environment within which Salvationist gender relations were forged. Beginning in chapters 3 and 4, these methodological and historical concerns are brought to bear on the primary source evidence. The third chapter focuses upon William Booth, who played such a pivotal role in the founding of the Salvation Army. Despite the fact that William made numerous references to women in his writings, his views on female ministry and equality have never been examined in any detail. It has been assumed by more than one scholar that he became a convinced feminist, won over to women's equality with men by his wife Catherine.[4] Here, however, I argue that his views on the subject were far more ambiguous than has been appreciated. Although William Booth came to accept female ministry, he continued to embrace a gender ideology that was incompatible with any widespread notion of sexual equality in the church or in the home. As chapter 4 demonstrates, this type of inconsistency was equally apparent in the thinking and practice of other Salvationist men, whose acceptance of female ministry did not imply any substantial rejection of conventional femininity. In their theological doctrines, personal beliefs and institutional policies, Booth and his male officers established a less than liberating environment for sexual equality.

Chapters 5 and 6 examine the part that women themselves played in the construction of the Salvation Army's gender ideology. The assumptions that governed their actions in public and domestic life, and the consequences that flowed from them, are highlighted in this section of the book. This line of inquiry begins with the life and thought of Catherine Booth in chapter 5, where the argument is made that Catherine's promotion of female ministry and equality, while extremely significant within the context of the Victorian age, did not unseat her conservative views about sexual difference, motherhood and wifely submission. In fact, Catherine Booth sometimes used the pulpit to advance her very conservative attitudes about a mother's role in the home. As chapter 6 contends, the tensions between these progressive and conservative beliefs about womanhood proved to be detrimental for the female officers who followed in Catherine's footsteps. Basing their own actions in private and public life upon a very similar understanding of sexual difference and evangelical headship, most married and single women in the organization increasingly found themselves in segregated positions, effectively marginalized by a male-dominated hierarchy. Very few women were able to assume authoritative public roles, given the numerous burdens and restrictions imposed upon them by their gendered environment. While this set of circumstances was in stark contrast to the Salvation Army's professed commitment to sexual equality, it reflected the perils of trying to establish a broad public ministry on the foundations of conservative womanhood.

Broadly speaking, the pages that follow underscore the importance of viewing early Salvation Army women in the light of several relationships and contexts. First of all, any serious assessment of this subject should consider how female experience was shaped by the organization's mapping of public and domestic spaces. How did these two geographies interact with one another, and how did a female officer's obligations in the one area have a bearing on the other? Heretofore this type of question has been ignored by most students of the denomination, given their primary interest in the more public activities of female officers. A central purpose behind this study is to address this shortcoming. Second, the nature of women's roles in the Salvation Army cannot be appreciated fully without exploring the thinking and behaviour of men like William Booth. He and other male Salvationists played a significant part in the successes and failures of women in acquiring and preserving a public voice in the organization. This insight, however basic, has often been forgotten by those with an interest in female ministry in the Army. By placing the views of men alongside those of women, this book sets out to correct this deficiency. Finally, and perhaps most significantly, there is a pressing need to analyse the relationship between the Salvation Army's stated aims and actual practice in the area of sexual equality. As the first to trace this issue in any depth, this book points to the wide chasm that separated theory from action and image from reality.

CHAPTER 1

Gender, Stratification and the Sacred

I F WE ASSUME THAT HUMAN INQUIRY is as much about interpretation as it is about facts, then a certain degree of transparency should be evident in our scholarship. Those interested in our research should be aware of our assumptions and analytical frameworks, whether or not they agree with the conclusions that we reach. This underscores the importance of articulating our methodologies in a straightforward manner. Allowing those who engage with our work to appreciate the sense and direction of our efforts can head off misunderstandings as well as generate new questions. Theologian J. J. Mueller draws attention to these concerns by defining a method as a tool that "extends our abilities, improves upon our limitations, reminds us of forgotten procedures, and allows others to see how we arrived at our conclusions."[1] Methods heighten our capabilities by serving as lenses through which to classify and channel our questions and insights about the data we encounter. While no theoretical model is able to account for everything, it helps to shape the raw material of research into a meaningful whole.

Part of the function of a methodology is to delve below the surface of a given phenomenon, searching for evidence that may be hidden from view. This type of critical illumination is especially needed to recognize the sexism that may exist within a particular setting, because gender discrimination can take subtle as well as blatant forms. While certain practices and statistics may point to obvious inequalities between the sexes, qualitative data sometimes need to be read against the grain in order to reveal unspoken assumptions and to expose contradictory viewpoints. This is particularly the case when considering the role of women in the early Salvation Army, since this evangelical body distanced itself from other denominations in Britain and elsewhere by claiming to give its female members equal opportunities to work alongside the members of the opposite sex. Its public

Notes on pages 161-64

pronouncements on the subject hardly suggested that sexism was either a theoretical issue or a practical problem within its ranks. Yet, beneath these impressive boasts were troubling beliefs and practices that seriously challenged women's right to an equitable place alongside men. In order to appreciate these dynamics, including the ways in which they found expression in the daily life of female Salvationists, we must be willing to move beyond received traditions and re-examine conventional assumptions.

Nineteenth-century Salvationists clearly knew something about challenging the established thinking of their day. Influenced by American evangelists like Charles Finney, who advocated novel techniques to reach the masses for Christ, the organization's leaders believed that they had to employ innovative strategies to reach the poor. These distinctive techniques included brass bands, ingenious advertising, military uniforms, lively audience participation, outdoor evangelistic meetings and female preaching. Facing accusations that these methods were vulgar and irreverent, the Army was forced many times to issue statements defending its practices. In one of these early defences, the Salvation Army declared:

> [M]any of our methods are very different to the religious usages and social tastes of respectable and refined people, which may make those measures appear vulgar, that is, in bad taste to them; but this does not make them wrong in the sight of God. On the contrary, we think this adaptation of measures to the state of the masses is abundantly justified by the extraordinary things which God set His prophets to do, in order to arrest the attention of the people.... And, if it can be proved from the results, that these methods lay hold of the ignorant and godless multitudes, compelling them to think about eternity, and attend to their souls' salvation, we think they are thereby proved to be both lawful and expedient.[2]

As this statement makes clear, the Salvation Army did not allow itself to be constrained by the ecclesiastical methods of its day. Instead of accepting preexisting measures that focused upon how to get the poor into the churches, Salvationists developed strategies that brought the church's message to the poor. The framers of this apologetic readily acknowledged that Army methods were different from those used in the more established churches. Yet, they did not consider a departure from conventional tactics to be a problem, believing instead that there was no definitive way of reaching the unsaved. This viewpoint was the logical consequence of seeing method as relative. Early Salvationists adopted and modified a variety of secular and sacred methods in an attempt to win the impoverished masses for Christ.

This type of methodological pluralism is evident as well in the work of feminist theorists, including those who analyse the roles, images and experiences of women throughout church history.[3] Feminist researchers employ social-scientific and theological concepts when examining the place given to religious women in public and private life. Central to this approach is a desire to understand how constructions of femininity are forged in various Christian settings, and how these contexts shape women's experiences and opportunities. How, for example, does gender influence our understanding of selfhood, authority and the sacred? Given the fact that religions routinely use gender to infuse human life with order and meaning, and typically delimit roles on such a basis, it is important to examine how gender identities are constructed and maintained.[4] Moreover, the gender and feminist categories outlined below provide ways in which to gauge the pervasiveness of sexual discrimination within an ecclesiastical setting. Since this methodological framework is applied throughout this book, it needs to be explained in some detail.

✤ Gender and Identity

Human identity is not formed simply by being born as a male or a female. Beyond the biological facts of our existence, however important they may be, are cultural and social definitions of what it means to be masculine or feminine.[5] In any given society, certain characteristics become associated with each sex in the course of male and female interaction. However unusual these sets of arrangements may be, they become deeply woven into the fabric of human communities.[6] Since these socially constructed realities are clothed with a certain legitimacy, divine or otherwise, and begin to be formed early in life, we often fail to recognize the extent to which these roles and beliefs are the products of our cultural world. As we perform expected roles, a certain transformation takes place. The social recognition and affirmation that we derive from acting out these parts help to change us—we become what we perform.[7] These constructed identities take on a life of their own, making our gender norms appear part of the natural order. Whether male or female, we tend to absorb the cultural expectations associated with a particular time and place. Functioning as self-fulfilling prophecies, these stereotypes become a part of our inner being.

Within almost all societies certain personality traits become associated with gender and weighed accordingly. As numerous scholars have demonstrated, certain clusters of assumptions about masculinity and femininity resurface time and again in Western culture.[8] Within this largely patriarchal context, men and women are placed within a system of binary opposites. Women tend to be branded as sentimental, fickle, submissive and meek, while men are viewed as logical, stable, independent and forceful. Underlying these supposed traits and expectations are a number of contrasting associations: (1) women are weak, men are strong; (2) women are emotional, men are rational; (3) women belong in the private sphere, men in the public realm; (4) women nurture, men dominate; and (5) women are passive, men are active.[9] These stereotypes often serve to support an ideology of separate spheres: the belief that the male role is to rule and order the world, while the female role is to nurture the young and perform the domestic chores. This dualistic framework is sometimes described in terms of complementarity, with masculine traits supposedly working in harmony with feminine ones, but this type of arrangement ultimately relegates men and women to separate ontological categories. Such a configuration constrains individual freedom, because in this seemingly natural order only certain options are available to men and women. Invariably, this sort of gender-specific division also leads to the male side being valued more highly than the female side.[10] Exclusion and domination become the defining features of this relational model.

Notwithstanding the persistence of these gender differences, and the values associated with them, they are reflective of a history. Although it is imperative to trace these developments in a concrete manner, the task is a challenging one given our tendency to reify the humanly created, gender or otherwise.[11] Reification takes place when human products (i.e., roles, rituals, institutions, etc.) are perceived as if they were non-human or suprahuman entities. This social process takes any number of things, including gender, and transforms them into timeless, immutable entities. A gender-defined function becomes part of a cultural heritage, often buttressed by authoritative canons. In the process, a society loses sight of the historical origin and manufactured nature of such a role. Following the work of historians like Joan Wallach Scott, we need to deconstruct gender and sexual difference, exposing the humanly crafted binary opposites that work to define femininity and masculinity.[12] In this process, gender itself becomes a category of historical analysis. If images and expectations of womanhood have been constructed in history, then they can also be deconstructed in history. This possibility exists, argues Gerda Lerner, if we learn to subject patriarchal assumptions, values and definitions to critical analysis.[13] In other words, the established modes of thinking and practice in our society need to be challenged and placed within the flux of historical change.

Given that these historical dynamics are forged in relational matrices, gender analysis entails more than simply an examination of the status of women. To treat women as a special problem separate from the wider social relations of the sexes serves only to marginalize them even further.[14] Fortunately, however, the bifocal nature of gender is able to incorporate men and women into its angle of vision. This analytical tool not only assumes that women's experiences are forged alongside those of men, but also provides a level of inclusiveness that leads to a greater understanding of both sexes. As feminist scholar June O'Connor points out succinctly: "[A] gender-alert hermeneutic ... offers the promise of a more complete, less distorted, less partial knowledge base because through it more is examined and less is assumed."[15] This type of reasoning lies behind the inclusion of Salvationist men in this study. In order to appreciate the roles and expectations associated with female officers in late nineteenth- and early twentieth-century Britain, we need to be aware of how men participated in the gendering of Army public and private life.

✤ Gender and Stratification

If gender gives rise to identities, it also reveals the degree to which status and power are associated with masculinity or femininity. Therefore, the chapters that follow pay considerable attention to the notion of social stratification. This sociological category is designed to chart the ways in which authority and advantage are correlated with gender.[16] The Salvation Army's espoused militarism, including its adoption of an extremely detailed system of rank during the late 1870s, makes the analysis of this relationship especially pertinent. The hierarchical nature of this organization, while often criticized by Victorians as despotic or "popish," provides an ideal laboratory for addressing issues of privilege and prestige.[17] The positions that an individual could hold, as well as the ranks and responsibilities that went along with them, were spelled out at length in the organization's earliest literature.[18] While scholars have typically chosen to ignore the ways in which these roles may have been tied to gender, this kind of analysis is crucial to determining how pervasive equality may have been in the early Salvation Army.

One way of mapping social stratification is to look at the question of status. Was status conferred in an equitable way on Salvationist men and women, or did one sex have a clear advantage over the other? Of particular interest here is the presence or absence of achieved and derived status among male and female officers in the early Army.[19] Did all officers possess equal opportunities to enhance their status or rank on the basis of variables over which they had some control, such as job performance or professional qualifications? In particular, were female officers just as able to achieve or earn their status as their male counterparts? Or did female officers—single and married—derive their status from their relationships with others (i.e., husbands, parents or other relatives)? Whether a married female officer's promotion through the ranks of the Salvation Army resulted from derived (familial) status, achieved status or a combination of the two will be addressed at various stages of this book.

Four specific sets of questions are especially pertinent if we wish to discover the extent of achieved and derived status in the early Salvation Army in Britain. Each of these questions seeks to unearth concrete evidence of women's social position in the life of the organization. Given the importance of these questions, I outline them here: (1) Were single female officers—notably those least affected by derived status—proportionately represented in the middle and upper echelons of Army leadership?; (2) Did married female officers ever hold more important jobs than their husbands, or hold positions of authority in the organization?; (3) How often did married couples receive separate appointments (assignments), and what were the nature of such postings? Conversely, if separate assignments were not given, who was awarded the appointment?; and (4) Were married couples ever given separate salaries for their work? If not, who received the wages? Together, these kinds of questions provide measurable ways to ascertain the degree to which women held achieved or derived status in the early Salvation Army.

In addition to assessing social status, social stratification also offers us a way to gauge how successful an individual is in advancing through the hierarchy of a religious body. An analysis of the relationship between gender and social structure makes it possible to evaluate a woman's freedom to move from one level to another. In other words, it raises the issue of social mobility. How much access female officers in the early Salvation Army had to middle and high ranks (i.e., Staff-Captain, Major, Colonel, Commissioner, etc.), as well as to important regional, national or international positions, is a vital concern here. Did married female officers have access to the jobs and prestige available to their husbands, or were these women relegated to subservient or stereotypical posts under their menfolk? Moreover, did single female officers enjoy the same positions as their male counterparts? To trace the extent of women's social mobility within the organization, I draw upon key statistics from relevant Salvation Army books and periodicals. Although this type of quantitative evidence has been available for some time, especially since the Salvation Army issued its first year book in 1906, scholars have generally shown little interest in analysing these statistics. More often than not, the strength of women's representation in leadership positions has simply been assumed by drawing attention to one or two high-profile female officers. Such a strategy may serve to bolster a public image, but it does little to provide a full appreciation of the actual figures. The correlation of gender with stratification is an attempt to address this shortcoming.

❖ Gender and Feminist Theology

As valuable as quantitative evidence may be, we need to do more than simply tabulate how many women occupy leading positions in a religious group.
A comprehensive examination of women and equality during the Salvation
Army's formative years also involves the analysis of qualitative data, especially the denomination's God-language and central doctrines. While the relationship between religion and gender is a complex one, there are at least two
general ways in which these dynamics interact.[20] First of all, religion serves
to structure gender relationships by delineating who does what in a religious
community. Within the Roman Catholic church, for example, high-status
roles, such as the priesthood, are open to males but forbidden to females.
Even in Protestant denominations, where women may have access to ministerial positions, it is typically the men who control the resources and leadership offices of their churches. By examining gender within a theological
context, we address not only obvious areas of discrimination, but also the
reasons behind these inequitable arrangements. This is because a second
function of religion is to infuse gender with a notion of what it means to be
human. Given that theological categories have been defined largely by men
throughout church history, gender analysis seeks to uncover how women
have been affected by this set of circumstances. What impact has the equation of male experience with human experience had upon the other half of
the Christian community?

One significant issue here is how the symbol of the deity functioned within the early Salvation Army. What metaphors and images were employed to
depict the Godhead, and how did they shape perceptions of a woman's place
in the organization? If the Supreme Being signifies the originating source of
our existence and worth, then the words we use to address the deity are not
without force. To equate God solely with the masculine is not simply an inno-
cent act of naming, but also a gesture of political and moral import. The exclusion of the female from this realm places an ultimate value on maleness and
legitimizes the subordination of women to men. Therefore, the question as
to whether Salvationists reinforced or challenged conventional masculine
representations of God is an important one. Feminist theologian Elizabeth
A. Johnson puts forward three probing questions that can be used to address
this concern in any religious community: (1) Is God exclusively designated
as male?; (2) Is God seen to be literally a father and king, thereby suggesting
that maleness is essential to divine being?; and (3) Is God typically referred
to as King, Lord and Ruler? Johnson contends that how we refer to God is
of central importance, because our ways of imaging the sacred serve to

reinforce or question patriarchal structures, values and behaviour.[21] An unquestioning acceptance of a male-defined deity helps to perpetuate societal systems that place men at the apex of authority, wielding power over all below them.

Two other motifs that have a particular bearing upon women are the doctrines of sin and holiness. These twin emphases, which address respectively the problems and possibilities of the human condition, have implications for women's self-identity, self-assertion and self-determination. For this reason, they form an important part of this investigation of female Salvationists. First, what did the Army view as the fundamental problem separating humanity from God? Was the human predicament described exclusively in the customary masculine language of pride, selfishness and self-assertion, or was reference also made to the traditionally feminine vices of over-dependence, self-abnegation and diminished personal agency?[22] In other words, did this religious organization ever appreciate the different temptations that men and women have been socialized to face throughout history, or did it generally define sin in terms of male experience? If the latter happened to be the case, what were the consequences for women? Second, how did the denomination's teaching on holiness, which stressed how a believer could achieve victory over a sinful nature, influence the role of its women? Did this doctrine give women the opportunity to develop and celebrate the self, or did it simply reinforce the stereotypical traits associated with women, such as obedience, humility and submission to authority? The extent to which the Army's understanding of the human condition created an unfavourable climate for women is of vital importance in the chapters that follow.

Informing this overall analysis is what theologian Rosemary Radford Ruether calls the critical principle of feminist theology. The purpose of this principle is to expose and challenge the sexism of a given theological tradition. Within Christianity, for example, it critiques beliefs and practices that make male thinking and experience the standards by which to judge all of humanity. In place of androcentric construals of reality, this feminist axiom embodies the biblical notion of *imago dei* (image of God). Feminists use this inclusive concept to affirm that women have the same capacity as men to mirror the divine, which the Judeo-Christian heritage reveals to be holy (i.e., righteous and just). It calls into question the androcentric assumption that only men share in the fullness of humanity. When utilized by those with feminist convictions, the biblical paradigm of *imago dei* becomes a critical standard by which to judge the liberating and oppressive aspects of the Christian tradition. Put negatively, the critical principle of feminist theology contends that "whatever denies, diminishes, or distorts the full humanity of women is ... not redemptive."[23] Thinking, behaviour and structures that, wittingly or unwittingly, distort women's reflection of the divine or limit their opportunities for self-actualization are labelled as sinful. In a positive form, however, this principle claims that whatever "promote[s] the full humanity of women is of the Holy ... reflect[s] the true nature of things, the authentic message of redemption and the mission of redemptive community."[24] This feminist criterion functions as a two-edged sword, uncovering the positive and negative aspects of Christianity's treatment of women. In the pages that follow I make use of this standard, exposing how women were affected by the various features of the Salvationist theological heritage.

Clifford Geertz's work in anthropology suggests that religious symbols have structural and psychological functions.[25] These signifiers provide a way of ordering the world objectively, as well as eliciting certain "moods and motivations" that serve to reinforce their assumed reality. This is especially true of theological images and associations that arise from our perceptions of God and the human condition. The language and metaphors that we construct through our experience with the sacred are potent, possessing the emotive power to justify relationships of exclusion or inclusion on divine and human levels. Our assumptions about gender can be seen in the way that we fashion these theological categories, including the moral and psychological values that we attach to them. We need to ask whose experiences have been reflected in conventional theology, and how these perceptions have shaped language for God, sin and holiness. These doctrinal themes reveal not simply the essence of a religious group's theological beliefs, but also the meaning and force of its convictions about gender, equality and inclusiveness.

A questioning spirit lies at the heart of all good scholarship, and this is especially true of feminist research. The methodologies that feminists employ are based upon a hermeneutics of suspicion, which challenges accepted axioms and conventional assumptions.[26] Beliefs and practices that oppress women, devalue their humanity or delimit their opportunities and responsibilities are subjected to critical scrutiny. Gender analysis, with its avowed purpose of deconstructing societal and religious images of femininity and masculinity, provides feminist scholars with a way to study identity formation, social stratification and theology. This kind of approach is especially relevant for those who wish to examine the Salvation Army, given its numerous references to women, rank and doctrine. Furthermore, this kind of methodology contends that constructions of femininity and masculinity have a past that can be examined. Once again, this approach has the potential to tell us a good deal about Salvationist gender relations, both during and after the nineteenth century. This historical objective is introduced in the next chapter, which concerns itself with the cultural and evangelical ethos that gave rise to the Salvation Army in Britain.

❖

CHAPTER 2

An Ambiguous Heritage: The Salvation Army's Victorian and Evangelical Roots

NEW RELIGIOUS MOVEMENTS do not arise out of a vacuum. Such phenomena, whether culturally accommodating or countercultural, involve some response to or reaction against their historical milieu. As a Protestant mission taking root in the complex soil of Victorian England, and nurtured by evangelical springs, the Salvation Army must also be understood within its time and place. More often than not, however, this basic insight has been lacking in official treatments of the organization's past. One central reason for this omission has been the Army's tendency, until recently, to view itself as the result of an act of divine creation, owing little to the era that produced it. An early article appearing in the Army's weekly periodical *The War Cry* expressed this sentiment clearly: "The Salvation Army is divinely originated. The General—God bless him!—was the human agent to bring it into existence, but it was born in the heart of God."[1] Presupposing their otherworldly roots, and separation from the world, Salvationists have been slow to appreciate the influences that came to make the denomination what it is today. However valid these theological assumptions may be in the minds of Salvationists, they have discouraged serious attempts to investigate the organization's concrete place within nineteenth-century Britain. This chapter begins to address this shortcoming by outlining the Victorian and evangelical ethos that gave rise to the Salvation Army. The social and theological themes of the period were complex, and often reflective of certain tensions and ambiguities in a number of areas, including gender. It is important, therefore, to understand the dynamics that helped to shape the thinking and behaviour of early Salvationists.

✤ Economic and Social Life

The economic changes that gave birth to the Industrial Revolution in the eighteenth century were to have profound implications for society in the century ahead. The transformations brought on by technological innovation and mass production provided the emerging middle class and skilled artisans with greater material prosperity, but they also resulted in financial hardship and dislocation for the lower working class. The plight of those in the latter category became the focus of the "Condition of England" question in the early to mid-nineteenth century, when parliamentary reports, royal commissions and popular literature grappled with the problems associated with the nascent, but unbridled, capitalist system: long hours, poor wages and occupational hazards.[2] In an effort to address these concerns, the British Parliament passed a series of Factory, Mine and Workshop Acts between 1819 and 1901, the purpose of which was to define minimum employment standards and protect workers from unscrupulous entrepreneurs. To some degree, therefore, the governments of the period were prepared to intervene in society, hoping to curb the worst instances of worker exploitation and abuse.

For much of the Victorian age, however, there remained strong opposition to the involvement of government in widespread reform. One author who captured the essence of this position was Samuel Smiles, whose book *Self-Help* became a best-seller after its publication in 1859. The central argument behind this popular work was the conviction that "where men are subjected to over-guidance and over-government, the inevitable tendency is to render them comparatively helpless."[3] For Smiles and others, the only guarantee of success and advancement in life lay with individual effort. A person's habits, especially thrift and discipline, were seen to be the keys to self-improvement. Moreover, those subscribing to this self-help philosophy felt that a certain amount of poverty was necessary in order to motivate the poor to rise above their circumstances. From this perspective, the advent of the Industrial age ushered in unparalleled opportunities for human economic betterment.

A sizeable portion of society did in fact benefit from the wealth generated by the new economy, and beginning in the late Victorian period the overall standard of living in Britain rose significantly. At the same time, however, those on the lowest rungs of the economic ladder were not so fortunate. Some indication of their miserable plight was underscored in October 1883, when the Congregationalist Andrew Mearns exposed the horrors of slum life in *The Bitter Cry of Outcast London*. In this influential pamphlet, Mearns highlighted the numerous evils associated with poverty: overcrowded and unsanitary

Slum conditions in the 1890s. Courtesy of The Salvation Army International Heritage Centre, London.

housing, pitifully low wages and high rents.[4] Numerous other studies and social commentaries would echo these findings in the years ahead, including William Booth's *In Darkest England and the Way Out*.[5] Published in 1890, this book laid out a blueprint for solving urban destitution through the establishment of city, farm and overseas colonies. Providing the poor with industrial and agricultural training, these centres would serve as bridges to better employment at home and abroad. While schemes of this nature drew considerable attention, and initially a good deal of support, the slums of London and elsewhere would persist well into the twentieth century.

There is no question that urbanization did much to intensify the plight of the poor. Industrialization and related factors transformed Britain from a predominantly rural society into one that was decidedly urban. Approximately one-fifth of the population lived in towns and cities in 1801, but by mid-century this percentage had jumped to half. This migration from countryside to city continued for the rest of the Victorian period, and by 1901 over three-quarters of Britain's population had been urbanized.[6] Enclosure Acts, which sought to prevent the rural poor from utilizing fields once held in common, added to the numbers flocking into the cities. Furthermore, the Irish potato famine of the 1840s had an impact as well, since it led many Irish poor to emigrate to populated English and Scottish centres like London, Liverpool and Glasgow. The consequences of this demographic transformation were profound, and they still engage the interest of many historians. In particular, this significant shift from village to metropolis put a burden on new and existing urban areas, and the poor often had little choice but to gravitate to the slums, with their inadequate housing, overcrowding, crime and disease.

One place that became notorious for its economic hardship, alcoholism and squalor was the East End of London. Those who ventured into this impoverished area quickly became aware of the numerous cases of human misery. A descriptive article appearing in the evangelical periodical *The Revival* in 1864 drew attention to the inadequate shelter and wages of those who inhabited this area.[7] It was not uncommon for a large family to live in a single room, where women and children worked side by side to assemble dolls and matchboxes for employers who paid a mere pittance. This kind of "sweated" labour was far too common during the nineteenth century. Exploitation of a different nature was apparent in the ubiquitous gin palaces and public houses lining the main thoroughfares like Whitechapel Road, enticing the labouring poor to squander their meagre income on alcohol. A reporter for *The Nonconformist*, describing this aspect of East End life in 1867, noted the thousands of people who entered these drinking establishments on every day of the week, especially on Sundays.[8] In order to address the economic, moral and spiritual destitution of this area, a number of evangelical missions were established there during the Victorian period, including William and Catherine Booth's Christian Mission, which became the Salvation Army in 1878.

Although the Salvation Army condemned the alcoholism and violence associated with East End working-class life, it was quite willing to adapt itself to certain aspects of this environment. One popular expression of East End life that the Salvation Army exploited in its efforts to win the masses for Christ was the Victorian music hall. This urban working-class institution—a hybrid of the theatre and the pub—became a venue for the organization's evangelistic meetings between the 1860s and the 1880s.[9] One particular feature of the music hall that the Army appropriated was the "free and easy," an unstructured evening of entertainment centred around audience participation and song. While a Salvationist "free and easy" had spiritual objectives, and obviously did not include alcohol, its emphasis upon lively singing and audience involvement mimicked the format of its secular counterpart.[10] In time, this type of outreach led to working-class conversions, with new recruits seeking to renounce the drinking and fighting that had exacerbated their impoverished existence in this part of London.[11]

If the changing economic landscape helped to create pockets of poverty and potential ministry, it also contributed to segregation of a different kind in the more prosperous classes. Britain's economic transformation moved most productive work from the domestic realm, invariably transferring it to the office or factory.[12] In the course of time, men became associated primarily with the public world of business, while women became identified largely with the demands of the household. From a capitalist viewpoint, this ideology of separate spheres meant that a middle- or upper-class woman's work was considered to fall outside the realm of economic production. Her usefulness increasingly lay in the care of children, the management of domestic servants and biological reproduction. Moreover, the advent of railways and trams made possible by capitalist expansion now allowed middle-class men to commute from their peaceful suburban homes to inner-city workplaces, a development that served to reinforce women's isolation from the male-dominated public world. Under these sets of arrangements most men grew to have little knowledge of or interest in household management, whereas many women became increasingly excluded from business and political affairs.

Women from the lower classes did not experience such a sharp dichotomy between private and public life, because the middle-class ideal of the male breadwinner was often unattainable.[13] In order to keep food on the table, they often had to find some kind of employment, even if this simply meant taking in piecework for a few shillings a week. Yet, even here, the ideology of separate spheres found expression, since women married to skilled tradesmen were increasingly under pressure to devote their energy to the home and children.[14] Working men with aspirations to middle-class respectability wanted to keep women and children out of the factory or mine. By the late nineteenth century the ideology of separate spheres was clearly defined, even if not always possible to maintain. Meanwhile, single working-class women possessed limited options, and they typically had to find employment as domestic servants. This part of the service sector employed the largest number of women in Britain between 1851 and 1911. Increasingly, however, respectable Victorians, including those in the working classes, viewed female paid labour as an embarrassment, a sign of poverty. Separate spheres, while originating with the middle classes, would become a reality for many in the working classes in the early twentieth century.

❖ Political Developments

On the political front, nineteenth-century Britain witnessed the gradual transition from privilege and paternalism toward democracy and self-help.[15] The first signs of change were apparent in the late eighteenth century, when lower- and middle-class radicals began to challenge an aristocratic state tied to the Church of England. Within this traditional mode of governing, those with power were linked to inherited wealth, the Anglican establishment and the Tory Party. Whigs and Radicals, often inspired by the actions of French and American revolutionaries, demanded parliamentary representation and access to the civic institutions of the land. Political agitators like Thomas Paine, who laid out the liberal agenda in *The Rights of Man* (1791-92), helped to contest the privileges of a largely conservative British state. The impetus for change also came from Dissenting chapels, where Baptists, Congregationalists and Unitarians sought to address the restrictions that the state imposed upon those who chose to worship outside the Anglican fold. Altogether, these demands for equal rights and representative democracy would lead to dramatic political changes during and after the Victorian era.

A number of nineteenth-century legislative measures went far in removing Dissenters' religious disabilities, reforming Parliament and expanding the vote. British laws that had banned Dissenters from Parliament, civil offices and Anglican universities were repealed, while other measures imposing certain obligations upon non-Anglicans were abolished. Furthermore, the Reform Act of 1832 increased the number of eligible male middle-class voters and initiated some restructuring of parliamentary boroughs. Additional Reform Acts in 1867 and 1884 enfranchised a number of urban and rural working-class men, respectively. While universal adult male suffrage would not take place until 1918, these liberalizing measures initiated the process of popular democracy. Some of the credit for the enactment of this legislation was due to the efforts of Chartists—working-class protesters during the 1830s and 1840s—who demanded the vote for the labouring man. Even though their own cause did not result in a parliamentary victory, it served as a symbol of protest against the ruling elite. Also of importance were the nouveaux riches, whose middle-class capitalist investments gave them the leverage to demand a voice in the governing of the country. These developments were significant, and helped to refashion the British political landscape.

At the same time, however, the relationship of certain groups in society to the changes brought on by political liberalism was ambiguous. Wesleyan Methodism, for example, never completely distanced itself from its roots in the Church of England. Its locus of ultimate authority, the annual conference, was dominated by autocratic figures, from John Wesley to Jabez Bunting. Those who opposed this conservative model were forced to separate from the parent body, forming new connexions in which clergy and laity had a more democratic voice. Given the Salvation Army's roots in Wesleyan and sectarian Methodism, which nurtured William and Catherine Booth in youth and early adulthood, it is not surprising that the Army mirrored some of these political tensions. On the one hand, it could use the language of liberalism to defend its right to parade through the streets and preach in the open air.

In this area, the organization sought to align itself with Nonconformists, arguing that it also fought for "the right of British citizens to worship according to the dictates of their conscience."[16] Furthermore, the Army was not above challenging British legislation, including the law governing the age of sexual consent, if it served to undermine evangelical moral standards.[17] On the other hand, the Salvation Army could also reflect a very conservative political ideology. Not wanting to leave the impression that it endorsed radical causes, the organization's early literature stressed that it taught "obedience to the laws and respect for the authority of the powers that be."[18] This right-wing outlook was also reflected in the sermons of Catherine Booth to the prosperous residents of London's West End. In her mind, the Salvation Army was a Christianizing and civilizing force, able to turn the masses into reliable employees and loyal citizens.[19] Even more significantly, the Salvation Army was avowedly autocratic in nature, even boasting of its ability to elicit unquestioning obedience from its members.[20] This central feature of the organization owed more to a conservative past than to a democratizing present, and helped to overshadow any affinity it had with liberalism.

The women's movement in Britain also reflected liberal and conservative strains.[21] One identifiable stream of thought came from those who followed the lead of Mary Wollstonecraft, whose treatise *A Vindication of the Rights of Woman* (1792) had applied liberal equal-rights reasoning to women. Unitarian and philosophical radicals like Harriet Martineau, William Fox and John Stuart Mill were among the earliest figures in this group. Mill, for example, argued for "a principle of perfect equality [between the sexes], admitting no power or privilege on the one side, nor disability on the other."[22] This type of reasoning also helped to influence women like Barbara Leigh Smith and Bessie Rayner Parkes, who began to forge concrete feminist strategies in London's Langham Place in the 1850s. These middle-class women pushed to enter the public sphere on an equal footing with men, and fought for changes to a married woman's legal and political status. A second stream of thought came from those who felt that women's maternal instincts and inherent virtues justified their wider involvement in society. Often couched in evangelical language, this viewpoint held that women's moral guardianship of the home justified their presence in the broader society when matters of conscience were at stake. The efforts of women like Josephine Butler to repeal the Contagious Diseases Acts, which sought to regulate prostitution, were reflective of this position.[23] At times, these two approaches overlapped, because some women combined liberal arguments with conservative assumptions. As will be seen in chapter 5, Catherine Booth could appeal to the language of rights and conventional images of feminine difference to justify female preaching. This uneasy alliance would have profound consequences for the Army's female officers.

❖ Philosophical Viewpoints

Alongside arguments of equality and difference, nineteenth-century Britain witnessed a philosophical contest between the mind and the heart.[24] On the one side of this debate were rationalists, who believed that reason was central to material progress, scientific advance and technological innovation.[25] Among the educated elite, these ideas were subsumed under the creed of positivism, which advocated an intellectual path to human betterment beyond outdated supernatural dogma. Those adopting this viewpoint argued that a scientific understanding of the laws of society would usher in a new age of prosperity and altruism. On the other side of the philosophical divide were romantics, many of whom drew attention to the negative effects of industrialization on Western European society. These cultural critics did not see reason as the saviour of the world.

While the origins of romantic thought could be traced back to Germany, romanticism spread throughout much of Western Europe during the late eighteenth and early nineteenth centuries. Transported to England through apostles like Samuel Taylor Coleridge, this philosophical and cultural movement contained a number of distinctive beliefs.[26] One of its central convictions was that the inward journey of the self held the key to appreciating the physical world. A full understanding of existence, animate and inanimate, was mediated through the imagination, mystery and feeling. The human will and heart were primary, taking precedence over the mind. For the romantically inclined, a related emphasis was the essentially spiritual nature of reality; the ultimately real was that which transcended the world of matter. Finally, in place of the atomistic and mechanistic view of the world put forward by Enlightenment liberalism, romantic poets like William Wordsworth pointed to the organic interrelationship of all things, human and non-human. In an increasingly industrialized and scientific world, with its propensity to divide and dissect, the romantics articulated a more inclusive vision of reality.

At the level of world views, the conflict between rationalism and romanticism involved two differing perspectives on reality—a word culture and an image culture.[27] The word culture was allied with rationalism. Influenced by the invention of the printing press, this metaphysical paradigm centred around knowledge disseminated in written form. It valued the analytical and the objective, but distrusted the emotional and the sentimental. Within this framework, mystery was seen as a problem to be solved rather than as something to inspire awe. Although the Anglo-Catholic movement, with its romantic stress on the senses and tradition, attracted a number of educated Victorians, many other educated Britons were more comfortable with a rationalist understanding of reality. Those within the lower classes, however, were more attuned to an image culture focused upon faith, mystery and emotion. Affected more by the senses than by the mind, and often only semi-literate, they appreciated emotion and drama more than theological sermonizing. The sensational and mysterious spoke more to their understanding of the world than the cold delivery of the written word in respectable churches and chapels.

The Salvation Army was never as successful as it claimed to be among the lower working classes, but it did articulate a theology that appealed to their dramatic and emotional tastes.[28] When, for instance, the Christian Mission became the Salvation Army in 1878, its identity and practice became increasingly image-centred. Referring to the Victorian age, historian G. Kitson Clark contends that the Salvation Army became "perhaps the most significant and notable product of this exciting period, for it used with great success all the elements of applied romanticism—the rhetoric, the melodrama, the music, the evocative ritual and [the] symbolism ... of war."[29] The organization's uniforms, brass bands and sensational attacks on the kingdom of the devil spoke to the lower working-class world of the physical and concrete. This was not the realm of intellectual abstraction and detachment. Even when the Salvation Army moved beyond its initial focus on the poorest of the poor, it retained a romantic orientation—the heart took precedence over the mind.

❖ **Religious Climate**

It would be an oversimplification to characterize the entire Victorian age as one of religious-mindedness. Although there was a good deal of truth behind this label, especially between the 1830s and the 1860s, the period as a whole experienced religious advances and retreats. It was, in the words of historian Gerald Parsons, an era of "crisis and confidence, faith and doubt, revival and decline."[30] On the one hand, the Victorian landscape gave rise to church and chapel expansion, revivalist campaigns, and a network of Sunday schools, mission halls and numerous church-based clubs to reach the urban poor. Furthermore, the major social movements of the period—including feminism, Chartism and socialism— appropriated biblical and theological themes to advance their causes. On the other hand, Victorian churches and chapels also witnessed a growing number of intellectual, social and financial challenges. Biblical criticism and the theory of evolution, while not always destructive of faith in general, served over time to weaken people's convictions about

the authority of scripture and dampen evangelistic outreach. Rising prosperity, and the new opportunities for leisure that went with it, also worked
to draw the middle classes and their money away from religious institutions.
Over time, these developments reduced the social and numerical significance of religion in British society.

Earlier in the century, however, religion still formed an important part of
middle-class life. On any given Sunday, respectable families could be seen
filling the pews of churches and chapels. J.W. Croker, a mid-nineteenth-
century Tory journalist, was one of many observers who noted "the fuller
attendance on every occasion of public worship and the multiplication of
these occasions—the more willing adhesion to reverential forms—the more
exact observance, both public and domestic of the Sabbath."[31] Meanwhile,
the church and chapel were often centres of fellowship and philanthropy
during the week. Undoubtedly, a mixture of social and theological reasons
lay behind middle-class involvement with Victorian religious institutions,
but one significant movement that helped to shape these beliefs and practices was evangelicalism. With its roots in European pietism and transatlantic
evangelism, this conservative and revivalistic expression of Protestantism
helped to set the tone of the age. Even though evangelicals never made up a
majority of Britain's population, they were found in political, cultural and
commercial circles, and did much to promote moral reform, pious home life
and Christian missions.[32]

Evangelical zeal was markedly apparent in the area of home missions,
which devoted particular attention to the rapidly expanding urban centres.[33]
As early as the 1820s and 1830s, inter-denominational mission halls were
being established in cities like Glasgow and London to minister to the masses,
and efforts were well underway to train lay assistants to distribute tracts,
bibles and material aid in poorer areas. Even so, there were many observers
who believed that even more needed to be done to evangelize the burgeoning metropolitan regions. The Census of Religious Worship, carried out on
March 30, 1851, did much to reinforce this growing conviction. When the census editor, Horace Mann, tabulated and interpreted the results of this survey, he described the labouring classes as "unconscious seculars"—a section
of the population alienated from religious life, and ultimately no different
from those in heathen countries.[34] Although Mann was wrong when he concluded that the working classes were largely indifferent to religion, there is
little doubt that the poor among them were not regular churchgoers.[35] Lacking
the resources to rent pews or buy Sunday clothes, and often associating religion with hypocrisy and privilege, they did not make weekly worship a part
of their lives.[36] Consequently, devout Christians redoubled their efforts to

reach this segment of society with the Home Mission Movement of the 1850s and 1860s. Behind this evangelical campaign was the belief that Britain's poor needed salvation as much as those in non-Christian countries. In order to win these souls for the Kingdom of God, the alliances and societies associated with this venture held meetings in theatres, halls, tents and the open air. One notable product of this evangelistic activity was the Christian Revival Association, a mission that eventually became the Salvation Army.

EVANGELICALISM AND GENDER

The theological convictions that lay behind evangelical activities at home and abroad were complex, and had a bearing upon a number of important areas. One of these spheres was the relation between the sexes. Certain assumptions and expectations went with feminine and masculine roles in the evangelical movement, and these responsibilities need to be charted in order for the Salvation Army's understanding of feminine gender identity to be appreciated. While a number of scholars have argued that evangelicalism had an ambiguous effect upon women between the late 1700s and the early 1900s, there has often been no attempt to relate these insights directly and systematically to the theological convictions that gave rise to the movement.[37] What is attempted here, therefore, is an overview of the cardinal beliefs of evangelicalism, and how these ideas influenced the role of women in a number of British religious settings. The overall task at hand is to understand the ways in which evangelicalism defined and structured gender roles.

At the heart of evangelical self-understanding were four theological tenets, each of which was held with a certain degree of tenacity by its followers.[38] First and foremost, this Protestant movement laid great stress on conversion. By placing their trust in Christ alone, people could be saved from their fallen state and sinful lifestyles. Since sin was believed to separate humans from God—ultimately sending the unrepentant to hell—evangelicals felt an urgency to preach the good news of salvation to the "heathens" at home and abroad. A second feature of evangelicalism was human effort and action. Most of those within the movement rejected the extreme Calvinist view that left the impetus for social and religious change to God alone. In particular, human effort came to be seen as an essential ingredient in revivalism, foreign missions and social betterment. A third distinctive feature of evangelicalism was a high regard for the Bible. It was believed to be the authoritative guide to all of life, providing a basis for morality, education and family life. In other words, evangelicals viewed the scriptures as the exclusive source for defining their relationship to God and the world. Finally, those within the evangelical tradition placed more weight on the death of Christ than on the broad features of his earthly ministry. Evangelical sermons and hymns pointed to Christ's sacrifice on the cross, and the burden of sin that he bore for humanity. Together, these central theological doctrines came to define the movement, as well as the opportunities available to women.

Conversion was doubly important in evangelical circles, serving as the vehicle of otherworldly redemption and the antidote to human suffering and poverty in the here and now. Given the urgency of these salvific concerns, the efforts of men were joined by those of women. This theological alliance of salvation and activism served to expand women's horizons in a number of ways during the eighteenth and nineteenth centuries.[39] One notable sphere of opportunity open to them was philanthropy, which expanded considerably during this period of economic upheaval. Anglican and Nonconformist charities provided female workers with paid and unpaid fields of service among the poor in the inner cities, distributing tracts, bibles and material aid. Women from various backgrounds were utilized as district visitors, and they provided valuable contacts between local churches and the labouring classes. Another avenue of ministry for women was found in the Sunday school movement, which began in the late eighteenth century to provide working-class children with the rudiments of a secular and religious education. By the early 1860s, women filled approximately half of the teaching positions in this movement.[40] These charitable and teaching roles often existed as well in the numerous sisterhoods that were established in the Anglican and Catholic communions during the nineteenth century. Although these roles gave Christian women a public presence in society, they did so by affirming conventional feminine associations with service and children.

Occasionally, however, the premium that evangelicals placed upon salvation and human effort could lead to more extraordinary female participation. Within early Wesleyan Methodism, for example, there was a pressing need to spread the gospel to the masses, whether this meant preaching in fields, barns or humble chapels. To meet the demands of these growing evangelistic endeavours, John Wesley gradually began to allow a few talented women to pray, testify and, later, preach in front of mixed assemblies. This was a significant move for Wesley, since he had initially believed that the New Testament clearly prohibited such public roles for women. Some of this reluctance was still apparent in 1769, when Wesley instructed Sarah Crosby, a gifted Methodist woman, to pray and witness in public but to avoid preaching (i.e., expounding on a biblical text).[41] Two years later, however, he began to allow Crosby and a handful of other women to preach in public. Here, in particular, Wesley was swayed by Mary Bosanquet, a close female associate, who suggested that God had called upon women to preach in unusual times. This line of reasoning was evident in a letter that Wesley wrote to Crosby in 1771, in which he justified female preaching by claiming that Methodism was an extraordinary dispensation, allowing for exceptions to St. Paul's injunctions on women's silence in the church.[42] Before Wesley's death in 1791, a number of female preachers became officially recognized by the Methodist Conference, and proved quite successful in ministry.

To his credit, Wesley provided a number of Methodist women with public opportunities far in advance of those offered in most other denominations. Nevertheless, there were signs, both before and after Wesley's demise, that these female gains were less than secure. First and foremost, Wesley never allowed female preaching to become a widespread practice in Methodism. He controlled the activities of the few women who preached, and he never formally appointed them to regular circuits alongside men.[43] As successful as these female evangelists may have been, they were always more the exception than the norm. A second problem, with even graver implications, lay in the fact that female preaching was subject to a male-controlled annual conference. This proved to be especially troubling for women after Wesley died, because his views on the subject were not widely accepted by most of the ministers in the Wesleyan connexion. This became strikingly obvious at the 1803 Wesleyan annual conference in Manchester, where it was resolved that if women felt an extraordinary call to preach they should address only their own sex.[44] Even then, women who wanted to do this had to gain the approval of the Methodist hierarchy. This severe curtailment of female preaching was justified on two major grounds: the substantial Wesleyan opposition to the practice, and an overabundance of male preachers. Now considered redundant, and garnering little support, female Wesleyan Methodist preachers were all but suppressed by the 1830s. In the end, the possibility of forging a new public role for women, and challenging the male monopoly of the pulpit, was lost within mainstream Methodism.

Women who wished to utilize their talents on the platform now had to look to some of the Methodist groups that broke away from the parent body. One significant product of this ferment was Primitive Methodism, established in 1811 by Hugh Bourne. Concerned about the declining revivalistic zeal and growing clerical control in the Wesleyan connexion, Bourne and other zealous Methodists began to hold unauthorized camp meetings to promote spiritual renewal and lay participation.[45] Their continued involvement in these controversial activities eventually forced them to form their own connexion. The group's initial focus upon revivalism and the laity was conducive to female preaching, and Bourne himself was a supporter of the practice. As early as 1808, he had written a pamphlet on the subject, entitled *Remarks on the Ministry of Women*.[46] In addition to addressing the passages of scripture that seemed to deny women a public role in the church, Bourne argued that Jesus had commissioned a number of women to preach the gospel, including the Samaritan woman and Mary Magdalene. An equally important component of Bourne's defence of female ministry was the success that attended the efforts of female preachers. Drawing upon his own experience, he testified to the ways in which God had used these messengers of the gospel to win converts for the kingdom. In light of this favourable climate, women like Mary Dunnel and Sarah Kirkland began to preach at the cottage and camp meetings where Primitive Methodists gathered to worship. In 1818 one out of every five preachers in the connexion was a woman.[47]

Yet, even with these seemingly impressive numbers, female preachers within this body were clearly subordinate to their male peers.[48] Single male preachers were paid almost twice as much as female preachers, and positions of authority were denied to women. In 1824, for instance, a conference ruling prohibited women from becoming superintendents and denied them the right to vote while serving on administrative boards. It was also the case that women could speak at quarterly meetings only if called upon to do so. This marginalization of women was apparent as well in Hugh Bourne's record of the connexion's early history, where he made only passing reference to the women who had done so much to establish the movement.[49] Furthermore, the movement's increasing respectability by mid-century made female ministry part of a controversial past that was best forgotten. By the 1850s, the Primitive Methodists were recruiting no new female preachers, and the few who remained often found themselves saddled with the burdens of marriage and motherhood.

The Bible Christians represented another expression of sectarian Methodism that was initially open to female ministry. Established in 1815 by William O'Bryan, this small band of religious enthusiasts, located in the southwest of England, provided an environment in which women could preach. The justification for this practice was set out by O'Bryan during the movement's earliest days.[50] Echoing a central argument used within Primitive Methodist circles, he believed that this public activity could not be wrong since God blessed the efforts of female evangelists. This type of rationale, based upon pragmatism and experience, underscored the importance that evangelical revivalism placed upon salvific activism. It was hard to oppose anything that proved to be successful in advancing the gospel during periods of intense spiritual renewal. In addition to this appeal to success, O'Bryan contended that New Testament passages enjoining female silence in the church referred only to women who usurped male authority. This latter argument had been used by the Methodist scholar Adam Clarke in his widely read biblical commentary, and later in the century it would be utilized by evangelical women themselves when justifying their public role in the church.[51]

With these foundations in place, a significant number of early Bible Christian women found an opportunity to engage in public ministry. Johanna Brooks, Hannah Row and Catherine Reed were just a few of the preachers who proved that success did indeed accompany female efforts. This fact was not lost on those who attended the movement's first conference in 1819, where the employment of women as preachers received unanimous approval. In the next few years, women filled approximately one-half to one-third of the group's itinerant preaching positions, and they played a key role in evangelizing urban centres.[52] Notwithstanding such opportunities, these female preachers did not enjoy a status equal to that of their male colleagues.[53] The women who served as preachers were simply called "helpers," while their male peers were designated as ministers. Female preaching might be biblical, but only insofar as it did not usurp male authority. Not surprisingly, therefore, the women who preached in the connexion played no role in its administration or annual conference. Bible Christian rules and regulations made it clear that governing was a male province. Moreover, a denominational policy of encouraging male preachers to marry their female colleagues also resulted in the decline of women preachers by the 1830s and 1840s, because the vacant positions that resulted were not filled by single women. At the 1844 conference, female preachers represented just under 6 percent of those in the itinerant positions.[54]

By the early 1850s, sectarian Methodism had largely closed the door on this liberating expression of women's ministry. In 1859, however, renewed revivalism in certain evangelical quarters in Northern Ireland and England once again created a climate conducive to female preaching. As historian Olive Anderson has argued, this period of spiritual fervour laid great stress on lay participation, sensational techniques and emotionalism, each of which served to legitimize the public activities of a few exceptional women.[55] The small number of women who began to preach during this revival, which lasted into the 1860s, were unordained preachers, attracted large crowds and conveyed a message that spoke to the heart. Furthermore, these female evangelists, from upper working-class and middle-class backgrounds, addressed respectable audiences in plain and modest attire. Geraldine Hooper, Jessie McFarlane and Catherine Booth were among the best known of these women, and they generated considerable attention. Hooper, an Anglican, was frequently a guest at Primitive Methodist tent meetings and Wesleyan chapels,

where she could preach to crowds of 3,000.[56] While this was clearly an interesting period in the history of female ministry, and deserving of more attention from historians, the popularity and acceptability of female preaching
did not last. When the American revivalists Moody and Sankey came to England
in the early 1870s, they only allowed women to address their own sex in public. Apart from in the Christian Mission, which became the Salvation Army
in 1878, female preaching was silenced during the late Victorian period. Most
denominations would come to terms with this subject only in the twentieth
century.[57]

There can be little doubt that the evangelical focus upon salvation and
human effort helped to open up several spheres of public service for women,
including preaching. In an age when most pulpits were closed to women,
and silence enjoined upon them, the authorization of female preaching in
Methodist and revivalistic circles was an exceptional phenomenon. Nonetheless, the theological rationale for this practice was problematic in the long
run. The continuance of female preaching depended upon the transitory and
fluctuating winds of revivalism, which more often than not provided the main
rationale for the employment of women in public roles. At such times, the
work of female preachers could be justified, because they were successful in
bringing sinners into the kingdom. Behind this line of reasoning was pragmatism rather than principle. Women might occasionally preach in Methodist and revivalistic circles, but they did not possess the right to do so. It was
a privilege dependent upon the zeal that Christians had for evangelism, not
to mention the dictates of a male-dominated hierarchy. Despite its own problems with female ministry, the Salvation Army was an exception here, since
it actually gave women the right to hold any office held by men. Even though
this precept was never applied in any widespread fashion, it was never so
poorly followed as to silence women altogether. In other denominations,
however, this kind of principle was absent. Furthermore, the evangelical association between female preaching and success represented a double standard. Female preachers had to be exceptional in order to preach, but there
is little indication that the same was true for the men who became ministers.
Evangelicalism's emphasis upon conversion and activism may have given
rise to female preachers, but its failure to institutionalize this ministry led to
its demise.

Similar possibilities and limitations surrounded the evangelical understanding of the scriptures. The Bible was held in high regard by those in the
movement, and they considered it a sacred responsibility to read its contents
carefully and prayerfully. It was not uncommon for evangelical children to
have read the Old and New Testaments several times before adulthood.[58]

For perhaps many women, a thoughtful and reverent searching of the scriptures was inspiring, since they recorded the exploits of a number of public female characters. Moreover, for the small number of women who wished to preach, the Bible could also provide the basis for action. Besides pointing to Jesus' liberating treatment of women, or passages like Galatians 3:28, which speaks of all being one in Christ, these women often turned to the prophecy-fulfilment passage in Acts 2:17-21. The Pentecostal experience outlined in the early chapters of Acts was viewed as confirmation of the prophet Joel's vision that, in the latter days, women would prophesy alongside men. Undoubtedly, the clearest instance of this argument was found in the work of Phoebe Palmer, a nineteenth-century American Methodist evangelist. Her 1859 defence of female ministry, *Promise of the Father; or, A Neglected Speciality of the Last Days*, contended that the bestowal of the Holy Spirit upon women at Pentecost gave them, and all subsequent Christian women, the authority and obligation to testify publicly in the church.[59] Not surprisingly, a good deal of attention was also directed at those biblical passages that seemed to prohibit women from assuming a public ministry in the church. Catherine Booth and Antoinette Brown, an American preacher, expended a great deal of energy on the relevant Pauline sections on women in 1 Corinthians and 1 Timothy. Both argued that these passages were only meant to correct the abuses associated with women's public role in the early church.[60] Along with Palmer and others, they believed that the Bible supported the public witness of women.

The desire to justify female preaching on the basis of scripture underscored the importance of biblical authority in evangelicalism. Texts that supported or questioned women's role in the church had to be examined with care. Scripture had to be compared with scripture, and harmonized rather than discounted.[61] Where the Bible gave explicit commands that appeared universal, evangelicals rarely disobeyed them. The injunction that wives should submit to their husbands, in passages like Ephesians 5:22-24, was a case in point. Scriptural authority was undermined when this command was violated. Henry Venn, an influential evangelical Anglican, believed that it was "nothing less than a proud self-exalting contempt of the word of God in a wife to affect to rule, or to refuse to submit to the authority of her husband."[62] For most of those who supported female preaching, this conviction remained normative. While maintaining that women should have a public role in religious life, they did not challenge scriptural commands on wives' submission to their husbands.[63] Their arguments for women's inclusion on the platform did not translate into equality in the home. With male headship left unchallenged, female involvement in the ecclesiastical realm depended upon the dictates of men.

Even when evangelical women espoused a degree of equality between the sexes, they still continued to be influenced by the Victorian biblical images of feminine dependence and masculine independence.[64] The idealized nineteenth-century woman was a helpmeet or supporter of man, but never a challenge to his authority. This widespread viewpoint was often grounded in the Genesis 2 Creation story, in which Adam was formed before Eve, and supported by St. Paul's contention in 1 Corinthians 11:7-10 that woman was created for man. Assertiveness by a woman was more than just unseemly; it transgressed the divine order. Women were expected, therefore, to pay heed to this pre-eminent expression of patriarchal rule. Interestingly enough, the substance of this belief was accepted by female exegetes like Antoinette Brown, Catherine Booth and Phoebe Palmer.[65] The abuses that they associated with the women in the early church included the usurping of male authority and other "unbecoming" female behaviour. Although they advocated a public role for women in the religious sphere, their commentary on passages like 1 Timothy clearly indicated that they believed it was inappropriate for a churchwoman to conduct herself in an assertive or domineering manner. Despite the fact that they entered a male-dominated public realm, evangelical women continued to promote a view of femininity that was tied to masculine governance.

Evangelicalism's fourth theological tenet, which centred upon the sacrificial death of Christ on the cross, also had a nebulous effect upon women. At times, this doctrine served to liberate women, leading them to assume a larger role in the church and society. For instance, the model of a suffering and sacrificial saviour figured prominently in the thinking of the few women who ventured to speak in front of mixed audiences. Harsh criticism and ridicule might accompany their controversial activities, but such women could take comfort in the fact that Christ commanded all believers to take up their cross and follow him. Suffering became a sign that female preachers were obeying God. Moreover, just as Christ had sacrificed his all for the world's lost, devoted Christian women might sacrifice their reputations and self-interest in the service of a larger cause. Phoebe Palmer, for instance, described her own ministry in this way: "I have given up my *reputation* to God"[66] [italics in original]. Catherine Booth could also associate her own preaching with the abandonment of reputation.[67] If female testifying and preaching destroyed a woman's respectability, she could find comfort in the fact that God expected Christians to deny themselves the things of the world in order to save it. Suffering and self-sacrifice, therefore, were themes that might enable women to justify their public roles within evangelicalism.

For many women, however, self-sacrifice was expressed primarily within the domestic sphere. This virtue might include mission and service to the world, but above all it was directed towards marriage and motherhood.[68] According to the biblical model espoused by most evangelicals, a woman was created as a helpmeet to serve man and train his children. This expectation of self-denying service was simply intensified by the evangelical model of Christ as a long-suffering and sacrificial lamb led to the cross to die for others. A Christlike selfless love did little to change Victorian men, who were often excused for being selfish, but it did provide further religious support for women's conventional identification with self-denial. Consequently, nineteenth-century women faced enormous pressure to put the interests of others ahead of their own. It was an oft-repeated saying during and after the Victorian period that no one respected a woman who neglected her home and family. This climate of feminine constraint did not preclude a limited public role for evangelical women, but it seldom encouraged them to pursue roles equal to those of men in the wider world. Evangelical culture did not motivate women to develop the self-interest and self-assertion necessary to fight for their rights in the ecclesiastical and secular world.

The parallels between selfless femininity and selfless religion also gave weight to the assumption that women were more religious than men. Unlike their husbands, who worked in the aggressive and acquisitive world of business and industry, women increasingly laboured in a domestic realm devoted to more virtuous pursuits.[69] The home came to be seen as the heart of all that was noble and sacred, and respectable women served as the moral and spiritual guardians of this sanctuary. Coventry Patmore, a nineteenth-century English poet, glorified this image of pious womanhood in his 1854 poem "The Angel in the House." Above all else, such a woman was the embodiment of purity and godliness. In addition to overseeing the religious education of their children, Victorian women were expected to exemplify angelic piety in the company of their menfolk. Although the concept of this type of feminine influence could justify a woman's entry into the public sphere, it often did not challenge evangelical and Victorian convictions about gender. The angel in the house may have ventured outside, but she remained an angel nonetheless.[70] Women assumed public roles largely consistent with service and piety, while men continued to fill positions of leadership and authority. Ultimately, Victorian gender arrangements had as much to do with belief as with geography. There were certain responsibilities and expectations for each sex, whether the setting was the home or the public arena.

By the end of the nineteenth century, evangelicalism had begun to lose its impact on certain sections of the British middle class. Its conservative theology did not mesh with the intellectual developments of the day, and growing leisure and prosperity made evangelical self-denial less attractive to those with more free time and money. At the same time, the growth of feminist activism and the emergence of the "New Woman" threatened the assumptions underlying the evangelical construction of female gender. Maud Booth, a prominent Salvation Army leader married to a son of the founders, was especially critical of the New Woman appearing in the mid-1890s.[71] Although Booth was supportive of a public role for women, she did not endorse this novel feminine ideal. The New Woman was the antithesis of self-sacrifice and dependence, because she rejected marriage and motherhood in favour of a career and self-indulgence. For Maud Booth and other evangelicals, a "true woman" pursued a self-sacrificing and Christlike mission of service to others. Sectarian bodies like the Salvation Army would continue to promote this Victorian and evangelical construction of womanhood well into the twentieth century. This model might include some public work, but it was especially centred upon marriage and motherhood.

The tensions between the possibilities of public work and the demands of the home and family underscored the ambiguous nature of Victorian culture. Numerous competing interests defined the age, and they were not always easy to reconcile with each other. On the economic and social front, wealth coexisted with poverty, while state intervention was pursued alongside self-help. Politically, the period gave rise to democratic demands and paternalistic solutions, not to mention equality as well as difference. Philosophically, the battle between the mind and the heart could be seen in the schools of positivism and romanticism. Even more significantly, this age was shaped by the principal theological tenets of evangelicalism, notably in the area of gender. For women, in particular, this movement provided opportunities and obstacles. The conversion of the world required the efforts of men and women, even in the area of preaching, but the pragmatism driving this activity did not ensure a place for women once the winds of revivalism abated. Likewise, the evangelical emphases on the Bible and Christlike sacrifice provided instances of female public service and domestic subordination.

Those who assume that the Salvation Army was set apart from its age—having its origins in the mind of God—have failed to appreciate how these complex societal and theological variables influenced the organization. This is strikingly apparent in the realm of gender, where uncritical and hastily drawn conclusions have been reached about the role of Salvationist women and men. What is surprising, for example, is how little research has been devoted to the views of William Booth on this subject. There has been no sustained attempt to examine the kind of equality he espoused, or the success with which he applied this concept in the life of the organization. The next chapter begins to address this shortcoming by examining his beliefs and practices in the area of gender and equality. This part of the narrative puts the life and times of William Booth into historical context, tracing the extent to which his views on women evolved over the course of his youth and adulthood. Whether or not William Booth ever arrived at "settled views" on female ministry and women's equality with men remains contested ground, since there has been no systematic treatment of these issues thus far, scholarly or otherwise.

CHAPTER 3

William Booth and Women: Settled Views?

CATHERINE BOOTH MAY HAVE DONE MUCH to shape the Army's stance towards women, but it was her husband, William, who reigned as the undisputed leader of the early Salvation Army. In this position of authority, William Booth had numerous opportunities to set the direction of the Army's views on female ministry and sexual equality. He had the power to implement these ideas, address potential inequities and establish a climate conducive to equality between the sexes. In light of this autocratic control, it is quite surprising that scholars have never systematically documented William's understanding of female gender and equality. At best, only highly selective aspects of his position on the subject have been presented. This deficiency, due in large part to an overemphasis upon the women of the Salvation Army, is addressed in this chapter. The following pages trace William Booth's attitudes and behaviour towards women from his early life to old age, seeking in the process to answer a number of questions. To what degree did William Booth mirror evangelical and Victorian ambiguities concerning women? How were Salvationist women affected by the variables that shaped their leader? In order to deal with the substance of these inquiries, we must turn to William Booth's early life, his Methodist background and his subsequent development of the Salvation Army.

✤ Early Life and Ministry

William Booth was born of working-class parents, Samuel and Mary (Moss) Booth, in the Midlands town of Nottingham on April 10, 1829.[1] Having a loose connection with the Church of England, the Booths had their son baptized at Nottingham's St. Mary's Anglican church on April 12, 1829. Two years later, after the birth of William's sister Emma, the family moved to the nearby village of Bleasby, where Samuel rented a small farm. It seems that Samuel's agricultural venture ended in failure, and the family moved back to Nottingham in late 1835. There is little indication that the household was especially religious, but William was sent occasionally to the local parish Sunday school. Samuel also enrolled his son at a school run by Sampson Biddulph, who was a local Wesleyan preacher. By all accounts, William was not an exceptional student, and his few years at this academy were uneventful. At the age of thirteen, however, William was forced to withdraw from the school when his father began to encounter serious financial problems.

Samuel Booth, a builder of houses for artisans, had become unable to pay the mortgages associated with his line of work and soon came to ruin. With the need for new sources of economic support for the family, William was apprenticed to a Unitarian pawnbroker, Francis Eames, in the Woolpack Lane area of Nottingham. This became a largely unpleasant job for William, since it put him in daily contact with the misery that forced people to sell their earthly possessions for a few shillings. To make matters worse, the Booth family was left nearly destitute when Samuel died in September 1842. With the family lacking any significant assets, William's employment in the pawnshop became all the more important. Even so, however, Mary Booth had to work as well, selling toys and household supplies in a small shop located in a poor section of the town. These early experiences, while not uncommon in an age of industrialization and economic uncertainty, put the surviving members of the Booth family close to the edge of Victorian destitution.

Fortunately, however, there were also a number of more positive influences working upon the young William Booth. Evangelical religion, in particular, became the focus of his life, providing him with a source of security and purpose beyond the mundane rhythm of daily existence. In late 1842, William left the Anglican fold and began attending the Broad Street Wesleyan chapel, where he underwent a heartfelt conversion experience. His commitment to God was deepened as well through a series of Methodist revival meetings held in Nottingham in May and June 1846 by the American evangelist James Caughey.[2] The vivid sermons of Caughey, which emphasized hell and judgement for those who rejected the gospel, served to alert all devout Christians of their responsibility to reach the lost. This climate of urgency was absorbed by William Booth and his close friends, and they began to preach to Nottingham's poor. Their enthusiasm, however, was not always appreciated by the more prosperous members of the Broad Street chapel, who felt uncomfortable around the destitute souls whom they brought to Sunday services. Consequently, this earnest group of young men began holding their own evangelistic meetings in the streets and cottages surrounding Nottingham.

One of these small cottages was the setting for William Booth's first sermon as a lay Methodist preacher.

It is quite likely that William first came into contact with female preaching at these cottage meetings. Women preachers had been silenced within Wesleyan circles, but they found acceptance in certain sectarian expressions of Methodism established in the nineteenth century. Primitive Methodism was one such body, and it was especially strong in the Nottingham area.[3] This working-class movement, founded by Hugh Bourne in 1811, held its services in barns and cottages, and had a significant number of female preachers. Given William's involvement with cottage meetings, it is quite probable that his first exposure to female preaching came from Primitive Methodism. What is certain, however, is that he was unimpressed with the first female preacher he encountered, in the mid-1840s. According to one early biographer, William disliked a certain unnamed female preacher's "masculine and dictatorial manner."[4] Perhaps he believed that, if women were to preach at all, they must do so in a strictly feminine manner appropriate to their sex. Whether or not William Booth opposed all female preaching at this time is not known, but his first association with the practice was not very positive.

The subject of female ministry would be raised more forcefully in the future, but in the late 1840s William Booth was preoccupied with other concerns. In 1848, his apprenticeship at the pawnbroker's shop was finished, and he experienced a lengthy period of unemployment. His plight was not exceptional at this time, because England experienced a great deal of economic unrest during the 1840s.[5] Believing that employment might be found in London, William moved there in the fall of 1849. Upon arrival in the English capital, he stayed with an older sister Ann and her husband Francis Brown, but they had become alcoholics and this environment soon became intolerable for William. With nowhere else to turn, he settled for a job in a pawnbroker's shop in the Kennington Common area of London. Notwithstanding the long hours associated with this job, William began to look for opportunities to preach at local Wesleyan chapels in London. After being assigned a place on the lay preaching circuit, he soon discovered that this arrangement amounted to little time in the pulpit. Always the pragmatist, William began to realize that the local streets would provide him with more opportunities to preach. He made his convictions known to the Reverend John Hall, the circuit superintendent, but Hall turned down the request, perhaps because he did not relish the idea of trying to supervise William's open-air preaching. In any case, William Booth's determination to engage in street ministry led to his expulsion from Wesleyan Methodism.[6]

After being forced to leave the Wesleyan fold in 1851, William was asked to join the Wesleyan Methodist Reformers.[7] This group had been established in 1849, largely because of clerical and lay dissatisfaction with the dictatorial leadership of Jabez Bunting, the Secretary of the Wesleyan Conference. When a series of anonymous pamphlets or "Fly Sheets" critical of Bunting was circulated in the 1840s, matters came to a head.[8] Three ministers unwilling to answer questions about these "Fly Sheets" were expelled, and approximately 100,000 clergy and laity followed them. According to his early biographers, William's love for authority did not make him an immediate supporter of the Reformer cause.[9] At the same time, however, he was impressed with the Reformers' evangelistic zeal, and he began to attend some of their meetings. These gatherings also presented William with an opportunity to occupy the pulpit on occasion. One leading Reformer, Edward Rabbits, became quite impressed with William's preaching abilities, and asked him to join the new movement in June 1851. Rabbits, who was a wealthy shoe manufacturer, went on to fund William's preaching between April and June 1852. This financial backing allowed William Booth to leave his employment at the pawnbroker's shop and preach full-time.

Edward Rabbits also played a role in bringing William into contact with people who would shape his views on women's ministry. It was, for example, at Rabbits' invitation that he attended a service at which a female evangelist, Miss Buck, preached the sermon.[10] Buck was a travelling preacher for the Primitive Methodists, and by all accounts very successful in ministry. She had been preaching for about fifteen years when William Booth heard her. He was apparently quite impressed with this gifted woman's preaching abilities, because he praised her efforts and vowed never again to oppose this expression of female ministry. This may not have signalled an enthusiastic endorsement of female preaching, but it showed that his views on the subject were beginning to change. His first encounter with a female preacher had been less than positive. Now, however, he promised not to place any obstacles before a woman who wished to engage in this practice. Even more significantly, William had Rabbits to thank for introducing him to Catherine Mumford, a young Reformer with strong views on female ministry and sexual equality.[11] William and Catherine had occasion to meet each other at a party hosted by Rabbits, and a more regular association began when William attended Reformer meetings where Catherine was present. An even closer relationship was cemented when William preached a sermon at Catherine's local chapel. Always a thoughtful observer of those in the pulpit, she was impressed with the young preacher's message and speaking abilities.

Catherine and William Booth. Courtesy of The Salvation Army National Archives, Alexandria, Virginia.

❖ New Commitments and Shifting Affiliations

A romantic relationship soon began to flourish between William and Catherine, and they were engaged in May 1852. On the ministerial front, however, things were beginning to look uncertain. Apparently a rift opened up between William and Rabbits, and the wealthy Reformer withdrew his funding in the summer of 1852. St. John Ervine, one of William Booth's more perceptive biographers, suggests that the cause of this breach lay in William's authoritative person- ality: "The Reformers, in their fear of priestly dominion, refused any author- ity to their minister, and William Booth was not, at any time in his life, easily able to subject himself to the rule of committees or councils."[12] A related rea- son for this separation lay in William's dissatisfaction with the limited oppor- tunities he had to preach in this nascent movement, since it encouraged the laity to share the pulpit with the clergy and full-time evangelists. There is some indication as well that William perceived the Reformers to have a less than certain future, and he was concerned about supporting Catherine once they were married.[13] At this point in his life William was seeking a less risky avenue of service. The break was made in June 1852, and for a brief period the couple's quest for new opportunities took them beyond the Methodist community.

The impetus behind this widening of horizons also lay with Catherine, who persuaded her future husband to inquire about a ministry within the Congregational Union.[14] Catherine herself was no stranger to this long-stand- ing religious tradition, which had emerged out of sixteenth- and seventeenth- century Puritanism. For a number of years she had occasionally attended a local Congregational chapel in London, and had become good friends with the resident minister, the Reverend Dr. David Thomas. Moreover, Catherine was well aware of the middle-class respectability and prestige associated with this ecclesiastical body, all of which could ensure a bright future for William in ministry. Given the schismatic climate within so much of Methodism at this time, there can be little doubt that such an environment appeared to offer the stability that Catherine and William desired. There was also some evidence that the Congregational Union had toned down its Calvinist doc- trine and might ordain a Wesleyan. This was clearly a possibility, since local congregations possessed the authority to choose their own ministers. Consequently, Catherine and William joined the denomination, and plans were made to allow William to study for the ministry. As things turned out, however, Congregationalist theology was more infused with Calvinism than William and Catherine had appreciated, and William quickly voiced his oppo- sition to the doctrine of election, with its assertion that God chooses to save only certain people. William Booth was a firm believer in the Arminian and

Wesleyan gospel of unlimited grace, which stressed that all could be saved by faith. Problems also lay with the course of study that William faced in order to become a minister, because he was not equipped to handle the academic requirements of the Congregational training program. In light of these insurmountable obstacles, William abandoned any hopes of securing a pulpit within this denomination.[15]

A ministerial offer from an affiliate of the Reformers brought William Booth back into Methodist circles in November 1852.[16] With no other prospects on the horizon, he now seemed willing to take his chances with this body. William was given its circuit at Spalding, Lincolnshire. Although this proved to be a short and uneventful appointment, one issue did create a good deal of friction between William and his future wife. It was while he was in Spalding that he and Catherine had their first serious disagreement over the equality of the sexes.[17] This subject had been of great interest to Catherine Mumford prior to her involvement with William. Not surprisingly, therefore, she soon expressed her conviction to William that marriages would not be perfect until women were educated as men's equals. In response, William contended that women might be emotionally superior to men, but they were inferior to men in intelligence. To reinforce his position he also quoted the aphorism that women had a fibre more in their hearts and a cell fewer in their brains. There was nothing unusual about William's reply, since he was merely reiterating very traditional assumptions about sexual difference.[18] Most Victorians were like him, believing that each sex had certain attributes superior to the other. Although Catherine herself continued to embrace certain aspects of this gender ideology, she could not accept that women were intellectually inferior to men.

Months before her marriage in June 1855, Catherine caused William once again to articulate his position on sexual equality and female ministry. By this stage he had left the Reformers and joined the Methodist New Connexion, an offshoot of Wesleyan Methodism. Edward Rabbits was now involved with the denomination, and he graciously sought a reconciliation with William and offered funds to support his work.[19] After some brief training in London under a Methodist scholar, William Booth became an evangelist with the New Connexion. William's campaigns kept him apart from Catherine for long stretches of time, so the young couple's letters became important vehicles for expressing their views on a number of subjects, including gender equality and women's ministry. The latter topics were raised when Catherine wrote to William shortly before his birthday in April 1855. Catherine expressed the view that a proper reading of scripture supported women's mental and spiritual equality with men, thereby legitimizing female ministry within the church.[20] While not referring to herself personally, she felt that women were needed in public church ministry. In closing, Catherine conveyed her desire, subject to William's approval, to write on the subject again in the future.

Having read Catherine's letter, William sent a brief reply on April 12, 1855. His correspondence was structured around two broad themes: the question of women's overall equality with men, and the appropriateness of female ministry. In the first part of the letter, William honestly disclosed his views on equality:

> From the first reading I cannot see anything in them to lead me for one *moment* to think of altering my opinion. You *combat* a great deal that I hold as firmly as *you* do—viz. her [woman's] *equality*, her *perfect equality*, as a whole—as a *being*. But as to concede that she is man's *equal*, or *capable* of becoming man's equal, in intellectual attainments or prowess—I must say *that* is contradicted by experience in the world and my honest conviction. You know, my dear, I acknowledge the superiority of your sex in very many things—in others I believe her inferior. *Vice versa* with man.[21] [italics in original]

William's understanding of women's equality with men revealed a certain ambiguity. On the one hand, he espoused the perfect equality of woman as a being. At some abstract level he was willing to concede a parity between the sexes. On the other hand, he also wished to maintain that, in concrete terms, men were intellectually superior to women. Perfect equality was ultimately a vacuous notion for William Booth, since it did not translate into gender equity in daily life. The contention that certain qualities were gender-specific seemed most important to William. It will be recalled that sexual difference had shaped his earlier thinking on the subject, including his first known argument with Catherine.

The topic of female ministry comprised the latter half of William's letter to Catherine. His thinking here revealed an unsettled perspective on the subject:

> I would not stop a woman preaching on any account. I would not encourage one to begin. You should preach if you felt moved thereto: felt equal to the task. I would not stay *you*, if I had power to do so. Altho', *I should not like it*. It is easy for you to say my views are the result of prejudice; perhaps they are. I am for the world's *salvation;* I will quarrel with no means that promises help.[22] [italics in original]

For the most part, the attitude reflected here was consistent with the remarks that William had made after hearing Miss Buck preach in the early 1850s. At that time he had vowed never again to oppose female preaching. Obviously, however, such a commitment was not an unqualified endorsement of female preachers. In this sense, William had not departed significantly from his earlier views. Yet, his pragmatic evangelicalism kept him from totally dismissing the viability of female ministry. Salvation was at the heart of evangelical theology, and Booth was not going to hinder anyone who had a desire to publish the gospel message.

Gradually, however, William's evangelical convictions, coupled with Catherine's influence, led him to encourage female ministry more openly. This became apparent while William was the minister of Bethesda Chapel, a Gateshead New Connexion parish.[23] In 1859, for example, William encouraged his wife to accept an invitation from the chapel's leadership to speak at an upcoming prayer meeting. Although Catherine declined the offer, it is noteworthy that her husband had urged her to undertake this public responsibility. Not long after this, William also stood behind Catherine's efforts to write a pamphlet in response to a minister critical of women's right to preach. He was pleased with the results of this booklet and urged his wife to address the issue at length. Even more significant were William's actions when his wife felt called to speak before the congregation on May 27, 1860. He not only allowed Catherine the opportunity to "say a word," but also announced that his wife would preach at the evening service. It is quite clear, therefore, that William played an important role in launching his wife's long and successful preaching career. Whether or not he had arrived at settled views on equality is less obvious, but he had come to appreciate and promote the public witness of women in the pulpit.

Female ministry became increasingly important within the Booth household when William and Catherine left the Methodist New Connexion in 1861. William had resigned his post when the conference leadership had denied his request to become a full-time travelling evangelist within the denomination. After moving in with Catherine's parents in London, William and Catherine received numerous requests to conduct revival campaigns throughout England and Wales. Although the revivalistic climate of the late 1850s and early 1860s has often been exaggerated, it was felt in certain pockets of evangelicalism.[24] It was undoubtedly stimulated as well by a number of American revivalists touring Britain at the time, including Charles Finney, James Caughey, and Phoebe and Walter Palmer. William and Catherine benefited from this revivalistic ethos, touring the United Kingdom as independent evangelists for the next four years.[25] For most of this period Catherine and William shared the preaching, but by 1864 they were in such demand that they embarked on separate campaigns. In the early part of the following year, Catherine's speaking engagements brought the family—which by now included six children— back to London.

❖ From East End Mission to an Army of Salvation

Catherine's preaching ministry in a southeast suburb of London in February and March 1865 proved to be the catalyst for William's future work among London's poor.[26] Her packed audiences included middle-class gentlemen fervently involved in the evangelization of poverty-stricken East Londoners. Two of these philanthropists, Richard Morgan and Samuel Chase, became aware of William's past experience in ministry after meeting Catherine. Morgan, in particular, was a member of the East London Special Services Committee, an evangelical organization arising out of the mid-nineteenth-century drive to convert the "heathens" at home. When one of the committee's regular evangelists became ill, Morgan asked William to conduct a campaign at a tent mission located in the Whitechapel area of East London. William accepted the offer, and in early July 1865 he began preaching in a place known for its aversion to organized religion.[27] The first few weeks of William Booth's evangelistic activities remained centred around the tent, which was pitched on an unused Quaker burial site. This canvas structure had been put up a few weeks earlier by the Christian Community, a non-denominational group previously tied to Methodism. The hundred or so members of this body were experimenting with new ways of reaching the lower classes, and were willing to welcome any evangelists sent by Morgan's organization.[28]

Neither William Booth nor those he worked with had any notion that he would establish a permanent mission among the area's poor. After a few weeks, however, his work was showing positive results. Consequently, Morgan and the East London Special Services Committee began to contemplate William Booth's future among them. Even more importantly, William was beginning to sense that God was calling him to this ministry. Such a conviction grew stronger as he perceived the extent of East London's spiritual poverty. True to his evangelical heritage, he felt an obligation to share the gospel with the unsaved. Years later, William Booth recalled this experience in the following manner: "I was continually haunted with a desire to offer myself to Jesus Christ as an apostle for the heathen of East London. The idea or heavenly vision or whatever you may call it overcame me, I yielded to it."[29] Therefore, late one night after a tent meeting, he returned home to tell Catherine of his growing sense of calling to the East End. According to Salvationist historiography, William Booth had found his destiny.[30]

To ensure the success of his new evangelistic venture, William was beginning to look beyond the Christian Community's tent. This makeshift shelter had to be put up and taken down on a daily basis, and the wind had blown it over on numerous occasions, resulting in costly repairs. As early as mid-August 1865 William proposed to establish a more permanent mission,

William Booth preaching in a tent meeting in the East End of London in July 1865.
Courtesy of The Salvation Army International Heritage Centre, London.

and he asked for the support of 100 people to join his Christian Revival Association.[31] Such a body would hold meetings in halls, theatres, chapels and the open air, and hopefully would retain a central facility for more intimate gatherings. William realized that such an undertaking would require stable funding, and he appealed to concerned Christians and organizations for financial assistance. Although he was unable to muster a large corps of male and female supporters, he began renting a Whitechapel dancing room for revival services in early September. This was a significant move, as William now needed a steady flow of donations to cover the rental payments. Funding worries would continue to plague him for years to come, but he was able to secure some initial support from a few wealthy patrons and the Evangelisation Society, a group financing many missions in the area. Meanwhile, Catherine began to preach in London's West End, and her influential audiences included numerous benefactors, some of whom gave William's mission needed assistance for a number of years.

William planned to train some of the converts he made to help with the expansion of the mission, while channelling the others into existing East End churches and chapels. The first part of this strategy worked out quite well, and William quickly learned the value of sending lower-class evangelists to minister to those of a similar background. It was impossible, however, to implement the second part of this strategy. As William explained years later, the poor would not go to the churches, and the churches did not want the poor.[32] This resulted, therefore, in the mission becoming a church for the lower classes, and helped to consolidate William's work. The number of rented facilities used by the organization, which became known as the East London Christian Mission, increased significantly between 1865 and 1868. More permanent quarters for the mission were also secured in October 1869, when William purchased an indoor market and transformed it into a central mission hall and headquarters. Around the same time, he changed the mission's name, now calling it simply the Christian Mission. This new designation reflected the fact that the work had begun to extend beyond the East End of London, with preaching stations in Croydon and Edinburgh.[33]

What was also becoming well established in the Christian Mission was female ministry. Undoubtedly inspired by Catherine Booth, section 12 of the organization's first-ever constitution, drafted in 1870, stated in part: "Godly women possessing the necessary gifts and qualifications shall be employed as preachers ... and they shall be eligible for any office, and to speak and vote at all official meetings."[34] This was a significant declaration, going far beyond the privileges given to the female preachers of past ages. It will be recalled from chapter 2 that female evangelists within Methodism never enjoyed constitutional guarantees of any nature, and were prohibited from assuming governing roles. Between 1870 and 1878 the Christian Mission was modestly successful in implementing these principles. First, the number of female preachers within the organization grew from a small handful in 1870 to comprise nearly half of the Mission's preaching staff by 1878.[35] Although this signalled a commitment to female preaching, these assignments rarely included female evangelists being placed in positions of authority over their male counterparts. Eliza Collingridge and Annie Davis were among the few gifted women who proved to be exceptions to this general rule.[36] Second, the percentage of eligible female voters at the Christian Mission's annual conferences grew from 17 percent to 25 percent of the total voting membership between 1870 and 1878.[37] Even though male Christian Missioners remained in the majority at annual conferences, and filled most of the Mission's administrative positions, these women had significantly more freedom than their sisters in other denominations. They enjoyed some control over the direction of the Mission, and found unparalleled opportunities to preach.

Significant changes were underway, however, as William Booth transformed the Christian Mission into the Salvation Army. Three distinct phases were apparent in this evolutionary process, which began in 1877 and continued into 1880. Changes in the Mission's semi-democratic power structure signalled the first major step towards a military system. The right of members, male or female, to have an equitable voice in the operation of the Mission was lost. At a Christian Mission meeting in January 1877, William Booth proposed autocratic rule instead of the committee system, which he considered to be ineffectual. This recommendation was ratified at the annual conference in June, after the following ultimatum from Booth was issued to all Christian Mission members: "This is a question of confidence as between you and me, and if you can't trust me it is no use for us to attempt to work together. *Confidence in God and in me are absolutely indispensable both now and ever afterwards*"[38] [italics in original]. This autocratic tone was evident as well at the Mission's annual conference in 1878, where Booth boasted: "We don't invite people to Conference as others do for the purpose of debating and legislation, because we take it that all here are in perfect harmony with us in purpose and design, for if they do not aim at the same thing and in the same way, they are not with us."[39] From this point forward, the organization would be controlled solely by one person.

Not long after these structural alterations, the Christian Mission adopted a new name and military terminology. This second phase of the Mission's metamorphosis reinforced the autocratic framework that Booth had put in place. Military metaphors, which had been employed at the Mission's preaching station in Whitby as early as October 1877, became a characteristic feature of the organization. Elijah Cadman, the head evangelist at the Whitby post, had called women and men to join "The Hallelujah Army." He also began to call himself "Captain" and to refer to Booth as "General" of the Hallelujah Army.[40] William Booth began to embrace the essence of this military symbolism, and started to refer to the Christian Mission as a Salvation Army in May 1878.[41] Within a short period of time this evangelical body became explicitly militaristic: preaching stations became corps, preachers became officers, members became soldiers, new openings became invasions, and William Booth's title of General Superintendent was shortened to that of General. The Mission had become an Army in both structure and substance.

This kind of paramilitarism served two purposes within the nascent organization. On the one hand, the Salvation Army sought to capture Victorian England's growing interest in the armed services, heroic soldier saints and distant battlefields. In particular, militarism had wide appeal among working-class men like Elijah Cadman, who wished to celebrate the physical side of life. Since the Salvation Army sought to reach the working classes, it wanted to adopt forms that resonated with this section of society. Salvationists were also following the lead of more respectable religious societies, which began to speak of the need for aggression and combativeness against sin, and to compose hymns with military imagery to describe the spiritual life.[42] On the other hand, Booth now possessed a convenient model through which to strengthen his totalitarian hold over his followers. The wider society was slowly moving in the direction of democratic reform, but Booth was moving away from the modest egalitarian beginnings of his Christian Mission. A hierarchical system gave him the kind of vehicle he needed to consolidate his position as leader, as well as a structure that would command the obedience of those below him.

The third and final phase of the Christian Mission's transformation into a Salvation Army concerned the need to recognize this new self-identity legally. The Foundation Deed of 1878, coupled with minor clarifications in 1880, sought to record the organization's history, purposes and theology.[43] Even more importantly, it legitimized William Booth's power. He was recognized by statute as the founder and sole head of the Salvation Army. All future policies, structures, appointments and procedures were in the hands of him alone. Surprisingly, however, the Foundation Deed of 1878 did not include any references to female ministry. This represented a striking departure from the organization's own constitutional heritage. Unlike the 1870 declaration, the 1878 Deed was silent on the subject of women's ministerial rights. Although women as well as men had lost any right to vote under the new structure, there was nothing of a legal nature preventing Booth from protecting the right of women to preach in the organization. Given his growing commitment to female ministry, and his wife's strong convictions on this subject, why were these ministerial rights left out of the new Deed?

Douglas Clarke, an Army theologian, has suggested that this omission merely bore witness to the fact that women had secured a permanent place in the life of the religious body, and therefore this did not need special mention in the Foundation Deed of 1878.[44] Given the influx of young women to the organization between 1877 and 1878, this explanation may have some credence. At the same time, however, such reasoning overlooks some important facts. For one, William Booth never offered any such rationale, and was in fact confused about this matter. He would often boast of women's legal rights in the organization, and make reference to the protection of these rights in the Army's constitution, when in fact such legal rights no longer existed. Moreover, if Booth had ever felt that female ministry was an established part of the organization, why did he continue to remind his officers of the need to uphold these principles?[45] In any case, legal rights of any kind would have been difficult to protect under the new constitution, given its legitimization of Booth's growing autocracy. The new structure did not give women a democratic forum in which to address possible violations of their public access to ministry, whether legally enshrined or not. The response to possible infringements of their ministerial opportunities would now be in the hands of William Booth and his predominantly male leadership regime.

✤ General Booth's Hallelujah Lasses

Initially, at least, the autocratic foundations being laid by Booth did not appear to hurt Salvationist women. There was no legal recognition of their rights, but the Army's first manual, entitled *Orders and Regulations for The Salvation Army*, began with a remarkable statement on gender equality: "[T]he Army refuses to make any difference between men and women as to rank, authority and duties, but opens the highest positions to women as well as to men."[46] By late 1878 the organization also had a growing number of young female evangelists, and they soon made up almost half of the Salvation Army's field personnel. These women, increasingly known as Hallelujah Lasses or officers, were sent out in systematic fashion to establish Army facilities throughout Britain and the world. Such success did not go unnoticed by William Booth, who boasted that "the prosperity of the work in every respect just appears more precisely at the very times when female preachers are being allowed the fullest opportunity."[47] When invited to address the Wesleyan Conference in 1880, Booth reiterated this viewpoint by arguing that female ministry was one of the key reasons for the Salvation Army's progress.[48] This kind of success was difficult to ignore, and Booth was willing to use any productive method to win the world for God. His salvific pragmatism, coupled with the influence of his wife, allowed the organization's female officers to promulgate salvation at home and abroad.

These pioneering efforts, which also included the work of many capable male officers, led the Salvation Army to grow substantially between 1878 and 1886. Although the organization may have been beset by decline in the East End of London, as Norman Murdoch has argued, it was expanding rapidly elsewhere.[49] In the United Kingdom alone, the Salvation Army moved into numerous towns and cities in the English provinces, Scotland, Wales and Northern Ireland. By the end of 1886, the Salvation Army had 2,271 officers and 1,039 corps in these areas, which represented a net increase of 2,183 officers and 989 corps since June 1878. Expansion also characterized the foreign field: it began with the United States, and went on to include Australia, France, Canada, India, New Zealand, Sweden and South Africa. At the close of 1886, the organization had 1,921 officers and 747 corps abroad.[50] The Army had become an international concern, and increasingly began to attract the attention of those in both the upper and lower classes.

This publicity, however, was not always positive. During these formative years the Salvation Army encountered a fair amount of persecution from both respectable and less respectable circles. Elite Victorians usually confined their displeasure to verbal and printed assaults upon the Army's practices.[51] A good deal of this opposition arose from the organization's invasion of public streets, where the Army created a commotion with its brass bands, flags and aggressive witness. In more than one town Salvation Army officers ran into trouble with local authorities, who often charged them with disturbing the peace. Middle-class opponents of the organization were also critical of the roles given to its Hallelujah Lasses, who were considered to transgress public spaces by parading down streets and preaching in public.[52] Working-class protest, however, tended to be more violent in nature. Certain elements within the labouring classes did not appreciate the Army's condemnation of their lifestyle, which included drinking, smoking and fighting.[53] The Army's puritanical theology was seen by some as an attempt to refashion their morality in more acceptable ways. This kind of hostility was especially apparent in the south of England, where "Skeleton Armies" were formed from working-class and local brewery groups to attack the Salvationist newcomers physically.

Success and persecution soon led the Salvation Army to expand its bureaucracy and further define its theological convictions. At a structural level, the organization kept control of its explosive growth by splitting up certain areas into divisions, each of which was supervised by a divisional officer directly responsible to William Booth.[54] In addition to this bureaucratic layer, the organization decided in 1880 to establish training homes for female and male converts who wished to engage in full-time ministry as officers. These training depots, initially accommodating between twelve and forty-six students, provided prospective officers with a practical and theological education, which was often compressed into just a few weeks.[55] Meanwhile, the Army continued to increase the staff and departments associated with its international headquarters in London. By 1891 this central facility had almost 600 personnel and over twelve departments.[56] At a theological level, the Salvation Army felt an increasing need to elaborate upon the simple doctrines recorded in its 1878 Foundation Deed. A hostile public might be more sympathetic to the organization if it understood its beliefs, and cadets entering the training homes required some theological knowledge for future ministry. Consequently, in 1881 William Booth published a small book entitled *The Doctrines and Discipline of The Salvation Army*. This modest document laid out the organization's convictions about the deity, as well as addressing distinctive evangelical themes like sin, salvation and holiness.[57]

One of the book's additional purposes was to articulate the Salvation Army's justification for female ministry.[58] William Booth devoted a section to this issue, and largely reiterated the biblical arguments that had been put forward by his wife and other evangelical exegetes. Booth began by arguing that St. Paul's injunction to the Corinthian Christians regarding women's silence in the church (1 Cor 14:34) referred only to their exclusion from debates, such as those that often took place in the Jewish assemblies. He did not believe that this passage was meant to keep women from preaching or testifying for Christ, since Paul described elsewhere the manner in which they could do so (1 Cor 11). Incidentally, Booth did not deal with 1 Timothy 2:11-12, another passage often used to exclude women from preaching. Having dealt with some of the supposed prohibitions of this practice, he went on to cite the numerous women who had been leaders and preachers in the Bible, thereby suggesting that such a practice was authorized biblically (Judg 4:4,10-11; 1 Kgs 22:14-20; Acts 21:8-9; Rom 14:12; 16:3; Phil 4:3). The book also made reference to Christ's resurrection commissioning of Mary Magdalene and "the other Mary" to share the gospel (Matt 28:9-10), and the outpouring of the Holy Spirit upon women at Pentecost (Acts 2:16,18). Booth concluded his defence of female ministry by alluding to Galatians 3:28: "The Holy Spirit ... states that there is neither male nor female, but that all are one in Christ Jesus, thereby affirming that, in the privileges, duties, and responsibilities of Christ's Kingdom, all differences on account of sex are abolished."[59]

While it is not clear that the foregoing appeal to Galatians 3:28 was taken to mean the abolition of all sexual differences in the secular realm, such a position did suggest that women and men were to enjoy equality in an ecclesiastical context. Given the domination of religious offices by men in other churches, such a declaration held radical implications. In the earliest days of the Salvation Army, this biblical principle was not only used to justify female preaching, but was also employed to sanction the administering of Communion by female officers.[60] George Scott Railton, an early associate of William Booth, drew explicit attention to Galatians 3:28 when asked to defend this highly unusual occurrence. He and others contended that if all were one in Christ, as this verse claims, then gender was no bar to the exercise of religious rituals. Sadly, however, the Salvation Army was to abandon this expression of equality by January 1883, when it set aside the traditional sacraments. In an age fraught with liturgical controversies, especially within the Anglican Church, William Booth saw this kind of ritualism as potentially divisive. Even more importantly, Catherine Booth was convinced that ceremonialism was the bane of the Christian church, believing that it caused people to seek empty forms rather than inward grace.[61] While perhaps the first Englishwomen to administer Communion, Army Lasses enjoyed this distinction for only a brief period.

The public roles given to female officers and soldiers in the Army proved to be a hindrance when the Church of England proposed a union with the Salvation Army in 1882.[62] A few Anglican bishops were sympathetic to the Army's work and were anxious to capitalize on its seeming success with the poor. These churchmen hoped that Booth would agree to place the Salvation Army under the auspices of the Anglican establishment. The fact that William Booth was even willing to enter into such talks suggests that he held the Church of England in some esteem. Even so, negotiations towards such a union were guarded at best, with issues like female ministry proving to be formidable obstacles. Church officials were unwilling to allow female officers to engage in prominent public roles such as preaching and administering the sacraments. These Anglican clerics simply held out the possibility that some Salvationist women could hold the position of deaconess, which had been introduced into the Anglican Church in 1861.[63] Deaconesses were paid a salary, but they were not allowed to preach or to take on priestly functions. Such a role was clearly inferior to the opportunities available to women in the Salvation Army. Given William Booth's love of authority, it is doubtful whether female ministry was the primary obstacle to any potential union with the Anglican Church, but it was clearly one major concern, and by early 1883 both sides had come to the conclusion that a merger would not be feasible.

Some indication of the possibilities that lay before Salvationist women was apparent with the publication of William Booth's first manual for officers in 1886. This book, entitled *Orders and Regulations for Field Officers of The Salvation Army*, reiterated the Army's official stance on women's rights. Although the book reflected an obvious androcentric bias—masculine pronouns were assumed to include men and women—it did express an official commitment to the equality of the sexes in the assignment of Army responsibilities, ranks and power: "In The Army men and women are alike eligible for all ranks[,] authorities, and duties, all positions being open to both alike. In these Orders, therefore, the words 'man,' 'he,' or 'his' must be understood to refer to persons of either sex unless otherwise indicated or evidently impossible."[64] This professed allegiance to gender parity in the offices and responsibilities of the organization was similar to Booth's 1878 statement on the subject, and clearly went beyond Booth's theological defence of female ministry, because it was less likely to be construed as a kind of spiritualized equality centred around the pulpit. Words like "rank" and "authority" carried secular overtones, and suggested that it was possible for female officers to acquire substantial power and status in the organization. In theory, women were being offered opportunities far in advance of those available to earlier Methodist female preachers, who had never been permitted to assume positions of authority. Altogether, this declaration seemed to indicate that Booth was pledging to foster a wide range of practices free of gender discrimination.

Unfortunately, however, there is little indication that William Booth ever really fostered a broad interpretation of the 1886 statement. The Salvation

William Booth. Courtesy of The Salvation Army George Scott Railton Heritage Centre, Toronto.

Army engaged in practices that clearly violated the tenor of this manifesto. This was notably the case with married female officers, who possessed a dubious status within the organization. In the early 1880s, for instance, these women were expected to be involved in the work of the corps or preaching stations, but their names were not recorded in the officer statistics. These women were supposedly joint officers with their husbands, but in practice officer rights resided primarily with the husband and only secondarily with the wife. In addition, the husband received the farewell orders when appointments were changed as well as any available salaries. A married female officer in the Army most often derived her status and economic support from her spouse. Another instance of discrimination lay in the Army's policy of paying single male officers between 15 and 40 percent more than their single female counterparts. Like their peers in other vocations, and consistent with the practices of earlier sectarian Methodist groups, female officers were expected to make do with less. All of these circumstances raised questions about the Army's willingness to pursue policies consistent with its radical stance on gender equality.[65]

Inequities in the area of salaries did not seem to trouble William Booth, as he never once addressed the matter. At the same time, however, he did express some concern over the problematic status of married female officers within this religious body. At a May 1888 meeting he identified the heart of the issue when he observed that "nearly every week there are two officers turned into one.... [B]y some strange mistake in our organization, the woman doesn't count."[66] This was indeed a troubling matter, because the Army's officers, who had often joined the organization during their teens and early twenties, were beginning to marry each other at a rapid rate. To complicate things further, the Salvation Army's sectarianism allowed officers to marry only other officers or soldiers, a practice that left fewer and fewer single female officers in the ranks.[67] In light of these developments, Booth proclaimed that married female officers should be counted the same as—perhaps even more than—their spouses. Such rhetoric aside, however, he did little to change the problematic status of married women, and it soon became apparent that his own policies and practices discriminated against them.

Throughout the late 1870s and the 1880s, William Booth's overall treatment of women in the Army was less than clear. On the one hand, some of his policies, practices and commentary seemed to suggest a commitment to equitable and liberating roles and identities for Salvationist women. His encouragement of female ministry, occasional willingness to put women over men, the 1878 and 1886 position statements, and some of his written comments on the subject of women were all trends in this direction. On the other hand, his other policies, actions and attitudes were vague at best and oppressive at worst for Army women. The exclusion of women's rights from the Army's constitution, inequitable pay scales and the problematic status of married female officers all seemed to suggest limitations upon and inconsistencies in William Booth's understanding of women's place in the organization. Given his autocratic hold over Salvationists, not to mention Army policies and practices, these problematic tendencies were sure to persist in the years ahead.

❖ Continuing Problems on the Gender Front, 1890-1912

William Booth's views on women continued to be difficult to reconcile with official Army principles after the death of his wife in 1890. In an address given in late 1890, Booth implied that women were the weaker sex, different from and subordinate to men. He felt that the Salvation Army was in need of the "more tender, feminine side of human character, as well as the more robust and masculine element" and that woman had "taken her place with man in the new kingdom as a helpmeet for him."[68] The emphasis upon a man's "robust" nature and a woman's "tender" disposition betrayed the traditional polarity between masculine strength and feminine emotion, as well as the Victorian notion of sexual difference. Such a viewpoint was typical of the period, but it was contrary to Booth's 1881 commentary on Galatians 3:28, where he claimed that oneness in Christ's kingdom rendered all sex-based distinctions meaningless. Booth's use of the word "helpmeet" was also troubling, since it was a word that symbolized the biblical subordination of a woman to a man. Just how this arrangement was going to allow women to have equal access to authoritative roles in the Salvation Army was left unanswered. Yet, in order for women to assume these kinds of responsibilities, they were going to have to function as more than mere helpers for men. Booth's remarks on gender revealed that he had never abandoned his earlier assumptions about sexual difference.

Further evidence of William Booth's vague position on women was contained in his influential 1890 publication entitled *In Darkest England and the Way Out*. While known chiefly for its advocacy of city, farm and overseas colonies for England's poor or "submerged tenth," this book also revealed Booth's attitudes towards women. It was a social commentary that illustrated both progressive and conservative views on women's roles in Victorian society. Perhaps the best example of Booth's advanced views on the subject of gender were found in his comments on prostitution. He criticized a society that placed the most burdensome consequences of prostitution on women, while leaving the male perpetrators unscathed: "The male sinner does not, by the mere fact of his sin, find himself in a worse position in obtaining employment, in finding a home, or even in securing a wife.... It is an immense addition to the infamy of this vice in man that its consequences have to be borne almost exclusively by woman."[69] Booth's critique was essentially an attack on the Victorian sexual double standard. This ideology held virginity to be the goal of both sexes, but "women were punished more severely than men for infringing it since, unlike men, they were said to lack sexual desires, and their action could, therefore, result only from their vanity or their greed for money."[70] Prostitutes, in particular, were the ultimate female symbols of sexual transgression, and considered to be "fallen women." Although Booth did not reject the image of fallen women, and had Rescue Homes to help them, he was willing to condemn the inequitable consequences of this punitive system and to draw attention to the sinfulness of the men who preyed upon these women.[71]

Other parts of *In Darkest England*, however, were more conservative on the subject of women.[72] In particular, Booth was annoyed with the Victorian educational system, because he felt that it was failing to train future mothers in the domestic arts of baking and washing clothes. He also blamed the factory system in England, contending that it destroyed domestic virtues and feminine duties. Women in factories, he noted, did not know how to bake, wash clothes and sew. Booth considered these "feminine" skills to be an indispensable part of his emigration scheme to alleviate poverty, and a necessary complement to men's abilities in the area of farming. At the same time, he implied that the women's rights movement, with its push to expand female opportunities beyond the home, was somehow flawed: "Talk about woman's rights, one of the first of woman's rights is to be trained to her trade, to be queen of her household, and mother of her children."[73] This kind of commentary suggested that women's chief responsibility lay in the private realm of the home, centred on conventionally female tasks. Views of this nature would prove problematic for Salvationist women.

One obvious question arises from William Booth's remarks about a woman's role in the home: if he believed that a woman's primary place was in the home, how did he reconcile such views with his wife's public role as a female preacher? The answer to this question was provided by Booth himself in an important address that he gave in 1891. Speaking before a large audience in the Australian city of Melbourne, he stressed that Catherine had in fact never put her preaching responsibilities before her domestic duties:

> She ministered ever to my needs.... She looked after my home; her public duties never interfered with those at home. In this relation

I never met with any one who was her equal; she could do everything from the bottom to the top of a house.... I mention this because
some people have a notion that when a woman is engaged in
public work she is bound to neglect her fireside duties. My
darling wife was a contradiction to such a notion.[74]

These comments underscored the double standard that women had to contend with in the Army and in the broader society: women who wished to work
outside the home still had to carry the bulk of domestic responsibilities.
Furthermore, Booth saw Catherine's role as that of a helpmeet rather than of
an equal, as he emphasized that she looked after his needs and his house.
Even more troubling was his suggestion that female ministry should not come
at the expense of a woman's obligations in the home.

It was within this context that Booth went on to praise his wife's efforts
as a preacher and role model for other Christian women. Of even greater significance, however, was Booth's recollection of his earliest arguments with
Catherine on the subject of sexual equality. As he told the Melbourne audience: "I had a sort of notion, *which I hold still to some extent*, that woman
was in some senses inferior to man, though in other senses his superior. I
used to put it in this phraseology: that women have a fibre more in their
hearts, and a cell less in their brains"[75] [italics mine]. Contrary to the views
of Salvationist historiographers, popular writers and some recent scholarly
research, William Booth's revelation here casts doubt upon the assumption
that he was ever completely won over to his late wife's position on women's
equality.[76] It may have been true that he had changed his initial views on
female ministry by 1859, but this evidence indicates that a similar development on the subject of sexual equality had not taken place. Obviously, he still
embraced certain views on nineteenth-century sexual difference, and he was
not completely willing to concede that a woman was equal to a man.

The ambiguities surrounding sexual equality in the Army were not merely
the result of Booth's adherence to the Victorian notion of sexual difference.
What was also working against any encouragement of gender equality and
liberation was the Salvation Army's autocratic and patriarchal structure.
Despite the fact that democratic tendencies were spreading throughout late
nineteenth-century England, the Salvation Army's locus of power was increasingly in the hands of William Booth. Asked to defend these totalitarian tendencies during an 1894 interview, Booth likened the Army to a family: "I stand
in the relation of Father to my people;—the children will resemble their
parents. My position and my duty have made me their instructor;—my
teaching has been, and still is, accepted, followed, and repeated until it
reaches every soldier in the most distant corps."[77] Even if Booth was over-

stating his power over Salvationists, it is highly significant that he described the Army's structure in such patriarchal language. Booth was the Army's father, and each soldier was his spiritual son or daughter. This "father-child" symbolism denoted a relationship of unequal power: childlike soldiers were dependent on Booth the father figure. He was the benevolent patriarch, seeking to guide and instruct those below him. Just how such an arrangement might support gender autonomy and equality within the Salvation Army was uncertain at best.

What allowed William Booth to justify this paternalistic social order? Part of the explanation obviously lay in his charismatic personality and seeming success as a leader. Less evident, but equally important, was how the doctrine of the Holy Spirit served to support Booth's hold over soldiers and officers. He explained the loyalty of his soldiery by referring to the influence of the Holy Spirit upon the Army and his leadership: "The loyalty of my Soldiers implies no mental servility, no soul-bondage. They believe in being influenced by the same Holy Spirit that influences their General, and in being led by the leader whom God shall raise up for them; and believing that God has raised me up to be their Leader, it is their joy to accept my direction."[78] Booth believed that his autocratic control of the Salvation Army was ordained by God, much as medieval monarchs had justified their reigns. Moreover, he implied that submission and obedience to the Holy Spirit meant submission and obedience to William Booth. For the Army founder, there could be no questioning of his authority, for it was ultimately derived from a sacred source.[79] To disobey William Booth was to rebel against God, since Booth felt that God had chosen him to lead the Salvation Army. There was, therefore, no strict separation between the authority of Booth and that of the divine. This, a striking illustration of religious social control, enabled William Booth to reinforce the paternalistic structure of the Army. At the same time, however, it raised doubts about the possibility of personal freedom and gender equality within the organization.

Additional concerns about the possibility of gender equality and freedom within the Salvation Army centred around the increasingly problematic status of married female officers. In late 1896, William Booth tackled the problem of their declining public presence in the organization. Once again his comments on the subject were vague. On the one hand, he criticized the practice among male officers of "relegat[ing] their wives to little more than the discharge of their household duties ... or at best only us[ing] them as mere subordinates."[80] Calling this situation unjust, Booth urged officers to consider their wives as friends and to provide them with "fair platform opportunities." On the other hand, Booth contributed to the ambiguous position of married female officers by identifying them here as merely "wives." In contrast, in this article he consistently referred to the men as "officers" or by rank (i.e., Captain).[81] The implication was that married female officers had less status than their officer husbands. Furthermore, Booth raised additional doubts about marital equality in the Salvation Army by giving the husbands the responsibility for finding their wives more public work. In spite of his 1888 commitment to counting women more than men, Booth demonstrated the reverse in practice. His confusing comments here only reinforced the uncertainties surrounding women's roles and identity in the Army.

The place of senior married female officers within the Salvation Army was also unclear, as was manifestly demonstrated by the publication of William Booth's policy guide for high-ranking officers in 1899. Under the title *Orders and Regulations for Territorial Commissioners and Chief Secretaries of The Salvation Army*, this manual described, among other things, the kinds of responsibilities that a husband and wife could undertake in senior leadership. Its major ambiguity centred around the opportunities it afforded women. The book allowed for the possibility of both spouses holding jointly the rank of commissioner, but it prohibited such an arrangement for lower-ranking chief secretaries and their wives.[82] A chief secretary's wife was to derive her rank from her husband (i.e., Mrs. Colonel, etc.), and she was not allowed to share "the duties of her husband, in the sense of being appointed joint Secretary with him."[83] Why did Booth consider equality between spouses acceptable in the former case, but unacceptable in the latter instance? The answer seems to lie with his family. Since only Booth daughters ever benefited from the opportunity of holding the position of commissioner jointly with their husbands, it is not unfair to conclude that Booth merely wanted to justify officially a practice that was common within his own family. Clearly, if Booth had been committed to gender equality, he would have allowed those other than his own children to hold the rank of joint commissioner, and he would have promoted the equitable sharing of the chief secretary's role. Yet, he never showed a propensity to do either.

When Booth wrote to his soldiers on the subject of female ministry in September 1901, his thinking once again exhibited a great deal of ambiguity.[84] A portion of Booth's letter seemed to support a very wide interpretation of gender equality. Quoting from his *Orders and Regulations for Staff Officers*, Booth referred to women's right to hold any office in the organization, including the position of General. To back up his point, he stressed that "married officers' wives" should assume more prominence at the corps level, especially on the platform. Referring to platform ministry, where Salvationists preached and led services, Booth went on to say: "Here at least shall there be

Liberty, Equality, and Fraternity. For on that blessed sanctified elevation there is neither male nor female. You are all one in Christ Jesus."[85] These latter comments, prefaced with the words "here at least," conveyed a much more restrictive understanding of equality, and seemed at odds with Booth's bolder declaration. He seemed to be suggesting that equality beyond the circumscribed boundaries of the platform was less of a priority. When viewed side by side, these remarks were ambiguous at best. Was Booth tacitly approving of an equality largely limited to the platform, or was he in full support of widespread opportunities for women, whether soldiers or officers?

In a letter that he addressed to soldiers two months later, Booth seemed to be leaning towards the former viewpoint, an equality limited largely to the corps platform. This correspondence, entitled "More About Women's Rights," focused on women's right to speak, sing and pray in public. After praising the blessings associated with this kind of ministry in the Army and in his own life, Booth indicated that the responsibility for exercising these gifts lay with women themselves: "We have by God's blessing opened the door of opportunity for woman, and made the platform for the exercise of her gifts. It is now for the sisters themselves to claim their privilege, to enter the door, and to fill the position."[86] Booth finished his pastoral letter with an exhortation to mothers to teach their children—especially the boys—the "duty and pleasure of treating woman as the equal of man."[87] But from all accounts, it seems that the kind of equality he had in mind was largely of an ecclesiastical nature, limited primarily to the pulpit. This itself may have represented a significant expansion of a woman's sphere in the church, but it was a far cry from the kind of egalitarian vision laid out in Booth's doctrinal and regulatory manuals.

Beyond the parameters of platform ministry, equality was an elusive concept in the early Army. It was especially difficult to define within the marriage relationship. On the one hand, William Booth seemed to promote egalitarian marriage relationships. In 1902, he published an important book on marital, domestic and practical affairs entitled *Religion for Every Day*. This lengthy volume was clear in its condemnation of marital arrangements that turned a wife into her husband's property or servant. Booth argued that such practices were wrong because they ignored women's capabilities, forced women to be subservient to men and led children to be disrespectful to their mothers. In place of such oppressive marriage arrangements, Booth advocated partnership marriages based upon equality: "The husband must regard his wife as his equal, and treat her accordingly.... The husband is responsible for giving his wife a position in the home answering to this equality.... If she is his equal, let him treat her as he would like others to treat him."[88]

With this kind of declaration, Booth seemed to be supporting enlightened marriages grounded upon sexual equality.

On the other hand, however, Booth also believed in a husband's headship over his wife. His acceptance of this view, which he felt was rooted in scripture and common sense, seriously undermined any notion he had of egalitarian domestic relations. A husband was to assume complete, albeit loving, control over his household:

> The head of the home is responsible for its good government. He must settle the rules and practices which are to prevail in it. While he gives every possible and kind consideration to his wife's wishes, it is his duty to regulate what goes on there, the visitors who are to be welcomed, the books which are to be read, the money that is to be spent, and many other important, if smaller, matters which will occur to all who have homes of their own. The true wife will accept this principle.[89]

A "true wife" was expected to obey her husband unconditionally. While Booth claimed to abhor marital practices that placed women in a submissive and demeaning light, his kinder version of marriage (i.e., rooted in love) had the same effects upon women. For Booth, this kind of patriarchal lordship also included the husband's mastery over his wife's body. However he wished to express this arrangement, it was a model based upon male dominance and female subservience, and reflective of Booth's continued allegiance to evangelical biblicism, with its scriptural admonitions on wifely submission. In any case, this explicit endorsement of male headship made Booth's notion of partnership marriages rather vacuous.

Male headship within Salvationist families had ramifications at the corps, administrative and constitutional levels of the Army. A married woman's role in the corps tended to be dictated more by her husband's position on female ministry than by any official policies on the subject. Moreover, apart from William Booth's own married children, officer couples rarely received an appointment where the wife held a position equal to or higher than her husband's.[90] As indicated earlier, a married man typically received the official appointment while his wife was usually left with a subordinate position. The male headship principle was notably evident as well in the 1904 amendment to the Salvation Army's constitution, which called for the creation of a High Council to elect a new General in the event of a serving leader's unfitness for office. This modification blatantly discriminated against married female officers. Senior female officers holding commands or commissions in the same country as their spouses could be members of the Council, but voting privileges favoured the husband: "One vote ... shall be given by the husband as he may think fit if he alone is present or both are present and shall be given by the wife as she may think fit only if she alone is present."[91] This amendment was a far cry from the Christian Mission's 1870 constitution, which had given women the right to participate in and vote upon all affairs affecting the organization.

What further threatened women's fair treatment in relation to men was William Booth's acceptance of both equality and difference. From the one direction, he encouraged his male staff to treat women as equal partners in the work of the organization, and he urged them not to allow their female colleagues to be kept back on account of their gender.[92] Near the end of his life, Booth left the impression that such advice had been followed, claiming that the Salvation Army had "welcomed [woman] to the platform and to the council chamber [and had] set before her an open door to every position of power and usefulness in [its] ranks."[93] From the other direction, however, Booth continued to espouse views which indicated that women were different from and inferior to men. In his mind, a man possessed superior strength and decision-making abilities, while women held a greater capacity for love, endurance and perception.[94] In particular, a married man was called upon to "champion [his wife's] interests, fight her battles, watch over her soul, and even die, if need be, as Christ died, on her behalf."[95] This type of chivalry revealed a relationship of masculine dominance and female dependence, which was only reinforced by Booth's tendency to portray women simply as wives, mothers and daughters.[96] Moreover, while the traits of love, endurance and perception were human values that could have been put to good use in the Army's leadership, Booth did not adequately acknowledge their place in the realm of decision-making. By identifying these characteristics solely with women, Booth marginalized female officers and devalued these attributes. In fact, he advocated the creation of special posts for women so that they could fulfil their "unique" abilities.[97] Booth's gender ideology of equal but different was self-defeating and translated into concrete inequality at all levels of the organization.

Overall, Booth's ambiguous views on women were reflective of his theological and cultural background. Theologically, he had moved from opposition and indifference to an open encouragement of female preaching, testifying and praying in public. True to his revivalistic convictions, which had been deepened upon marriage, Booth sought any means, however bold, to attract sinners to hear the gospel message. Women were needed alongside men to publish the message of the gospel to a world bound for hell. His early exposure to female preachers, and subsequent marriage to an outstanding evangelist, solidified his position on the subject. At the same time, however,

Booth remained part of a tradition that held clear views on male headship within the home. Biblical injunctions on a wife's responsibility to submit to her husband (e.g., Col 3:18; Eph 5:22-24) were still valid, even if those that seemed to enjoin her silence in the church (e.g., 1 Cor 14:34-36) were not. Booth's attitudes and behaviour towards women suggested that female ministry, while certainly valid, was subordinate to the husband's rulership in the home. Even when married women did assume a public role, it was usually as wives, mothers and daughters rather than as autonomous individuals fully equal to men. Moreover, any authority that women occasionally possessed in the organization was increasingly curtailed by the patriarchal and autocratic structure put in place by William Booth. This authoritarian framework was only strengthened by Booth's assumption that he alone had been chosen by God to lead the Salvation Army. There was little room to address infringements of gender equality within such an environment.

Any professed commitment to women's equality alongside men in the denomination was further undermined by William Booth's acceptance of certain cultural beliefs about gender. Here, in particular, he embraced the three pillars of Victorian ideal womanhood: (1) sexual difference, through his conviction that women possessed unique abilities and responsibilities; (2) separate spheres, since he emphasized a woman's special duties as a mother within the home and as an adjunct to her husband; and (3) women's moral superiority, because he portrayed women as angelic beings who possessed a great capacity for love and virtue.[98] Booth's adherence to these gender-based differences suggests that his views on sexual equality had changed very little from those of his youth. He still justified gender-specific distinctions, even if his appeal to passages like Galatians 3:28 contradicted this. Such a viewpoint helped to foster conventional images of women, including that of domestic mother and submissive wife. These cultural assumptions, when coupled with Booth's theological beliefs about masculine authority, ensured that women would experience little equality beyond the pulpit.

The scholarly neglect of William Booth's understanding of gender has given rise to uncritical conclusions about what he accomplished for the women of the Salvation Army. It has been assumed that he constructed a liberating environment for female officers, and promoted egalitarian partnerships in the home and in the public sphere. As the story goes, he was "won over" to complete equality between the sexes upon his marriage. In reality, his views on gender and equality were much more problematic and complex than this mythology suggests. This becomes apparent, however, only when we pay as much attention to the views of men as we do to those of women. With this in mind, the next chapter continues to explore the masculine side of the gender equation by looking at how Salvationist men understood femininity between the 1880s and 1920s. For instance, how did their Victorian background and evangelical convictions shape their perceptions about and behaviour towards female officers? To what degree were their thoughts and practices conducive to female ministry and leadership in the Salvation Army, as well as consistent with the organization's avowed commitment to sexual equality? The answers to these questions form the substance of chapter 4.

A Gendered Geography:
Male Salvationists and Women

BRITISH WOMEN FOUGHT for and won a number of significant economic and political victories between the late Victorian period and the 1920s, including control over their personal assets, suffrage, and access to higher education and the professions.[1] Although these advancements represented important milestones for British women, they did not immediately alter the average person's beliefs about femininity. Victorian and evangelical assumptions about sexual difference and separate spheres for men and women continued to be espoused in numerous circles, especially as the working classes increasingly absorbed societal expectations about "mothercraft" and "housewifery" by the early twentieth century. Notwithstanding their brief experience with traditionally male jobs during the First World War, most women throughout this period were defined in terms of marriage and motherhood.[2] Poor pay, limited employment opportunities and marriage bars—designed to prevent women from combining marriage and a career—only reinforced the dominant conviction that women belonged in the home, looking after the needs of their husbands and children. Consequently, women's legislative emancipation did not necessarily entail freedom from restrictive feminine expectations and conventional roles.

The themes of advancement and restriction also figured prominently in the experience of female Salvation Army officers during this period. On the one hand, they possessed the right to preach and to hold authoritative offices in the organization, even the position of General.[3] The denomination's official regulations and pronouncements claimed that gender was not a determining factor in an officer's advancement through the ranks. On the other hand, women encountered beliefs and practices that sought to circumscribe their public position in the organization. Cultural and theological assumptions, working in conjunction with institutional policies, ensured that the

Salvation Army's expansion to six continents did not coincide with an enlarge-
ment of female roles and responsibilities. This chapter highlights how masculine perceptions about gender, ministry and doctrine created an uncertain
environment for women. One individual who receives special attention is
George Scott Railton, since he is often credited with helping to expand the
opportunities available to Army women. Consideration is also given to how
the Salvation Army's important theological doctrines often failed to foster a
climate conducive to female experience. Finally, the chapter looks briefly at
the institutional policies that discriminated against female officers.

❖ George Scott Railton and Women

One early figure who contributed a great deal to the emerging Salvation Army
was George Scott Railton, the son of Methodist missionaries. Railton was first
made aware of the organization through his brother Launcelot, who met
William Booth while recuperating at a facility for Methodist clergy with health
problems. Launcelot told his brother that Booth needed an assistant for his
Mission in East London. Upon reading the booklet *How to Reach the Masses
with the Gospel*, in which William Booth outlined his strategy for spreading
the gospel among the poor, George Scott Railton headed to London in October
1872 and joined the fledgling Mission. By late 1873 Railton had become the
General Secretary of the Christian Mission and was living in the Booth home.
For the next several years, Railton was to remain within the inner circle of the
evolving Army's leadership, helping to shape the ministry and theology of
the organization. His stature among the Booths was apparent when he was
chosen to officially open the Salvation Army's work in the United States in
1880. Even though Railton became somewhat marginalized after the mid-
1880s, due in large part to his criticisms of William Booth's social and fundrais-
ing schemes, he continued to shape the organization in countless ways prior
to his death in 1913.[4]

According to various writers, one of the chief contributions that George
Scott Railton made to the Christian Mission and the Salvation Army lay in
his support of women's equal opportunities in ministry.[5] Bramwell Booth,
the second General of the Army, was perhaps the earliest promoter of this
viewpoint, suggesting that Railton was the key influence behind the placement of some women over men during the early days of the Mission. Years
later, biographer Bernard Watson went even further by making the claim that
Railton "was a leading protagonist, perhaps the decisive influence, in caus-
ing William Booth to give women equal place with men in Salvation Army
commands."[6] Even though Watson overestimated Railton's impact in this

area, since Catherine Booth was clearly the decisive figure behind female ministry in the Salvation Army, this kind of claim underscores the extent to which George Scott Railton has been construed as a liberator of Salvationist women. What is surprising, however, is how little has been done to examine the strength of these statements. Much more light needs to be shed on Railton's thinking and behaviour in this sphere before these judgements can be accepted. As a way of better understanding Railton's views on women, this section examines his beliefs and practices in the areas of female ministry, sexual equality and domesticity.

FEMALE MINISTRY

Four related elements lay behind George Scott Railton's position on female ministry. First and foremost, his own personal history predisposed him to accept the legitimacy of women preachers. After a failed attempt to bring the gospel to the Moors in northern Africa in 1868, Railton returned to England and began work in the lead mines of Cornwall. While in the Cornish region, he began to worship with the Bible Christians, a Methodist offshoot with a long history of female preaching. Even though the role of women in this sect had declined significantly by the late 1860s, there were still a few women preachers in this area, which was the birthplace of the Bible Christian Connexion. There can be little doubt that these seasoned evangelists had a positive impact upon Railton, who was always open to anything that would advance the cause of the gospel. The continuing influence of the Bible Christians upon Railton was apparent years later, when he argued that God had owned the labours of women preachers throughout church history. This kind of argument had been used by the founder of the Bible Christians, William O'Bryan, who justified female ministry by pointing to the divine blessing that accompanied the efforts of pious women.[7]

A second distinctive element that shaped George Scott Railton's understanding of female ministry was evangelical revivalism. British Methodism, in particular, owed a great deal to this revivalistic ethos, which not only played a role in John Wesley's Methodism, but also lay behind the formation of the Primitive Methodists and the Bible Christians. Much of this evangelical enthusiasm had been brought to Britain from America, where a series of emotional and protracted frontier camp meetings had spread the revivalistic message to respectable churches on the east coast in the early nineteenth century. This spirit of renewal was transported to Britain throughout the nineteenth century, when American evangelists from Lorenzo Dow to Charles Finney and Phoebe Palmer helped to revive certain sections of conservative Protestantism.

One of the central features of this revivalism was the use of novel measures to attract the masses to Christ. Finney, in particular, believed that attention and action were essential to the spread of the gospel: sinners had to be made aware of salvation, and it was the duty of all pious Christians to seek out the unsaved, presenting them with a fresh and dramatic expression of the good news.[8] As Finney knew quite well, this type of approach had been mastered by Methodist offshoots like the Bible Christians, which sought whatever means possible to win others for the kingdom. For those with a revivalistic spirit, these measures included female testifying and preaching in front of mixed audiences.[9]

George Scott Railton absorbed these revivalistic principles from the Bible Christians and the writings of Charles Finney. He shared their spirit of innovation and salvific activism, all of which he took with him to the Christian Mission in 1872. In one of his early articles in the Mission's periodical, Railton emphasized the importance of unconventional methods, arguing that the millions of people dead in their sins needed to be awakened by an "earthquake of sensation."[10] An evangelical passion for souls was clearly manifest in Railton's musings on the subject, and the urgent tone of his message suggested that he was open to any practices that would accomplish the salvation of those headed for hell. Not surprisingly, therefore, he sought a partial justification for female preaching in the revivalistic principle that Christians must employ bold and dramatic strategies in order to win the world for God.[11] Not unlike William Booth, Railton believed that women would revolutionize the Christian Mission if employed in this manner.

Even with this revivalistic rationale for female ministry, George Scott Railton also sought a third justification for this public practice. As with other evangelical supporters of women preachers, he relied upon scriptural authority to make his case. One verse that Railton appealed to constantly was Galatians 3:28, the New Testament declaration which suggested that unity in Christ made distinctions based on gender irrelevant. This biblical proclamation supported his conviction that the female had "as much right to preach the Gospel, to exercise any sacred office, as the male."[12] Although Railton did not elaborate upon what he meant by "sacred office," he may have been holding out the possibility that women could in fact assume authority over men. What is clear is that he utilized this scriptural principle in an effort to defend the early Army practice of allowing female officers to administer Communion to their congregations.[13] While it would be wrong to assume that Railton ever abandoned his pragmatic approach to female ministry, his interpretation of Galatians 3:28 held radical implications for women. Female preaching was not merely a means to salvific ends; it was also based upon a biblical right to

George Scott Railton. Courtesy of The Salvation Army National Archives, Alexandria, Virginia.

proclaim salvation. As will be seen in chapter 5, Catherine Booth had used the language of rights to defend a public ministry for women, and obviously Railton had been influenced by her in this area.

The final element underlying Railton's support for female ministry was the Victorian notion of sexual difference. Like many other nineteenth-century individuals—including William Booth—he considered women to be the more attractive and emotional sex, possessing traits that gave them a special aptitude for drawing crowds and saving souls. For Railton, Army women, in particular, possessed a certain compassionate and sentimental force, which fitted them for moving the hearts of sinners: "The Salvation Army woman, at a street corner, can get and hold as large a crowd by even giving out a hymn, as the most eloquent of its male officers. The power of the woman's speaking, as her own heart melts and her tears flow at the sight of the lost around her, streams of tears from eyes that never wept for sin before, heaving breasts and broken hearts attest it, a million times, every Sabbath-day!"[14] The mere presence of a woman, however simple her gestures and words, was seen by Railton to always be an effective means of reaching the romantically inclined working classes. Railton's Victorian assumptions about female gender, which also owed a great deal to evangelicalism, were thereby intertwined with his revivalistic pragmatism. His evangelistic strategies depended upon an appeal to the senses, and women appeared ideally suited to make the most of such methods.[15]

The notion of sexual difference also lay behind Railton's praise of the female officers who commanded corps in the earliest days of the Salvation Army. There can be little doubt that he approved of the placement of women in positions of spiritual authority, but he continued to associate emotion and influence primarily with women:

> The women are generally more popular than men. They more readily gain everyone's sympathy and so enlist help of every kind, for which men could not decently appeal, and which no appeal would procure for them. It is not that women are usually gifted with extraordinary organising ability or business skill, but they can command those who have these gifts.[16]

The identification of women with governance at the corps level was significant for the nineteenth century, since British churches and chapels were largely male-dominated institutions. At the same time, however, Railton based such an unusual practice upon a tenuous foundation. He was right to value sympathy and influence in corps leadership, but wrong to identify these traits primarily with women. This kind of gender typing suggested that it was inappropriate or unnatural for men to display emotion, and implied that women were somehow deficient in the areas of business and organization. Neither sex was seen as capable of full personhood under this typology. Moreover, any endorsement of these gender-specific characteristics was ultimately problematic, since they could just as easily be used to justify separate spheres for each sex beyond the pulpit. According to the patriarchal assumptions behind Victorian gender relations, sympathy might be valued in corps ministry, but it would not be seen as indispensable in the administrative offices of the denomination.

Sexual Equality

It is clear that George Scott Railton enthusiastically endorsed the placement of women in ministerial leadership positions. Was this viewpoint, however, reflective of a clear commitment to equality between the sexes? The answer to this question is much less obvious, since Railton's thinking and practice in this area were rather ambiguous. He seemed to suggest that gender was both a meaningful and a meaningless category. On the one hand, his understanding of Galatians 3:28 implied that sexual identity was no longer relevant for the Christian: "It makes no matter to what family or sex any one belongs now."[17] On the other hand, he also maintained that women's unique emotional nature suited them for the tasks of preaching and corps leadership. Railton was an advocate of both sexual irrelevance and sexual difference. While such an inconsistency was not uncommon during the Victorian era, with even feminists themselves arguing for equality and difference, Railton leaned closer to the latter notion. He favoured the idea of sexual difference more than any principle of sexual equality, given his contention that the Salvation Army had "demonstrated its confidence in God's power to lift up the weakest [i.e., women] to the uttermost degree."[18] Overall, he tended to view women as either the weaker or the superior sex, but neither of these emphases reflected a clear commitment to sexual equality.

Where equality was stressed by Railton, it was primarily spiritual in nature. This was clearly apparent in an article he wrote on the subject of men's rights within late Victorian society in the September 1875 issue of *The Christian Mission Magazine*. Although affirming men's legal rights and their equality of opportunity, Railton felt that these concerns could "never be fully adjusted on earth."[19] He went on to state that "there is a Judge and King enthroned on high who is reigning and judging alright ... [and] all unjust inequality here will be put right in the world to come."[20] Furthermore, he believed that it was "a comparatively useless task to deal with the claims made for equality in [its] various respects" because all people were already equal in a spiritual sense: equally guilty, saved, called to service and judged by God.[21] This being the case, Railton claimed that it was short-sighted to worry about earthly inequality—to do so might distract Christians from taking hold of the privileges of spiritual equality. Besides the obvious fact that women were not included in this exposition on equality, Railton's conception of equality did not foster a critical concern for or a safeguard against possible concrete inequities within the emerging Salvation Army.

This relative disregard for temporal equality provides the necessary background against which to judge the claim that Railton was wholeheartedly committed to sexual equality. One piece of evidence offered to support this assertion is found in a letter that Railton sent to G. Thursfield, a Mission supporter, in 1876. In this correspondence, he implied that female evangelists should have the same pay as male evangelists: "If women can do the work and can raise the money they should have the same [salary] as men."[22] As remarkable a statement as this may have been, there is no evidence to indicate that Railton ever acted upon this claim. Moreover, by the mid-1880s the Salvation Army was regularly paying its female officers less than their male counterparts, and there is no indication that Railton ever spoke out against this discriminatory practice. This silence can hardly be explained away by arguing that he was not in a position to express his indignation. Railton was known to voice his opinions with force when he felt that something was wrong, as his bold opposition to the Salvation Army's evolving social programs clearly shows.[23] He was willing to cross William Booth over perceived threats to the organization's spiritual objectives, but he failed to address obvious instances of sexual inequality.

Railton's role in placing certain women in command of Mission preaching stations by 1875 represents the best evidence we have that he believed in equality between the sexes. As noted at the beginning of this section, Bramwell Booth cited this fact as proof that Railton was a radical proponent of women's equality with men. Clearly, George Scott Railton deserves some praise for encouraging this practice, which was indeed a bold move during the Victorian period. At the same time, however, the stations to which these women were sent were not considered to be important ones. This was admitted by Railton in 1886, when he noted that the first Christian Mission post held by a woman was "a little out-lying station," and that the few other women given similar assignments were sent to "small stations."[24] While these women were given remarkable opportunities, and undoubtedly did well at these postings, they did not necessarily enjoy equality with their male colleagues. The more important Mission stations, as well as the Mission's administration, remained in male hands. To say this is not to suggest that Railton was a lukewarm promoter of female ministry. He clearly was not, and shortly before his death in

1913 he expressed the hope that Army women would never "be content to do their work only 'behind the scenes.'"[25] Nevertheless, he fostered an understanding of equality that was primarily spiritual in nature—what he called the "equality of souls."[26] He lacked, therefore, the necessary commitment to practices that would have enabled Salvationist women to enjoy an equitable place alongside their male comrades.

DOMESTICITY

George Scott Railton's comments on domestic life shed additional light on his understanding of sexual equality and female ministry. There is no indication that he ever advocated egalitarian partnerships between a husband and wife within the confines of the home. In fact, he reflected the belief that women were both socially inferior and spiritually superior to men. On the one hand, a woman was a helpmeet to her spouse in the domestic sphere. Her mission in the home was to "minister to the ease, the rest, [and] the comfort of man." On the other hand, Railton contended that it was legitimate for wives to usurp their husbands' authority if the objective was spiritual in nature: "Is it not time somebody [woman] usurped authority over all the millions of professedly Christian men, who stand idle while the world is perishing?"[27] For Railton, women were naturally adapted for saving men's souls, and therefore it was permissible for them to assume spiritual authority over men. The efforts of pious Christian women, argued Railton, were a vast improvement over male mismanagement and stupidity in this area.[28] If men were negligent in the proclamation of salvation, then it was incumbent upon the opposite sex to take matters into their own hands. When viewed in tandem, these contrasting positions indicated that women could be elevated above, as well as subordinated below, their husbands, but in either case this did not denote an equal partnership within the home.

A woman's domestic responsibilities might infringe upon her public preaching opportunities, but there was no inherent incompatibility between these two areas of activity. George Scott Railton readily acknowledged that a woman's vocation was not limited to the kitchen, but he also echoed the sentiments of William Booth and others when he asserted that a woman's public ministry should not lead to "the neglect of home duties."[29] Apparently, however, this principle was taken too far in the Railton household, because Railton's wife Marianne became so wrapped up in the care of her family that she was unable to take an active role in public life. While George Scott Railton circled the globe to scout out new fields of Army service, his wife remained at home tending to the training and education of their children.[30] Like other men of his era, he assumed that the domestic sphere was a feminine one. Not surprisingly, therefore, Railton employed domestic language to describe Catherine Booth's work on the platform. From his perspective, Catherine had established a "simple homely system of public ministry … [where] as a mother [she] might talk to her children."[31] This kind of description minimized the contributions of the Army's cofounder, but it grew out of Railton's belief that women's preaching represented an extension of their work in the home.

In an overall sense, George Scott Railton's views on women fell somewhere between the Victorian images of "the Angel out of the House" and "the Female Saviour."[32] These models justified women's involvement outside the home on the basis of their pure and godly characteristics, but the latter image could also challenge certain aspects of male leadership in society. "The Female Saviour" had the task of ushering in an era of fuller humanity or salvation, something that the male half of humanity had been unable to accomplish. Facets of these two feminine constructions converged in Railton's assumption that female ministry made use of women's emotional and spiritual qualities, both of which legitimized women's public role as well as their usurpation of male spiritual authority. To some degree the "Railtonian" woman was radical, because she broke through the barriers of a male-dominated church. At the same time, however, she did not challenge patriarchal authority beyond the pulpit or push actively for sexual equality in the wider society. Moreover, her responsibility for the domestic realm could threaten her public ministry, given the fact that she could not forsake the obligations that she had to fulfil in the home.

It is only fair to point out that female ministry in the Salvation Army owed a great deal to men like George Scott Railton. He helped to promote a public role for Army women. Nevertheless, his alleged role in forging an atmosphere of gender equality in the organization is ambiguous. Railton's past history, revivalistic convictions and adherence to the notion of sexual difference had the most to do with his justification of female preaching. When he occasionally dwelt upon the subject of equality, his understanding of the principle was much more obscure and confusing. At times, he implied some semblance of sexual equality by claiming that women and men were one in Christ, and by advocating equitable salaries for female evangelists. Yet, he never seemed interested in addressing the obvious instances of sexual discrimination in the Army. Furthermore, his comments on gender often suggested that certain stereotypical differences defined the sexes, making women both inferior and superior to men. Perhaps George Scott Railton was closer to Catherine than to William Booth in his support of female ministry, but like William he held to a vision of womanhood based upon sexual difference and domestic subordination.

❖ Other Male Visions of Womanhood

Queen Victoria's death in 1901 may have signalled the official end of the Victorian period, but the cultural and evangelical assumptions about gender that had been consolidated during her long reign did not necessarily disappear. Some well-educated Edwardians may have rebelled against certain features of the Victorian era, including its constraints upon sexuality and gender, but most men and women continued to entertain nineteenth-century convictions about the female role in society. Part of the reason for this continuity lay in the late Victorian and Edwardian fear that Britain was losing her stature in the world. Confronted by Britain's declining industrial strength, dismal performance in the Boer War and urban poverty, many observers believed that a renewed emphasis upon motherhood and domesticity would help to save the British Empire.[33] Furthermore, groups like the Salvation Army increasingly became the preserve of conservative theological and cultural beliefs about female gender. The Salvation Army men who occasionally addressed the subject of women between the 1900s and the 1920s espoused beliefs and engaged in practices that reflected this milieu. Like William Booth and George Scott Railton, they did not necessarily deny that women had a public role to play in the organization, but such assertions were often overshadowed by assumptions about a woman's particular role behind the scenes or within the home as a mother and wife. These male Salvationist viewpoints underscored the persistence of the notion of sexual difference as well as the belief that women were ideally suited for work of a less than public nature.

WOMEN AND THE PRIVATE SPHERE

Some indication of the Salvation Army's views on women and the private realm was given by its opposition to married women's employment in the workforce. This was aptly illustrated on the front pages of an early edition of *The Social Gazette*, a British Salvationist periodical. The lead story, written by James Barker, a high-ranking officer, openly criticized married women who—often out of economic necessity—attempted to supplement their husband's wages. Barker maintained that "the married woman gains in every way who stays at home, makes the most of her husband's earnings, and properly trains her family and cares for her home."[34] This message, aimed primarily at the working classes, demonstrated the growing pressure upon men to become the sole breadwinners in their families. Barker went on to voice a common Victorian and Edwardian assumption, fuelled by the rise of domestic science and eugenics, that wives who worked outside the home put their husbands and children at risk. This was made even clearer by another early article appearing in the Salvation Army's newspaper *The War Cry*, which suggested there was a strong correlation between high infant mortality rates and a mother's work outside the home.[35] Such alarms were taken seriously around the turn of the century, when motherhood was increasingly tied to the progress of empire and race.

Further insights into the relationship between female gender and the domestic sphere could be gained from the qualities that a Salvationist man wanted in a wife. One short advice column in an Army periodical was headed boldly "Wanted, a Wife."[36] After reminding women that a man's success depended on his spouse, the author of this piece went on to describe the ideal wife as a guardian of the home and a good housekeeper. Judging from these comments, the perfect wife did not pursue any kind of public ministry. These same sentiments were expressed by William Gilks in a 1916 article on how a wife should treat her husband.[37] He made it clear that a man's happiness in the home depended upon his wife, who should make the domestic realm a place where a husband felt important. Yet another article on the same theme appeared years later in the "Women's Section" of *The War Cry*, and expressed many of the same domestic expectations. Required duties for a wife included keeping the house clean, training the children and making sure that meals were served promptly when the husband returned from work.[38] Apparently, however, a hard-working wife could participate in weekly corps activities if she met all her obligations at home. This type of female servitude was only reinforced by the Army's *Orders and Regulations*, which advised a male officer to seek "a wife capable of keeping his home, preparing his food, and training up a family to serve God and help Jesus Christ in the fight."[39] These expectations pointed to the patriarchal nature of Army marriages, and underscored how difficult it was for women to enjoy an equitable ministry alongside their menfolk.

Theological convictions about gender also served to keep Army women from undertaking significant roles outside the home. This was strikingly apparent in an article with the revealing title "Woman's Life Behind the Scenes," which appeared in a 1924 issue of *The Officer*, a journal intended solely for the Army's commissioned personnel. The male author of this short article echoed the widespread sentiment that a woman's influence lay in the background, and he admitted that this was especially true for mothers: "It is the lot of most mothers to toil unceasingly and self-sacrificingly behind the scenes; only very few come before the public."[40] These comments were not unusual for the age, but clearly troubling in an organization that claimed to support female ministry. Even more problematic, however, was the author's belief that this arrangement was divinely sanctioned: "The menial tasks are just as much [a] part of God's will for us, as are the greater responsibilities, and they are as sacred as are our prayers and songs of praise."[41] Beyond the fact that he associated the home with the menial, the author of this article simply reinforced the view that the female role was self-effacing and domestic, all of which discouraged women from pursuing ministerial and leadership roles in the organization. They were told that they were exactly where God wanted them.

Much of the same thinking was expressed by James Hay, a senior officer in the organization, when he addressed the subject of motherhood in 1929.[42] Against the backdrop of an increasingly promiscuous Western culture, he wrote of the important spiritual obligation that mothers—the allies of the Holy Spirit—had to nurture the souls of their children. In particular, Hay reminded Salvationists of the great influence that Army mothers possessed in the training of the organization's future leaders: "Not one-hundredth part has yet been told of what the mothers of officers have wrought towards the salvation of the world, and it is so in the lives of thousands of our soldiers."[43] Yet, for James Hay, this significant maternal influence was essentially hard to measure, often so inaudible that it could not be heard beyond a few feet of the home. Although acknowledging the contribution of Army mothers, Hay's comments unwittingly revealed the problems associated with a mother's role in this religious body: she was to influence but not to lead; she was to carry out most of her tasks at home rather than in the public realm; and from the perspective of men her overall contribution to the public life of the organization was hard to quantify. Once again, sacred motherhood served to dictate the nature and scope of a married woman's work within the Salvation Army.

Whether or not motherhood was the theme under discussion when Edward Higgins, another senior officer, addressed a large audience of women in 1914 is uncertain, but he did make it clear that women had an important role in the less than visible areas of the Salvation Army.[44] Higgins believed that the most powerful influences in life were often exercised behind the scenes, and he went on to assert that women far surpassed men in this realm. Women, he argued, were often behind the plans put forward by Army men, and their feminine role of persuasion in the private sphere should not be underestimated, since it had steered the Salvation Army in the right direction over the years. Ironically, however, these depictions of women as hidden powerful influences upon public men were juxtaposed with other seemingly contradictory statements that Higgins made earlier in the same speech. He actually began his address by praising the female leaders he had served under in the past, all of whom were highly visible figures! Moreover, in the very same speech he also suggested that gender should play no part in the selection of leaders. What Higgins failed to appreciate, however, was how his own assumptions about gender sent the opposite message. His belief that a woman's role was a hidden one called into question both his own praise of female leaders and his comments on sexual equality. Strangely, Higgins effectively discouraged his female audience from emulating the very leaders and principles he seemed to admire.

SEXUAL DIFFERENCE

The evangelical and Victorian understanding of gender was largely binary, which meant that some traits or characteristics were seen as feminine while others were considered masculine. As part of this overall sex-based ideology, women were believed to possess certain qualities ahead of men. Perhaps the chief of these gender-specific associations was between religion and the feminine, as women were perceived to be spiritually superior to men.[45] Evangelicalism, in particular, had much to do with this connection, because it advocated a religion of the heart that was conventionally feminine in nature. In an evangelical body like the Salvation Army, this angelic feminine image justified a woman's spiritual work at home and on the platform. This aspect of sexual difference allowed female officers to preach, but it also reminded them of their maternal role in the home as the spiritual and moral guardians of the young. Consequently, this understanding of gender did little to undermine patriarchal authority or traditional gender stereotypes. For the most part, women's alleged superiority in the spiritual realm translated into modest and limited opportunities for them, and merely reaffirmed conventional feminine representations. Male officers, in particular, embraced this conception of womanhood in a number of ways.

Evangelical religion, with its emphasis upon the sacrifice of Christ on the cross, made selflessness and sacrifice into cardinal theological virtues, but women were believed to possess these traits much more than men. This conviction was illustrated by Edward Higgins in his speech to women in 1914:

> I can but recognize that *God has endowed woman with special gifts, which make her influence supreme in many directions. In the spiritual realm she is capable of accomplishments beyond man, as in the physical realm man is capable beyond woman....* [She] *has been largely instrumental in keeping alive the spirit of self-sacrifice in The Army....* Her forgetfulness of self and self-interests in her anxiety for others has produced a list of heroines of which the whole world is proud.[46] [italics in original]

The distinction that Higgins made between the spiritual and the physical realms was telling, because for Victorians and Edwardians the latter sphere was where men competed with each other in the largely secular workforce. For Higgins, however, women had special God-given abilities associated with the spiritual arena, the chief of which were selflessness and self-denial. He believed that these feminine characteristics had shaped the ethos of the Army, and had produced a number of women pioneers.

Assumptions about feminine selflessness and self-denial did not keep women solely in the private sphere, as Victorian and evangelical women utilized such traits in order to participate in religious and philanthropic work. Likewise, these gendered notions could motivate Salvationist women to assume certain public roles within their organization. This was notably the case during the Army's earliest years, when Hallelujah Lasses willingly sacrificed reputations, comfort and safety to carry the Salvationist message through the streets of British towns and cities. Nevertheless, the close association between selflessness and femininity was ultimately counterproductive within the Salvation Army. Feminine self-denial provided a narrow and unstable justification for public work, because whatever a godly woman did had to be consistent with selflessness. This expectation was problematic on a number of fronts: (1) it hardly encouraged female officers to maintain their visibility in an organization that often violated its own principles of sexual equality; (2) it fostered female public roles based upon service and submission; and (3) it pressured women to put the cares of family and the home ahead of their own interests. Ultimately, the problem here lay not so much with self-sacrifice and selflessness as with their intimate connection with female gender. Officer women needed to develop self-assertion and self-interest as much as men needed to nurture self-sacrifice and selflessness. The cultivation of these human qualities was important if female Salvationists were to protect their gains and move into the middle and upper ranks of the denomination. Unfortunately, however, the Army continued to foster more restrictive conceptions of gender.

The association of motherhood with the sacred represented a second way in which women were perceived to be holier than men, and this conviction underscored how feminine sacrifice could be directed inward as well as outward. This motif was particularly evident in an article appearing under the title "Mothers—A Great Need." The author of this article made the connection quite explicit: "[A]fter the word '*God*' there is not a more sacred word than '*Mother*.' ... [A] good mother is the most perfect representation of God's great love for this poor world"[47] [italics in original]. This article, which was designed to be read at women's meetings, went on to draw a common parallel between motherhood and a moral society: "We need good mothers in order to have good citizens. As mothers are nobler in character, the greater and nobler the nation becomes."[48] Unlike proponents of maternal feminism, who sometimes used this kind of argument to extend a mother's role into the public realm, the author of the above did not situate his reasoning within a broad context.[49] Army mothers were called upon to use their pious position to train their families and raise future leaders for the organization, but these were tasks that ensured their confinement to the home. Sacred motherhood translated into domestic bondage.

Frederick Booth-Tucker, a prominent officer in the Army's early days, illustrated a third way of understanding women's supremacy in the spiritual realm. Echoing the sentiments of William Booth and George Scott Railton, he suggested that a woman was often more successful than a man at saving souls:

> [V]ery often the woman can do with a word, a look, a smile, a tear, an invitation, a casting of the net on the right side of the ship and the enclosing of a great multitude of fish within its meshes—what the husband, the father, the brother, the son, could not accomplish with their most strenuous efforts.... God loves to work with these simple and apparently insufficient agencies and means.... [They have] the spirit and humility and non-self-consciousness of a child.[50]

Although Booth-Tucker's remarks were meant to acknowledge the importance of a public role for women—one that he felt was declining in the organization—his views highlighted the unsettling ways in which Army men characterized the opposite sex. Underlying these comments was a subtext that perpetuated stereotypes about women. To begin with, Booth-Tucker associated female ministry with appearance and emotion rather than with acquired ability or intelligence. He may have believed that this gave women a magnetic spirituality, but his approach did little to dispel the Victorian belief that men were somehow more rational than women. Furthermore, Booth-Tucker's portrayal of women as "simple agencies" and childlike in spirit served to devalue their public contributions to the Salvation Army. Condescending labels such as these left the impression that a woman's ministry was actually less significant than that of the opposite sex. The equation of humility with women also continued the suggestion that any self-assertion upon the part of female officers was unwomanly. When taken together, these assumptions disclosed the constraints under which Salvationist women operated.

The motifs of domesticity and pious womanhood, both of which had been nurtured within evangelicalism and Victorian society, were not forsaken by the male officers of the Salvation Army. These men, following the lead of

William Booth and George Scott Railton, maintained what were essentially troubling attitudes towards women. A public preaching ministry might be possible for some female officers, but they were more likely to be reminded of their obligations and expected roles behind the scenes. The value that men attached to this private realm might vary, but Army men of high and low position agreed that this arena was a feminine one. Although the Army's biblical and regulatory principles declared women to be equal partners with men in ministry and leadership, female officers found themselves constrained by a gender ideology that glorified sexual difference and equated certain tasks and spaces with the feminine. Overall, these tensions did little to construct an equitable place for women in the public or private life of this religious organization.

✥ The Secondary Status of Female Ministry

Given the domestic demands placed upon women in the Salvation Army, and the constraints associated with their femininity, it should not be surprising that their officer status could be problematic after marriage. The comments that male Salvationists made on the subject suggested as much. A certain logic, whether subtle or otherwise, left the impression that married women were wives, mothers and homemakers first, and officers or public figures only second. This kind of reasoning, even when placed alongside assertions of women's equality with men, represented a serious obstacle for women who wished to pursue a public ministry comparable to that of their husbands. Ostensibly, marriage in the Salvation Army was not supposed to hinder either spouse's opportunities for ministry, and this conviction was even incorporated into the vows exchanged at Army weddings.[51] In reality, however, a married female officer rarely found this to be true. A clear double standard emerged: a married woman's public status and opportunities were tied to the home in a way that her husband's status and responsibilities were not.

Alex M. Nicol, a senior officer addressing the topic of married female officers in 1908, unwittingly revealed the problems in this area. His written remarks began with the assertion that the Salvation Army, unlike the wider society, was already firmly committed to sexual equality within marriage: "Partnership with man, instead of slave to him, is an ideal that is coming gradually nearer realisation [in society.] ... But The Army has ever contended that woman is neither the inferior nor the superior of man, but his equal."[52] At a time when the movement for female suffrage in Britain was becoming increasingly visible and vocal, Nicol left the impression that the Army was at the forefront of women's rights. Yet, the substance of his argument, which revolved around a case study of a young married officer couple whom he had visited recently, conveyed a message of inequality. Nicol, for example, referred to the woman in question as "Mrs. Adjutant" or as "one of our Adjutant's wives," whereas he described her husband as the "Commanding Officer." Unlike her husband, this woman was a spouse before she was an officer. Her status was dependent upon and derived from the rank given to her husband. Moreover, her officer role was subordinate to her spouse's position in the corps, since he was the officer in charge. To make matters worse, Nicol's characterization of this female officer as "a busy housewife and partner to an officer ... who give[s] the lie to the false notion that public service is incompatible with domestic and family obligations"[53] suggested that her responsibilities within the home were of greater importance than her public ministry. Ironically, this case study underscored the extent to which married female officers were, in both status and responsibility, devalued and restricted in ways that their husbands were not.

The subordinate place of female ministry within married life was emphasized in less subtle ways in a 1910 article entitled "Army Wives and Mothers." The writer, an anonymous male officer, believed that his spouse or "helpmeet" was fulfilling the role that God had chosen for her. She was, according to the implied logic of her husband, primarily a wife and mother, and only secondarily an officer:

> As a wife I have found her ever ready to sacrifice for my comfort, ever ready to cheer me.... God has blessed us with four boys and one girl; thus I have had some experience of how my wife has discharged her sacred duties as a mother.... In spite of the numerous duties of home and children (and the brightness of our home and the appearances of our own children testify to the fact that these are not neglected) yet she has always found time to do a certain amount of visiting and to attend nearly all the Indoor, and many of the Open-Air, Meetings. She takes her turns with me in giving the Bible lesson, and as I have sat and listened to her stirring addresses ... [I] have known how they have had to be prepared, to a great extent[,] in the rush and toil of the home work.[54]

The fact that this woman had a public life at all was remarkable, given the demands placed upon her. Her work as an officer came only after the completion of her "duties" in the domestic sphere, which included looking after five children and a husband. This was obviously not a concern for her husband, who boasted of her attentiveness to his needs. His comments underscored the fact that self-sacrifice for a woman often meant the sacrifice of her needs to those of her spouse. Mutual sacrifice in this marriage did not seem to be in evidence, since it was the wife who had to look after the housekeeping and the children.[55] Although it was permissible for this married female officer to miss the occasional corps function, she obviously did not have the same liberty to set aside her arduous work in the family. This double standard revealed the extent to which a married woman's officership was governed by the domestic expectations placed upon her.

A further indication of the problems associated with a married woman's status as an officer was apparent in the comments made by Bramwell, the Booths' eldest son, in his book *Servants of All*. This volume, which described the work of Salvation Army officers, included a revealing chapter on marriage and officership. In this section of the book, Bramwell began by asserting that a woman retained her commission as an officer upon marriage. At the same time, however, he went on to admit that in the majority of cases the man was the "chief gainer by the union."[56] This set of circumstances, Bramwell explained, lay in the fact that women's duties behind the scenes, involving the sacred obligations of the house and children, prevented women from taking on much of a role in the public realm. Far from considering this situation to be unjust, Bramwell felt that the Salvation Army owed these women a great deal for their self-sacrificing efforts in this area. This was indeed a troubling sign for women, since Bramwell Booth was in a position to address this diminution of a married woman's officer status. Yet, as the leader of the worldwide Salvation Army from 1912 to 1929, he never resolved this matter.[57] Like other men in the organization, he believed that the responsibilities of the home and the training of children were feminine tasks.

These assumptions were also factored into Bramwell's assessment of his own mother's public ministry. One of his initial tributes to Catherine, written shortly after her death in 1890, was striking in the manner in which it domesticated her considerable preaching career and other public achievements. He suggested that Catherine's faithful discharge of her domestic duties had enabled her to be successful in the public sphere, adding that "Mrs. Booth was before everything a mother."[58] Bramwell conveyed a very similar sentiment shortly before his own death in 1929, suggesting once again that Catherine's public opportunities came only after her responsibilities in the home:

[S]he did a great work for her sex, vindicating their call to preach the Gospel of Christ … [but] the remarkable thing is that despite all these labours and interests she fulfilled, and more than fulfilled, every obligation of wife and mother.… Her home sympathies were never dulled by the claims of the platform … her own home was never neglected for what some would call—I doubt whether she would have so described it—the

> larger sphere. Both alike had been opened to her by her God. She saw His purposes in both. In the humble duties of the kitchen table ... or in the nursery ... or at the bedside ... she was working for God's glory.[59]

It is clear that Bramwell admired his mother's public accomplishments, but he placed them within a largely domestic framework. He hesitated to associate her preaching with the public sphere, electing instead to see her ministry as simply an extension of her work in the home. Moreover, the word "neglect" was used in reference to the home rather than to the platform, implying that forsaking domestic obligations was more of a feminine transgression than abandoning the pulpit. Altogether, the more visible and unconventional aspects of Catherine's life and thought were somehow lost in the conservative image by which Bramwell best remembered her—the "Army Mother."

Given the cultural expectations concerning a mother's role in the home during the late nineteenth and early twentieth centuries, it is not surprising that Bramwell Booth and other Salvationist men tended to assume that a married woman was a mother before she was a public figure. Unfortunately, however, their acceptance of these societal norms was at odds with the Salvation Army's claim that it was based upon "the right of woman to an equal share with man in the great work of publishing salvation to the world."[60] A conservative model of motherhood, founded upon domesticity and feminine piety, was hardly compatible with a liberal principle devoted to sexual equality. No married female officer could be expected to meet domestic obligations in the home and then assume an equal part in the public life of the organization. Her status as an officer was threatened in a way that a man's was not, since she bore the responsibilities of the household and had to satisfy demands in this arena before she could take her place on the platform.

✤ Salvationist Theology and Female Gender

The factors that created a less than liberating atmosphere for female ministry and leadership in the Salvation Army were not simply cultural in nature. In addition to the societal assumptions about a woman's duties in private life and her opportunities in public work, male Salvationists nurtured certain theological values and convictions that often fostered a negative environment for female officers. These variables—God-language, sin and holiness— have been alluded to already, but it is important to examine them in a little more detail since they have had a profound impact upon women throughout church history. Both institutional and individual Salvationist texts addressed

Bramwell Booth. Courtesy of The Salvation Army George Scott Railton Heritage Centre, Toronto.

the nature of God and the human condition at some length, and such material provides insights into the challenges and possibilities that these themes presented for women. Particular attention is given to the institutional or official Salvationist theological manuals of the period, because they were designed for the training of officers. What becomes clear in this analysis is how closely the Salvation Army's theology articulated the conservative evangelical concerns of the period.

GOD-LANGUAGE

The language that Christians employ for the sacred is of historical significance, since conceptions of the Godhead not only serve as sources of worship but also mirror the values of a given age. To some degree, the evangelical tradition, with its focus on the heart and the emotions, reflected religious values that were conventionally feminine and romantic in spirit. The hymns of the period included references to both a personal saviour with traditionally feminine traits and a benevolent and gracious fatherly God, but this ostensible feminization of religion did not unseat exclusive and literal masculine depictions of God.[61] Elizabeth Cady Stanton and the other female exegetes behind *The Woman's Bible*, which appeared in 1898, were well aware of this fact. Stanton, in particular, believed that the first step in the elevation of her sex was the recognition of the divine as both a heavenly mother and a heavenly father. Referring to the first chapter of Genesis, she contended that being made in God's image was an inclusive act, incorporating the male and the female. Stanton saw this initial Creation motif as a declaration of the equality between the sexes.[62]

Despite its dramatic and passionate style of preaching, as well as its tendency to associate women with angelic qualities, the Salvation Army also reflected the kind of patriarchal God-language that Stanton and others sought to challenge. Neither the Army's earliest doctrinal booklet nor its more extensive *Handbook of Salvation Army Doctrine*, which appeared in 1923, allowed or suggested that the Godhead could be envisioned as female.[63] In fact, the overriding image that these volumes employed to describe God was that of "Father." The depiction of the Godhead as solely male had much to do with the organization's roots in conservative evangelicalism, which espoused a method of interpretation bordering upon a literalistic reading of scripture.[64] In particular, the *Handbook*'s references to God as "Father" and Jesus as "Son" implied that maleness was essential to the divine nature, as the following passage indicates: "The *First Person* in the Godhead is especially *the* Father.... He is *the Father of His Son*, Jesus Christ. His designation of 'The

Father' is due to this eternal relationship.... He is *the Father of all men*....
He is, in a peculiar sense, *the Father of those who become His true followers*"[65]
[italics in original]. The use of the words "is" and "eternal" suggested that the
relationship between God and Christ was literally and immutably
masculine in nature. In the use of such words, Salvationist God-language
effectively excluded the feminine from imaging the divine.

Exclusively male God-language was not conducive to the promotion of
sexual equality within the Salvation Army, because it encouraged male rule
over females. Male Salvationists were, by the nature of their gender, tied to
an authoritative and powerful masculine deity, an association that made it
naturally fitting and theologically appropriate for them to assume the highest offices in the organization, as well as headship within the home. As early
as 1890, Bramwell Booth noted that the Salvation Army's "government is
based upon the Divine authority of fatherhood. The authority claimed, in its
system of discipline, over its officers and soldiers, is derived from the same
source as that of the father over his son."[66] William Booth, it will be recalled,
likened his own leadership to that of a father, a connection that also strikingly paralleled the role of divine fatherhood. Just as God the Father ruled
over the world, the fatherly Booth ruled over the Salvation Army. Even after
William Booth's death in 1912, the organization continued to base its patriarchal structure on "the government of the family, where the father is the
head, and his directions are the laws."[67] This kind of symmetry suggested
that female leadership was unnatural at best—somehow a transgression
of the divine ordering of life. Furthermore, the Army's sexist God-language
called into question women's human dignity. Solely masculine depictions
of God suggested that women were unable to image the divine, the originating source of goodness in Christianity. Wittingly or unwittingly, Salvationist
God-language served to subordinate women and discourage them from
developing a positive self-identity.

THE DOCTRINE OF SIN

An additional theological concept that fostered a troubling environment
for female officers was sin and the Salvation Army's understanding of it. The
way in which this doctrine was conceived spoke more to male than to female
experience. Most of the space devoted to this subject described sin in the
conventionally masculine language of selfish ambition and wilful acts of
rebellion against God. The organization's doctrinal manuals laid great stress
on sin as pride and selfishness, arguing that these were the essence or root
of all other evils. As the *Handbook of Salvation Army Doctrine* sought to

emphasize: "The essence, root, or underlying motive of all sin is selfishness; that is, pleasing self without due regard to the glory of God or the welfare of others."[68] Bramwell Booth was especially concerned to identify iniquity with self-love and self-satisfaction, both of which he called the "deadly enemies of the soul."[69] Only rarely did the Army mention that sin also included the failure to do what God required, a transgression that was most applicable to female officers, given that their burdens in the home could tempt them to neglect their public ministry.[70] The predominant view of sin as self-interest and worldly ambition was unhelpful for women, because it merely reinforced their traditional identification with self-sacrifice and self-forgetfulness. This kind of theological interpretation hardly encouraged them to pursue their own interests in the denomination.

The equation of sin with selfishness in Salvationist circles was prone to affect women adversely, because this theological construct failed to account for the types of vices that they were likely to experience in their lives. As part of a culture and religious tradition that glorified female service and sacrifice, especially within the family, female officers heard yet another call to put others before themselves. Moreover, the men in their lives largely failed to appreciate this problem, since they continued to affirm that the home and children were feminine areas of service. The societal and evangelical expectation that women were "helpmeets," created to serve the needs of men, suggested that any associations between sin and selfishness needed to be directed primarily at men. Among the dangers that women faced were the failures to assert and affirm themselves.[71] Self-assertion and self-confidence were the qualities that Salvationist women needed to cultivate if they were to enter and remain within the public arena. This was something that Army men recognized only occasionally, when they admonished women to "boldly rise up [and] enter the door of opportunity" or fight for their rights.[72] More often than not, however, any exhortations in this direction were overshadowed by the demonization of self-interest and ambition. A call to self-denial may have been heard by both sexes in the Salvation Army, but it was women who were most often called upon to heed this cry.

TEACHING ON HOLINESS

Holiness was an influential tenet of many evangelical groups, addressing the believer's need to overcome the remnants of sin in her or his life. The sincere Christian was expected, after conversion, to renounce worldly habits (e.g., fashionable dress, alcohol, secular entertainment) and demonstrate a willingness to serve God without reservation. Throughout this process of consecration, the Holy Spirit worked within the heart and mind of the Christian, providing cleansing from and power over sin. Salvationists, in particular, were among the chief advocates of this deeper work of God. This was due in large part to their roots in Methodism, which from the time of John Wesley had expounded the belief in Christian perfection or holy living.[73] American Methodists like James Caughey and Phoebe Palmer were especially fervent promoters of teaching on holiness, claiming that holiness was within the reach of all sincere Christians. This zeal for holiness found its way into the Salvation Army's earliest doctrinal texts, one of which spent seven chapters on the subject.[74] Like the organization's expositions on God and sin, this ubiquitous teaching also had a bearing on women's roles. Its effects, however, were potentially more liberating for women. The doctrine of holiness was capable of both liberating and subordinating women, because it had the potential to challenge and to reinforce the prevailing societal and cultural norms.

There has been no shortage of studies on the relationship between nineteenth-century evangelical women and the doctrine of holiness, and various historians have drawn attention to how an appreciation for the work of the Holy Spirit could lead to the expansion of women's roles in religious groups from Methodism to Pentecostalism.[75] These evangelical bodies believed that the Holy Spirit could anoint any Christian, male or female, trained or untrained. After experiencing such a consecration or cleansing, believers often felt empowered to serve God in new ways. Revivalists like Charles Finney not only urged their audiences to seek the Holy Spirit actively, but also encouraged men and women to exercise the gifts that the Spirit had bestowed upon them.[76] For some women, the appropriation of pneumatic power and authority included testifying before mixed audiences. One notable example here was Phoebe Palmer, who felt obligated to share her faith in public after receiving the blessing of holiness.[77] Often, this perceived call to witness was realized only after a period of struggle, but once women obeyed the voice of the Spirit they inadvertently challenged Victorian assumptions that they belonged in the private sphere, not to mention theological interpretations concerning feminine silence in the church.

This kind of empowerment could be seen to some degree in the Salvation Army as well. Catherine Booth, for instance, not only explained her own call to preach within the context of holiness, but also stressed the role of the Spirit in the public lives of the Army's Hallelujah Lasses.[78] She believed that the power of the Holy Spirit helped to explain the success of these women, many of whom came from humble backgrounds. A very similar kind of reasoning was also apparent in the Salvation Army's doctrinal handbooks, which considered one of the fruits of sanctification to be an eagerness to speak in public.[79] There is little indication that female Salvationists used this kind of authority to demand equitable access to the Army's administrative offices or to subvert headship in the home, but the power of the Spirit did provide these women with a justification for preaching on the platform—a public realm traditionally dominated by men. To some degree, therefore, female Army officers subverted the gender norms of nineteenth- and early twentieth-century British society. Holiness was never so radical a doctrine as to overturn the notion of sexual difference or the power inherent in a patriarchal hierarchy, but it could provide Salvationist women with a public voice.[80]

In other ways, however, the Salvation Army's conception of holiness was less than empowering for women. The liberating possibilities of the Spirit could be overshadowed by the organization's desire to situate holiness within an authoritative framework that served only to reinforce conventional views about women. This was best illustrated in the Army's *Handbook of Salvation Army Doctrine*. To begin with, this volume largely defined holy living in terms of the conventional feminine traits of self-abasement and humility, while equating self-love and ambition with an ungodly life. Virtue consisted of self-denial and submission, but these traits clearly did not motivate women to challenge societal or Salvationist gender discrimination.[81] Nor did such qualities encourage women to seek leading roles in the Army system. Even more unsettling, this book highlighted the extent to which teaching on holiness bolstered the Salvation Army's authoritarian structure. Addressing the issue of holiness and obedience in officers, the text noted: "They ever put the interests of God's Kingdom and The Army before their own ease and advantage, and are, therefore, always to be relied upon to carry out instructions heartily."[82] Because of their traditional association with submission and obedience to patriarchal leadership, women had the most to lose from this theological argument. By discouraging assertiveness and a questioning of authority—both of which were needed to overcome instances of sexual discrimination—the Salvation Army encouraged women to be satisfied with modest roles under the authority of men.

Although historians of evangelical women have been quick to point out the ways in which holiness empowered these women, they have tended to ignore the more unsettling features of conservative evangelicalism. This kind of oversight is unfortunate, since such scholarship fails to appreciate the complex interaction between theology and female gender. The Spirit may have liberated female evangelists, but androcentric conceptions of God, sin and submission could just as easily restrict them. Within the Salvation Army, this kind of ambiguous relationship was clearly in evidence. Alongside an empowering conception of holiness was a patriarchal structure supporting male rule and a masculine notion of sin that made self-interest and ambition problematic. Assertiveness, self-interest and ambition were construed as aspects of a fallen humanity—vices that Salvationists were told to forsake if they wanted to be holy. Yet, these were the very qualities that women, especially, needed if they were to have a substantial public presence in the organization. The Army's doctrine of holiness was insufficient in itself to protect this area of ministry, because the very same theological concept could just as easily be used to consolidate the patriarchal model of governance adopted by the denomination.

✛ Institutional Discrimination

These theological doctrines, coupled with the various cultural beliefs about womanhood outlined earlier, help to explain why the Salvation Army engaged in a number of institutional practices that discriminated against female officers. One clear expression of this sexism was found in the economic realm.[83] Between the 1880s and the 1920s, the Salvation Army's salary policies favoured men over women on a consistent basis. In the case of married officer couples, for instance, the husband received any wages provided by the Army. This arrangement was contrary to the organization's principle of sexual equality, but it was consistent with an evangelical model of male headship, as well as with the societal assumption that the husband should be the family breadwinner. By the early twentieth century, this principle of the male breadwinner was becoming increasingly evident in working-class households. Furthermore, single male officers received between fifteen and forty percent more in wages than single female officers. Pay disparity along the lines of gender was typical of the historical period in question and had been practised in Methodist circles where women were employed as preachers, but once again it underscored the Salvation Army's failure to maintain equal standards for women and men.[84] In the area of finance, both married and single female officers were treated inequitably.

Inequities of a different nature were evident in the Salvation Army's method of assigning responsibilities to its married officers. Most often, the organization's system of deploying personnel to new commands did not include the officer wife. This revealed the fact that officer wives were not generally given their own official appointments; instead, their duties were left largely in the hands of their husbands. It will be recalled from the previous chapter that this was a problematic arrangement, since, as William Booth admitted, some husbands discouraged their wives from assuming a prominent ministry. It was expected, however, that married women, upon entering a corps, would assist the leader of the Home League, a group created to train women in child and home management.[85] But the situation was far worse for the married female officers not involved in corps work. When a married man was appointed to a position at headquarters, his officer wife might be left without any official role. One announcement of appointment changes at the Army's international headquarters in London was a case in point. This news bulletin made extensive reference to the careers of the male appointees, but it concluded by noting that these officers' wives "do not take any important part in the particular Departments [to which their husbands are assigned]."[86] These women were seen to have the unofficial role of "increasing [the] usefulness of their respective husbands."[87] At best, married female officers were expected to assist their husbands, while at worst they were given no specific function outside the home.

Few married female officers were fortunate enough to receive their own appointments. This was a fact that the Salvation Army acknowledged in a 1915 statement on the position of its women: "In some circumstances, a woman officer, after marriage, may hold separate responsibilities from those of her husband."[88] The words "some" and "may" highlighted the degree to which this was not the general practice of the organization. Furthermore, an even smaller number of women were given public duties that approached, met or exceeded those of their husbands. On the rare occasions when this did occur within the senior ranks, it was confined largely to women who, by birth or marriage, were related to Catherine and William Booth. The Booths' daughter Emma and daughter-in-law Maud both held posts equal to those of their husbands, while Lucy Booth-Hellberg, another daughter, was given a position that placed her over her spouse. Florence Booth, Bramwell Booth's wife, also assumed important senior commands that carried a great deal of power, although never any postings that challenged the authority of her husband. Those not associated with the Booth name, however, were less privileged. The few married women actually given appointments at the administrative levels of the Army generally filled posts that were clearly beneath those given to their husbands. High-ranking female officers, including the wives of chief secretaries, were never allowed to encroach upon the administrative roles given to their husbands.[89]

The way in which the Salvation Army allocated ranks to its married officer couples further enshrined women's subordination to men. In theory, women retained their full officer status after marriage, but in practice this was seldom the case.[90] Their officer commissions were undermined in two fundamental ways. First, married women tended to derive their designations from their husbands. A married man was always addressed by his rank and name (e.g., Captain William Jones), but his title never indicated his marital status. For married women, however, the situation was different: they were always identified primarily by their marital status, and only secondarily by their rank and name (e.g., Mrs. Captain Jones or Mrs. Captain William Jones).[91] The derivative nature of a female officer's public title was even more striking when she married a lower-ranking officer: she was forced to assume her husband's inferior rank. Second, the widespread practice of classifying a married woman as an officer's wife left the impression that she was not even an officer at all.[92] At the concrete level of Army life, a woman's officer status was either subordinate to that of her husband or questionable altogether.

Additional strain was placed upon a married woman's officership by the belief that she was a mother and wife before she was an officer. This assumption not only was held by individual male officers, but became part of the Salvation Army's institutional policy. Officer manuals reminded administrative personnel of the unique working conditions faced by married female officers: "All necessary forbearance and patience must be exercised towards woman in view of the drawbacks under which she labours in public life from marriage relationships, family cares, and other burdens which she is specially called to bear."[93] These instructional books went on to assure leaders that the irregular working hours of a married female officer were fully compensated by her "personal influence and remarkable gifts."[94] Such directives were, undoubtedly, sincere attempts to accommodate the reality of a married woman's work in the home, but they did not recognize the larger problem at hand—wives, unlike their husbands, were expected to put their domestic responsibilities before their officership. This kind of official arrangement hardly provided married women with equal opportunities to engage in the sort of public work performed by their spouses.

Institutional practices of the foregoing variety illustrate the extent to which Army men's perceptions of gender were guided more by conservative societal and evangelical norms than by any widespread application of sexual equality. Male commentators shared William Booth's Victorian and theological presuppositions about womanhood. Collectively, they justified female ministry by resorting to woman's stereotypical nature, especially her domestic, emotional and spiritual qualities. Positively, this interpretation afforded Salvationist women a public presence in advance of their sisters in other denominations. In particular, early Salvationist men are to be commended for providing women with the opportunity to preach. Negatively, however, Army men legitimized such activity on a basis that was less than liberating for women. Stereotypical femininity was not conducive to the maintenance and expansion of women's ministry and leadership in the Salvation Army. The evangelical and Victorian pillars of this construct, most notably the association of women and theology with self-sacrifice, functioned to discourage female aspirations beyond those of home and motherhood.

How female Salvationists learned to cope with, accept or redefine this image of womanhood is the subject of the next two chapters. If the negotiation of gender issues is a collective affair, then the beliefs and practices of women also need to be taken seriously. This area of inquiry begins in chapter 5, where the life and thought of Catherine Booth are examined at length. Catherine, like her husband, deserves to be treated separately, given her role in the founding of the Salvation Army. The central task in this section of the book is to place her views on gender and equality alongside her understanding of public ministry and domestic life, a juxtaposition that has seldom been attempted by students of Catherine Booth. Most treatments of this evangelical woman have pursued the public and radical features of her life at the expense of a consideration of her more conventional understanding of gender and the home. This is unfortunate, because Catherine was a much more complex figure than such portrayals suggest. Moreover, such accounts fail to appreciate the full significance of the legacy that Catherine Booth bequeathed to the women who followed her.

CHAPTER 5

Catherine Booth:
A Public and Domestic Legacy

T HE SALVATION ARMY was a relatively young organization when Catherine
Booth died in 1890, but its existence and expression owed a great deal to
her life and thought. Minnie Carpenter, a Salvationist author writing in 1945,
captured well the significance of Catherine's influence in this area by suggesting that her beliefs and convictions had been woven so deeply into the
foundations of the denomination that her unseen presence continued to
guide Army affairs.[1] While Salvationists continue to debate the precise nature
of Catherine Booth's contribution to the origin and development of the Army,
a number of recent scholarly studies have confirmed Carpenter's general thesis.[2] They have highlighted the ways in which Catherine Booth moulded and
shaped Army theory and practice. In particular, it has been argued many
times that Catherine's pre-eminent legacy to the Salvation Army lay in her
defence of women's right to minister alongside men in the public work of the
organization. Various students of this Victorian woman have shown that the
Army's professed commitment to gender equality in ministry was fashioned
upon her convictions and animated by her example. Even those unwilling to
recognize Catherine as the cofounder of this religious body have accepted
this contention.[3] Few would wish to challenge the assertion that she was
responsible for making female preaching one of the organization's distinctive features.

As significant as this legacy may be, and it clearly should not be underestimated, very little scholarly attention has been paid to the less public side
of Catherine Booth's life and thought. This is unfortunate, because her public responsibilities were intimately related to her duties in the domestic realm.
Minnie Carpenter seemed to realize as much, noting that "[i]n her home,
between household duties, [Catherine] thought out and prepared mighty
addresses, which held and moved congregations of thousands."[4] One would

not wish to "domesticate" her public achievements, as her son Bramwell seemed to do, but the fact remains that Catherine Booth's life can be adequately understood only by an appreciation of her roles as a public figure and as a wife and mother. To do this is to acknowledge that Catherine's institutional legacy was public and domestic in nature, and served to influence the roles that female Salvationists would adopt in public and private life. Therefore, the pages that follow look seriously at Catherine's assumptions about the public and domestic spheres, and how they reflected and challenged her Victorian and evangelical surroundings.[5] By considering the basis of her convictions about female ministry as well as her beliefs about selfhood, marriage and motherhood, we can arrive at a more comprehensive picture of Catherine Booth's contribution to the organization.

❖ Early Years and Formative Influences

Catherine Booth's views on a woman's place in the church and the home owed a good deal to what she learned as a child and adolescent growing up in early to mid-nineteenth-century England. Catherine was born on January 17, 1829, at Ashbourne, Derbyshire, a small community situated in the East Midlands.[6] She was the only daughter of respectable working-class parents, John and Sarah Mumford. Her father was a carriage builder by trade, and an occasional lay preacher within Wesleyan Methodist circles. The family's association with Methodism was not surprising, given the strength of this religious movement in the region. Even more interesting was the prominence of the Primitive Methodist Connexion in the East Midlands. As noted in chapter 2, this sectarian expression of Methodism had emerged in 1811 when Hugh Bourne and others became disenchanted with the lack of revivalistic fervour within mainstream Wesleyanism. These zealous dissenters held camp meetings and employed travelling preachers, a significant number of whom were women. Some of these female preachers were quite active in Derbyshire, including Sarah Kirkland, Mary Dunnel and Mary Hawksley, and Bourne himself travelled to Ashbourne on more than one occasion.[7] Although Catherine Mumford was a Wesleyan Methodist at this time, and left Ashbourne in 1834, she and her family undoubtedly absorbed something from this revivalistic group. Moreover, the Primitive Methodists were active in other parts of the East Midlands as well, including the Lincolnshire area where the Mumfords lived for the next ten years. In later life, when about to embark upon her own preaching career, Catherine lamented that, had she been brought up among the Primitive Methodists, she would have been in the pulpit long before.[8] Perhaps, however, she underestimated the influence of this connexion on her own life, since it was a significant part of the Derbyshire and larger East Midlands landscape.

Equally important, however, were Catherine's earliest years in the Mumford home. Catherine had four brothers, but only one survived beyond early childhood, and after her remaining brother left home at the age of sixteen, she became the sole child of the household. This was an especially isolating period for her, since her mother did not allow her to associate with the neighbourhood children, believing that they might teach Catherine bad habits. Perhaps Sarah Mumford's actions were extreme, but they were motivated largely by religious conviction. Sarah was a person for whom religion was life itself and, like the seventeenth-century Puritan writer John Bunyan, she believed in a Christian's literal separation from worldly people and popular amusements.[9] Viewing this earth as a place of preparation for the next, Sarah Mumford was suspicious of anyone or anything that might distract her family from this heavenly destination. In particular, she was afraid that Catherine's friendships with other children might lead her to cultivate self-indulgent habits such as novel reading and fashionable dressing, rather than the evangelical virtues of self-denial and self-restraint. The latter were seen by pious evangelicals as the concomitants of true Christianity. Consequently, Catherine Mumford's social relations beyond the home were curtailed because of her mother's aversion to worldliness.

The fact that this evangelical concern for Catherine's soul was expressed chiefly by her mother was reflective of evangelical and nineteenth-century mores. Pious Christian mothers, while not generally employing the extreme tactics of women like Sarah Mumford, were expected to play the central role in the religious education of their sons and daughters.[10] In large measure, this gender-specific undertaking grew out of the feminization of religion in the eighteenth and nineteenth centuries. Liberal and conservative Christianity, influenced by the subjective emphases of European pietism and romanticism, began to associate the sacred and the moral with the traditionally feminine areas of the feelings and the heart. This close correlation between women and religion made women appear to be the natural candidates for instructing children in religious and moral matters. William Wilberforce, a prominent evangelical writer and politician, captured the essence of this viewpoint, arguing that the female sex was naturally "more favourably disposed than [the male sex] to the feelings and offices of Religion; being thus fitted by the bounty of Providence ... [for] the education of our earliest youth."[11] Moreover, as women's conventional identification with Eve the temptress gave way to that with angelic Mary, the mother of Jesus, spirituality and morality became the defining characteristics of Victorian motherhood. These developments served increasingly to place the burden of children's religious education upon women.

In the case of Sarah Mumford, however, the maternal role in educating children was taken one step further. Despite the fact that the early Victorian school system was ecclesiastically based, she was determined to oversee Catherine's entire education. Once again, this decision reflected a compulsion to separate her daughter from ungodly influences, whether in the form of classmates or teachers. Thus, when the Mumford family moved to Boston, Lincolnshire, in 1834, Catherine was taught at home by her mother. Not surprisingly, the Bible was central to this academic curriculum, and Catherine's reading skills developed steadily as she read through the entire scriptures a number of times. This was not an uncommon accomplishment within evangelical circles, as children were expected to read the Bible from cover to cover once each year from the age of seven.[12] In 1841, Catherine's field of study was broadened when a close friend of the family convinced Sarah to enroll Catherine at a highly respected local school. Within this setting, the twelve-year-old child studied history, geography, English and mathematics. According to her biographers, Catherine was a conscientious pupil. Unfortunately, however, spinal problems forced Catherine to cut short her formal education in 1843.

Although she had acquired less than half the average schooling of her upper-working-class contemporaries, Catherine remained eager to learn.[13] In fact, while confined to her bed for an extended period of time, she displayed a remarkable interest in theology and church history. It was unusual for laymen, let alone laywomen, to explore these subjects, because they were typically the preserve of Victorian clergy.[14] Moreover, it was believed that a woman's emotional nature made her incapable of any prolonged rational inquiry.[15] The conventional wisdom of the period suggested that women would suffer physical and mental exhaustion if they engaged in such rational pursuits. Yet, assumptions of this nature did not deter Catherine, who ventured into works like Joseph Butler's *Analogy of Religion*, an early eighteenth-century response to deism. This religious byproduct of the Enlightenment held, among other things, that God no longer had an active and personal interest in the ongoing life of the world. By delving into this kind of material, Catherine challenged prevailing assumptions about what the members of her sex could accomplish.

The less abstract works of other religious figures were even more influential in Catherine Mumford's theological development. Of significance here were the life and work of John Wesley, the principal founder of Methodism. Even though reason played a role in his theological system, Wesley's approach to religious faith was essentially experiential and subjective. Such an understanding reflected his association with the Moravians, a pietist community that fostered a warm and experiential Christianity.[16] Wesley had encountered this group while serving as a missionary in the American state of Georgia. Returning to Britain in the late 1730s, he increasingly stressed that religion must speak to and transform the heart. This theme became a defining feature of Methodism in the eighteenth and nineteenth centuries, and contributed a great deal to Catherine's spiritual formation. The strength of her beliefs on this subject were evidenced years later in her book *Life and Death*, in which she asserted that God's Spirit worked through human subjective experience: "When a person begins to *feel*, it is a sign that the Spirit is striving"[17] [italics in original]. This sentiment was echoed in Catherine's other writings, wherein she laid great stress upon the "faith of the heart" and a "salvation that renews the heart."[18] Religion that spoke only to the head was, according to Catherine, a counterfeit form of Christianity.

A second Wesleyan theme that shaped Catherine Mumford's spiritual life was the doctrine of holiness. John Wesley taught that holy living, by which he usually meant a perfect love for God and others, was a scriptural command binding on all Christians. Even with the help of the Holy Spirit, however, this righteous ideal was seldom attained easily. The blessing of holiness came only after believers conquered the remaining sin in their lives, which often meant winning a battle against pride and selfishness. Writing in her diary in November 1847, Catherine Mumford described the struggle that typically accompanied this quest for sanctification: "I believe the blood of Jesus cleans from all sin, and yet there seems something in the way to prevent me from fully entering in. [B]ut I believe today at times I have had tastes of perfect love, and that these may be ... an overwhelming shower of saving grace. [M]y cheif [*sic*] desire is holiness of heart."[19] A number of years elapsed before Catherine experienced the state of holiness, but the agonizing inner conflicts leading up to this sacred goal became the lens through which she understood her own entry onto the platform in 1860. On more than one occasion, she suggested that her struggles with pride and selfishness lay behind her own reluctance to speak publicly before others in the church.[20] In this way, Wesleyan teaching on holiness proved to have a significant impact on Catherine's later public life.

Besides the Wesleyan emphases on holiness and the heart, Catherine Mumford gained a good deal of inspiration from the writings of Charles Finney, a nineteenth-century American revivalist. She especially admired his *Lectures on Revivals of Religion*, published initially in America in 1835, and then subsequently in Britain by 1837. This popular text, with several hundred thousand copies in circulation in Britain by the late 1840s, was regarded by

Catherine as the "most beautiful and commonsense work on the subject [she had] ever read."[21] Although Finney's volume was concerned primarily with the question of how to stimulate revivals in nineteenth-century society, it also advocated ideas that were conducive to female ministry.[22] To begin with, the book's inclusive ecclesiology underscored the New Testament notion of the priesthood of all believers. While this principle had been revived briefly by Protestants during and immediately after the Reformation, it eventually receded into the background as distinctions between the clergy and the laity grew. Finney challenged this division by defining ministers simply as "soul-winners," a label that in fact he gave to all Christians. This egalitarian thrust was reinforced further by his belief that revival meetings should "exercise the gifts of every individual member of the church—male and female."[23] This lowering of ecclesiastical and gender barriers by Finney and other like-minded evangelists encouraged some women to assume a public ministry.

Even more central to this brand of revivalism was its unconventional methodology; it was not slavishly bound to traditional ways of promoting religion. Following the lead of Methodists on the American frontier, Finney wrote of the need to employ "new measures" or innovative strategies to draw the interest of the spiritually indifferent. He held that God had set down no prescribed method of reaching the unsaved. Experimentation was therefore seen to be legitimate: "As sure as the effect of a measure becomes stereotyped, it ceases to gain attention, and then you must try something new."[24] Pragmatism of this nature justified a number of controversial measures, including female testimony before mixed audiences. New ways of presenting the gospel seemed to take precedence over traditional policies regarding women's silence in the church.

Although Catherine's defence of female ministry rested more upon biblical principle than pragmatism, and encompassed more than just female testifying in prayer meetings, she did retain much of Finney's methodological perspective. The debt she owed to this American revivalist was illustrated in striking fashion many years later when she spoke of the need to present the gospel in novel ways to sinners:

> Adaptation is the great thing we ought to consider. If one method or agent fails, we should try another.... It is here, I conceive, that our churches have fallen into such grievous mistakes with reference to the propagation of the Gospel in our own times. We have stood to our stereotyped forms, refusing to come down from the routine of our forefathers, although this routine has ceased to be attractive to the people.... [I]f you would benefit and bless them, you must interest them.[25]

Methodological freedom remained a distinctive element of Catherine's life and thought, and through her became a key feature of the early Salvation Army. Customary ways of sharing the Christian message were fruitless if they could not gain the attention of sinners. Catherine's conviction that a measure must attract sinners had, in turn, some bearing on how she viewed the public ministry of female Salvationists. While she did not consider Army women to be typical means of reaching sinners that could be employed and then abandoned when no longer useful—in her mind, women would always be able to attract an audience because they were suited by nature to preach—she did speak occasionally of her Hallelujah Lasses as "female agencies" or agents whose success lay in drawing numerous sinners to Christ.[26] From Finney she learned that successful measures, as long as they did not compromise the essential truths of Christianity, were reason enough to abandon man-made conventions of the past.

In addition to these theological features, Catherine Mumford also learned skills that would prove invaluable to her later ministry and leadership role in the Salvation Army. Prior to her illness, for example, she was associated with the temperance movement. This largely evangelical cause aimed to restrict or ban the sale and consumption of alcohol in Victorian England. Through this group Catherine gained exposure to the art of debate and learned to develop her own leadership abilities. In particular, the Mumford home became a central meeting place for Boston-area residents to discuss the pros and cons of the drink issue. Although only a child at the time, and therefore unable to grasp every aspect of the discussions, Catherine probably absorbed something from this stimulating atmosphere of debate.[27] The necessity of defending one's convictions with reasoned arguments against those with opposing views was perhaps the key lesson that she learned from this early exposure to the temperance cause. Catherine's logical defence of female ministry years later was traceable in part to this childhood environment. Moreover, Catherine became the secretary of the local Juvenile Temperance Society at the age of twelve. This position afforded her an opportunity to gain valuable leadership skills and to develop her self-confidence. Altogether, these early experiences made lasting contributions to Catherine's life.

Methodist chapel life was another factor in Catherine Mumford's social development, especially after her family moved to the London area in 1844. Once settled in her new surroundings, Catherine joined the Brixton Wesleyan Chapel and began to attend the class meetings designed for members of the congregation. These classes, which had emerged within Methodism in the 1740s, provided an intimate setting for spiritual nurture and study.[28] Usually convening on a weekly basis under the direction of an appointed leader, the dozen or so Methodists who attended a typical class meeting were expected to search their souls and engage in extemporaneous public prayer and testimony. Attendance at these classes was important, as it helped to define one's membership in the connexion. The more spiritually advanced members of a class would often find themselves placed in more select groups or "bands," where they were urged to seek the blessing of holiness. This pious environment not only stimulated the spiritual growth of Wesleyans, but also gave the laity a place to foster their self-confidence as they shared openly with one another.

Women, in particular, benefited greatly from the way in which class meetings were organized. Female Methodists demonstrating leadership qualities were urged to head these classes, which were such a crucial part of the religious body's system of instruction. Those who assumed this responsibility cultivated their interpersonal and public speaking skills, and thereby increased their self-confidence.[29] Catherine Mumford witnessed this kind of female leadership when she joined the Brixton chapel, since she was placed in a class under the direction of a Mrs. Keay. Seeking to be true to the ideals of this intimate grouping, Keay encouraged her class members to speak of their religious experience. This woman, however, found it difficult to persuade a timid Catherine to testify and pray in front of others. According to biographer William Stead, Catherine "pleaded in vain that the excitement and the strain of the effort made her ill."[30] Keay continued to urge Catherine to utilize the gifts that God had given her. While acknowledging that this class leader may have pressured Catherine relentlessly, Stead claimed that without this prodding "Catherine Mumford would never have been Mrs. Booth, and the Salvation Army might have still been a thing to dream of."[31] Perhaps this statement was an exaggeration, but there was some truth behind it. The Methodist class atmosphere not only demonstrated to Catherine that women could assume a public role in religion, but also forced her to confront her own fears about speaking in front of others.

An incident that took place within Wesleyan Methodism in 1849 ultimately led Catherine away from the denomination where she had gained her first exposure to female ministry. By the mid-nineteenth century the autocratic Secretary of the Wesleyan Connexion, Jabez Bunting, had orchestrated a campaign to purge his denomination of so-called agitators: freelance revivalists and democratically inspired clergy and laity.[32] Matters came to a head when three ministers suspected of being behind published attacks on Bunting were expelled. Those who sympathized with these ministers and their "Fly Sheets" seceded from the parent body in 1849, and a number within this group established a body known as the Reformers. When the schism occurred, chapel leaders warned their members to avoid contact with the secessionists. This was not something that Catherine could do, however, because she was sympathetic to the ideals of this breakaway faction. She supported the Reformers' demand that chapels should have more local autonomy, and, more importantly, she viewed the Reformer emphasis on revivalism as the antidote to a Methodism that had grown spiritually cold. Consequently, when Catherine attended the Reformers' meetings and defended their views, she was expelled from the Wesleyan fold. Soon after this expulsion, she joined the Reformers' chapel on Binfield Road, South London, where in 1852 she assumed leadership of a Sunday school class of teenaged girls. The timid girl whom Mrs. Keay had urged to speak just years earlier was now assuming a public role herself.

Many factors shaped the early life of Catherine Mumford, but the overriding influence in her life was Methodism. As an important branch of Victorian evangelicalism, this religious denomination nurtured her both within and outside the home. Domestically, Catherine learned quickly that the Christian life was one of self-denial and separation from the world, and that mothers bore the responsibility for their children's upbringing. Publicly, through Methodist social causes like temperance and Wesleyan classes and Sunday schools she was afforded the opportunity to confront her fears about public speaking and to develop her leadership abilities. Significantly, however, the domestic and public aspects of Catherine's life left her with two unresolved issues: how to develop self-confidence while maintaining self-denial; and how to promote female ministry while remaining committed to evangelical motherhood.

✥ Female Ministry and the Public Sphere

It will be recalled from chapter 3 that Catherine Mumford met her future husband, William Booth, through a mutual friend and Reformer by the name of Edward Rabbits. Not long after the young couple became engaged in May 1852, Catherine began to put forward her own position on female ministry. Whether or not this was the first time that she had done so is uncertain, but clearly her reading as a child, and her later exposure to a modest version of female ministry within her own Wesleyan chapel, contributed to the shaping of her convictions. Moreover, William's initial opposition to female preachers undoubtedly played a role in motivating Catherine to clarify and defend her notion of women's ministry. This process of refinement only intensified as she encountered much more hostile critics of female ministry in the years ahead. To a great extent, it was Catherine's background and the critics she faced that led her to defend and expand upon her views on women's role in the church. She would soon formulate arguments to justify a woman's right to preach and teach, and eventually she would begin her own public ministry in Methodist circles.

The extent to which women's historic role in the preaching life of Methodism had been eroded was the backdrop against which Catherine set out her earliest views on female ministry. Wesleyan Methodism of the eighteenth century and sectarian Methodism of the early nineteenth century had given a number of women the authority to preach and teach before mixed audiences.[33] Preaching, in particular, had expanded a woman's public role well beyond the parameters of the small Methodist class meetings, where a woman typically addressed just a few members of her own sex. A female preacher spoke before entire congregations and outdoor audiences of unsaved men and women. By the early 1850s, however, Methodist women found themselves within an environment that largely discouraged female preaching. Wesleyan Methodism had long since banned female preaching before mixed assemblies, and sectarian Methodist groups like the Primitive Methodists and the Bible Christians were gradually closing their doors to the practice. Within Methodism as a whole there was a growing conservatism among religious leaders, most of whom wished to adhere to supposed biblical injunctions against female preaching as well as to Victorian assumptions about a woman's place in the domestic sphere.

Catherine Mumford's earliest comments on women's role in the church were made within the context of this stifling environment. She was well aware of how the ecclesiastical arrangements of her own religious tradition were increasingly discriminating against the members of her own sex. Believing that God had, in both the Old and the New Testaments, made use of women in public ministry, Catherine considered it "cruel for the <u>church</u> to foster prejudice so unscriptural, and thus make the path of [female] <u>usefulness</u> the path of untold suffering"[34] [emphasis in original]. This conviction was evident in her first article, which she submitted to *The Methodist New Connexion Magazine* in 1854. While addressing the question of how to retain converts within the church, Catherine found time to criticize Methodism openly for abandoning its progressive stance on female ministry: "Why should the swaddling-bands of blind custom, which in Wesley's days were so triumphantly broken, and with such glorious results thrown to the moles and the bats, be again wrapped round the female disciples of the Lord Jesus?"[35] By invoking the name of John Wesley, the principal founder of Methodism, Catherine was challenging mid-Victorian Methodists to return to the core ideals of their own religious movement. Female ministry was not only biblical, but also part of the Wesleyan heritage. Those within the Methodist New Connexion, especially, needed to hear this message, because it was a branch of Methodism that had traditionally encouraged women to remain "lovely examples of domestic piety."[36]

Female ministry remained an important topic for Catherine after she married William Booth in 1855. However, it was not until four years later, when she was stationed with her husband at a Methodist New Connexion chapel in Gateshead, that she defended the practice at length. The circumstances surrounding her more detailed analysis of the issue were connected with the arrival of the American revivalists Phoebe and Walter Palmer in the neighbouring city of Newcastle in early September 1859.[37] Phoebe and her husband had just commenced a four-year evangelistic campaign in Britain to promote holiness and to awaken the spiritually cold members of the church. What made the Palmers' revivalism unique was the fact that Phoebe took an active role in these endeavours, addressing both men and women publicly. Even though she never claimed to preach in a technical sense by entering the pulpit to speak, Phoebe's public testifying and biblical expositions were consistent with her scriptural understanding of the practice. For Phoebe Palmer, all people were called upon to preach the gospel, since the biblical notion of preaching was simply the proclamation of the good news. This broad definition also included testifying and prophesying, which she associated with the outpouring of the Holy Spirit upon men and women in the book of Acts. By acting upon these convictions, Phoebe challenged the mid-Victorian belief that women should remain silent in the church.[38]

Already familiar with Phoebe Palmer's books on holiness, Catherine Booth told her parents in mid- and late September 1859 that she hoped to attend one of Phoebe's revival meetings.[39] Frederick Booth-Tucker, one of Catherine's earliest biographers, claimed that she never found the opportunity to do so, but Phoebe Palmer did return to the area in 1860, spending five weeks in Gateshead beginning in June.[40] Perhaps, therefore, Catherine found the opportunity to hear her then. In any event, Catherine followed Phoebe Palmer's initial activities in the region quite closely. When, therefore, a nearby independent minister, the Reverend Arthur Augustus Rees, criticized Phoebe Palmer for preaching, Catherine was incensed. Rees's remarks, which were addressed initially to his own Sunderland congregation and then published in the form of a pamphlet, meant to show that Phoebe Palmer's preaching was a violation of the Apostle Paul's directives to the church.[41] Appealing to 1 Corinthians 14:34-35 and 1 Timothy 2:11-14, Rees argued that, since sin had entered into the world through Eve, all women were to remain silent in the church. He therefore considered it unnatural for a woman to assume any role other than one of quiet submission to the men of a congregation. Not only was Catherine angered by these comments, which she felt were demeaning to all women, but she also was unhappy with the various attempts to defend Phoebe Palmer against Rees's charges. Consequently, in December 1859 Catherine decided to refute Rees herself by writing her own pamphlet on the subject of female ministry.

This pamphlet, given the lengthy title *Female Teaching: Or, the Rev. A.A. Rees Versus Mrs. Palmer, Being a Reply to a Pamphlet by the Above Gentleman on the Sunderland Revival*, put forward a threefold argument in favour of women's right to preach and teach in the church.[42] First of all, Catherine furnished a response to Rees's charge that it was unnatural or unfeminine for a woman to preach in a religious assembly. While conceding that it was not customary or usual for women to do so, she claimed that the members of her sex were suited by nature to preach: "God has given to woman a graceful form and attitude, winning manners, persuasive speech, and, above all, a finely-toned emotional nature, all of which appear to us eminent *natural* qualifications for public speaking"[43] [italics in original]. This being the case, Catherine went on to argue that women's exclusion from public ministry was simply the result of prejudicial customs that prevented them from employing their God-given gifts. These man-made restrictions gave the impression that a public ecclesiastical role for women was unnatural, when in fact the very opposite was true. For Catherine, God had endowed women with a nature that gave them the right to engage in female ministry.

Given the world in which she lived, it is not surprising that Catherine argued that women's subjective qualities—emotionality, gracefulness and persuasiveness—suited them for preaching. To begin with, her own Wesleyan heritage equated religion with the heart or subjective aspects of human nature. To emphasize a woman's subjective characteristics was to underscore her compatibility with the essence of religion, and thereby present her as an ideal candidate for preaching the gospel message. Moreover, the emphasis that Catherine put on the subjective side of a woman's nature was not meant to imply that women were by nature intellectually inferior to men. Elsewhere in *Female Teaching* she argued that any inferiority that women displayed in the realm of the intellect was due to their inadequate training and unequal access to education.[44] Catherine did not believe that a woman's emotional characteristics came at the expense of her intellectual abilities. This was strikingly apparent in the way in which she presented this first argument. Rees and other Victorians might claim that a woman's emotional nature suited her to a secondary role in the church, but Catherine turned such reasoning on its head: a woman's subjective qualities made her the logical choice for the pulpit! Although she employed this line of reasoning with great skill, Catherine was not the first person to justify female ministry on the basis of a woman's nature. Phoebe Palmer's lengthy defence of female ministry, *Promise of the Father*, had appeared a few months before Catherine's pamphlet, and had incorporated this theme within its overall argument. Phoebe Palmer argued that women were ideally suited to public ministry, because God had endowed them with "the power of persuasion and the ability to captivate."[45] Catherine certainly agreed, and used this kind of argument to good effect.

Above all else, however, Catherine Booth believed that her defence of female ministry had to be justified biblically. Her evangelical conviction that the Bible was the authoritative guide to all of life, divinely inspired and infallible, led her to recognize the gravity of this task.[46] Consequently, the scriptures became the focal point of her second general argument in *Female Teaching*. The heart of her strategy here was to show that the Bible, when interpreted and applied properly, supported a public role for women in the church. It followed from this premise that opposition to female ministry resulted from a mishandling of the biblical text. The overall charge that Catherine levelled against Rees and others was that they took "isolated passages, separated from their explanatory connexions."[47] More specifically, she claimed that (1) they severed scriptural texts from their contexts, and (2) they failed to use the "plain and unmistakable" portions of the Bible to shed light on the more difficult sections.[48] Once the biblical texts were handled in a more responsible manner, a strong case for female ministry could be made. With this in mind, Catherine devoted the body of her pamphlet to the key passages related to the subject.

One part of this strategy rested upon a reassessment of the two New Testament texts most often used by conservatives to prohibit women from preaching and teaching in the church. The first passage in question, 1 Corinthians 14:34-35, was taken by most Victorian believers to prescribe women's silence in the church. What Catherine argued here was that the Apostle Paul, the assumed writer of this text, could not possibly be commanding women to remain completely silent, because he had just described, in chapter 11 of the same epistle, how women should pray and prophesy publicly. To claim that he enjoined absolute silence upon women was to make his earlier comments meaningless: "[I]f the Apostle refers in both instances to the same thing, we make him in one page give the most explicit directions how a thing shall be performed, which in a page or two further on, and writing to the *same* Church, he expressly forbids being performed at all"[49] [italics in original]. Catherine's hermeneutical method of comparing scripture with scripture, and her assumption that the Bible could not contradict itself, led her to conclude that 1 Corinthians only precluded women from engaging in "a pertinacious, inquisitive, domineering, dogmatical kind of speaking" that might "bring them into collision with the men … ruffle their tempers, and occasion an unamiable volubility of speech."[50] This reinterpretation, although encouraging no direct challenge to male authority, had the potential to subvert the traditional male monopoly of preaching.

The second text that opponents of female ministry often cited was 1 Timothy 2:11-14, which conveyed the message that women must remain silent in the church because of Adam's priority in Creation and Eve's priority in sin. Rees, in particular, drew upon this passage to argue that women's silence in the church was a punishment for Eve's role in bringing evil into the world. Catherine's major tactic here was to question the assumption that these verses referred at all to a woman's deportment in the church.[51] She put forward the views of commentators who suggested that this passage, when studied contextually and grammatically, was aimed simply at wives who usurped the authority of their husbands in the home. Catherine also weakened the argument linking women's silence to the Fall, because, while acknowledging that woman was the first to sin, she reminded Rees that man bore equal responsibility for introducing sin into the world. She argued additionally that, even if one were to place any moral significance on woman's temporal position in the Fall, this was now overshadowed by the primacy of woman's role in redemption: "If, through her, sin first entered, through her also, without the concurrence of man, came deliverance."[52] The fact that Christ had been born of the Virgin Mary, and had upon his resurrection appeared first to women, was more than sufficient evidence to counterbalance the dishonour associated with the female role in chapter 3 of Genesis. Although Catherine's main concern was to call into question the relevance of this Pauline passage to an ecclesiastical setting, she also helped to undermine the rationale used by church leaders to keep women silent.

After reinterpreting these so-called problematic texts, Catherine put forward the positive biblical case for female ministry. Two dominant contentions emerged from her appeal to various portions of scripture. First, Catherine argued that a public role for women in religion had divine sanction. Women like Miriam, Deborah and Huldah had been commissioned by God as leaders and prophetesses in the Old Testament, and the Samaritan woman and Mary Magdalene were among the first individuals in the New Testament to receive authority from Christ to spread the message of salvation in a public manner.[53] Each of these instances proved that God endorsed a public ministry for women. Also significant for Catherine was the book of Acts, especially the second chapter, because it revealed that upon Christ's ascension to heaven the Holy Spirit was bestowed equally upon male and female believers, authorizing them to prophesy publicly. Moreover, Catherine claimed that the prophesying referred to in Acts was equivalent to preaching: "The prophesying spoken of was not the foretelling of events, but the *preaching* to the world at large the glad tidings of salvation by Jesus Christ"[54] [italics in original]. It was apparent, therefore, that when Acts referred to women prophesying—such as Philip's four daughters in Acts 21:9—they were in fact preaching. On the basis of these biblical texts, she contended that God's Spirit authorized women to preach.

Catherine's other major rationale for female ministry rested upon Galatians 3:28. She took this passage to mean that in the church all cultural and sexual divisions were to be set aside: "If this passage does not teach that in the privileges, duties, and responsibilities of Christ's Kingdom, all differences of nation, caste, and sex are abolished, we should like to know what it does teach, and wherefore it was written."[55] From this text she drew the conclusion that a woman's gender could not be used to disqualify her from a public ministry in the church. All believers, male and female, should therefore have the freedom to utilize their gifts, including those of preaching and teaching, within the Body of Christ. Old distinctions, even those between the clergy and the laity, were to be superseded by oneness and liberty in Christ.[56] That the gospel signalled a new dispensation of freedom under which men and women could minister together was apparent, Catherine claimed, from the Apostle Paul's letters to the Roman and Philippian Christians, in which he identified a number of women as his co-labourers in the Lord (Rom 16:3-4, 7; Phil 4:3). These relationships hardly revealed women's subordination to men in the church: "To be a partner, coadjutor, or joint worker with a preacher of the Gospel must be something more than to be His waiting-maid."[57] In other words, a woman's role in the Christian religion was not to work for men, but to work with men. Overall, Catherine viewed Galatians 3:28, and its subsequent application in the earliest churches, as the expression of authentic Christianity.

Thus far, Catherine's defence of female ministry included appeals to a woman's nature and to the Bible, but near the conclusion of her pamphlet she presented a third and final argument. Here, she claimed that success accompanied the efforts of female preachers. Quoting extensively from Phoebe Palmer's book *Promise of the Father*, Catherine documented the positive results achieved by the female preachers and missionaries of the eighteenth and early nineteenth centuries. It was clear from these accounts that numerous holy women had been "owned of God in the conversion of thousands of souls, and the abundant edification of the Lord's people."[58] This appeal to a woman's success in ministry was also an important pillar of the arguments of Hugh Bourne and William O'Bryan. Bourne, in particular, concluded his pamphlet *Remarks on the Ministry of Women* with a personal affirmation of the ways in which "the Lord has set his seal to a woman's ministry, by converting sinners to himself."[59] Catherine agreed, reasoning that this success was, according to the Apostle Paul, evidence of a divine call. In closing, Catherine asked her Victorian readers to ponder "whether the circumscribed sphere of woman's religious labours may not have something to do with the comparative non-success of the gospel in these latter days."[60] For her, there was no doubt about the answer.

This pamphlet's threefold argument, set within the context of a woman's right to preach, represented a bold challenge to male privilege in the church. Yet, the assertive tone underlying this justification of female ministry was not transferred as easily to Catherine's everyday life.[61] She struggled at a personal level, as she had during the 1840s, to assert herself publicly by speaking in front of others. The nature of this problem had been illustrated clearly in a letter she wrote to William in 1853: "I want to serve God as He requires, but I fear to err in my judgment and my nature shrinks from singularity and publicity."[62] Catherine had garnered enough confidence to speak before a group of young temperance supporters by late 1857, but she continued to display an ambivalence towards her own public ministry. Writing to her mother soon after she had given this lecture, she stated: "I felt quite at home on the Platform[,] far more so than I do in the Kitchen!! … [B]ut I must not be too sanguine. I perhaps may lose my confidence next time"[63] [emphasis in original]. Here, Catherine was beginning to discover her gift for public speaking, but self-doubts lingered on. Two years later, however, on the eve of the publication of *Female Teaching*, even Catherine's tempered enthusiasm for public work was no longer apparent. When asked by the leaders of her Gateshead chapel to address a special prayer meeting, she turned down the request. Describing this incident to her mother, Catherine exclaimed: "[O]f course [I] declined. I don't know what they can be thinking of."[64] Although Catherine's writings encouraged women to assume a public role in the church, she was reluctant to take on this role herself.

When Catherine Booth finally found the courage to preach for the first time in the late spring of 1860, she did not justify her own entry into the pulpit with the assertive language of rights or on the basis of self-determination. Instead, her own motivation for ministry grew out of an intense religious experience. On a Sunday morning in May, while sitting among the one thousand or so members of her husband's Gateshead chapel, she sensed two inner voices. The first of these urged her to fulfil a recent vow that she had made before God to testify in public, telling her that it would bless her own soul as well as the souls of those in the congregation. Even so, Catherine was initially

Catherine Booth. Courtesy of The Salvation Army International Heritage Centre, London.

unwilling to respond affirmatively: "No Lord, it is the old thing over again, but I cannot do it."[65] Immediately after this divine prodding, Catherine seemed to hear another inward voice, that of the Adversary, tempting her to remain silent: "And then the Devil said, 'Besides, you are not prepared to speak. You will look like a fool, and have nothing to say.' He made a mistake. He overdid himself for once. It was that word which settled it. I said, 'Ah! This is just the point. I have never yet been willing to be a fool for Christ, now I will be one.'"[66] With this, Catherine moved out of her seat, went up to the front of the chapel and told her bewildered husband that she wanted to "say a word."[67] Turning to the assembled crowd, she confessed that she had been resisting God's will for some time by refusing to speak publicly in the church. Once this admission had been made, William Booth announced that his wife would be the preacher at the evening service. This Gateshead experience marked the beginning of Catherine's long and successful preaching ministry.

Over the course of the next twenty-eight years Catherine Booth not only became a popular preacher throughout Britain, but also helped to establish and run the Christian Mission and Salvation Army. In addition, she sought many times to defend the nascent organization against its critics, and through her sermons and books she provided it with some of its basic theological foundations.[68] Many Victorian observers of the Salvation Army considered her preaching and teachings to represent the best the organization had to offer.[69] Yet, despite these impressive accomplishments and accolades, Catherine rarely took the credit she deserved. She based her own preaching on a denial or deficiency of self rather than on her gifts and her right to utilize them. Her own call to preach arose out of submission to God and self-sacrifice—or what she had to yield to or give up rather than what she had to offer. At times she even placed her own preaching within the context of human weakness, arguing that God "loves to use the weak things, that the excellency may be seen to be of God."[70] Catherine experienced periods of illness throughout her life, but she too easily subsumed her own preaching talents under the theme of human weakness. Furthermore, when the Christian Mission evolved into the Salvation Army and adopted military titles, Catherine did not take one. Her husband was known as the General, whereas she was simply "Mrs. Booth" or "Mrs. General Booth."[71] Such a title gave the impression that Catherine derived her status from her husband William, when in fact this was not the case at all. Altogether, Catherine never took sufficient credit for her role in the founding of the Army.[72] In so doing, she devalued her own contributions to the Salvation Army.

What is the explanation for Catherine Booth's reluctance to affirm her own abilities and acknowledge her significance in the creation and maintenance of the Army? To some extent, she was protecting the fragile ego of her husband. As Norman Murdoch has noted perceptively, Catherine's early success as a preacher and author, all of which gained her a good deal of coverage in the international press, was more than "an insecure husband could cope with."[73] Perhaps even more significant, however, was Catherine's strict evangelical upbringing. She grew up in a home where the concepts of submission to God's will and self-denial were of paramount importance. This kind of environment hardly encouraged her to take credit for anything she did. The subordination of one's will to God, which was necessary to overcome sin, meant that self had to be renounced. To allow a part of self to survive was to remain in bondage to sin. It is apparent from Catherine Booth's own writings that she never abandoned this evangelical perspective. In her early correspondence with William this understanding of selflessness was expressed clearly: "I must get *self* destroyed, and then the Lord may trust me to do good without endangering my own soul"[74] [italics in original]. Another instance of this notion of self-abnegation surfaced in an article that Catherine wrote on pastoral visitation. She asked her readers if they were "*willing* to trample on self"[75] [italics in original]. Weak or selfless individuals were God's chosen vehicles for ministering to a lost world. Then in her book *Papers on Godliness*, Catherine identified self with the epitome of sinfulness: "[God] hates selfishness—selfishness is the devil, the very embodiment of him. You must get out of self."[76] These evangelical beliefs about self had a great deal to do with the way that Catherine interpreted her own life and place within the Salvation Army.

In the end, the public legacy that Catherine Booth left to Salvationist women was an ambiguous one. On the one hand, she was fearless in her writings, challenging male prejudice in the church and demolishing arguments that sought to keep women silent in the church. Furthermore, the fact that she placed her defence of female ministry within the context of a woman's right to an equal role alongside men in the church was groundbreaking for her time. Not only did she go beyond the early Wesleyan practice that based female preaching on an exceptional call, but she also refined and expanded Phoebe Palmer's arguments for female ministry. A female preacher was neither the product of unusual circumstances (Wesley) nor a preacher without a pulpit (Palmer), but rather someone possessing a God-given right to occupy the platform. In turn, this conviction found its way into the Salvation Army's *Orders and Regulations*, which laid down the principle of sexual equality in ministry. On the other hand, the ways in which Catherine Booth interpreted her preaching and other contributions to the Salvation Army were less than liberating for women. The placement of her own abilities and accomplishments within the evangelical context of self-denial, weakness and submission was problematic for female officers. This side of Catherine's life seemed to convey the twofold message that it was illegitimate for women to celebrate their own strengths and abilities and wrong for them to pursue a public ministry on the basis of self-expression and self-determination. Selfhood remained a rather suspect category for Catherine, and seemed at times to be much less important than female self-sacrifice and selflessness.

❖ Domesticity and the Private Sphere

By the 1850s, Victorians were categorizing certain roles and responsibilities on the basis of gender. Men and women were assumed to possess different traits, the substance of which suited them for unique tasks and callings. Underlying these societal convictions, which had a great deal to do with evangelicalism, was an ideology of separate spheres: the world of business and politics was a masculine preserve, while the home was a feminine realm. Although the domestic sphere was not the sole realm for middle-class women, who engaged in philanthropy, and rarely the only one for working-class women, who had to supplement family incomes, it continued to be defined in terms of female submission, morality and motherhood. The Victorian home was largely a feminine geography, and women were expected to nurture a domestic environment that served their husbands and provided education for the young. In evangelical households, in particular, the wife had a sacred obligation to serve as a helpmeet to her husband and a guardian of her children's spirituality and morality. As many pious Victorians were known to assert, no one respected a woman who neglected domestic affairs for the sake of wider interests. Even though these feminine ideals were challenged by the more radical members of the nineteenth-century women's rights movement, they remained normative beliefs for the vast majority of British people well into the twentieth century.[77]

Looking simply at the public legacy of Catherine Booth, it may appear that these societal mores had little to do with the way in which she thought and lived her life. It is true that her own public ministry on the platform helped to blur the distinction between a masculine public realm and a feminine private realm, but did she endorse a view of womanhood that sought to remove such boundaries altogether? Judging from her assumptions about marriage and motherhood, the answer is no. Catherine strove to expand the opportunities afforded to women, but she had no time for women who wished to forsake their duties in the home. Her own evangelical upbringing, in particular, had taught her about the great importance of a woman's place within the home. While she felt justified in pursuing a public life of preaching, she continued to support the Victorian pillars of domesticity: feminine submission in marriage and maternal obligation in the home. Evangelicalism may have provided Catherine Booth with a public life, but it also reminded her of the duties she had towards her husband and children.

VIEWS ON MARRIAGE

Catherine's earliest views on marriage appeared in correspondence she sent to William when he was stationed on the Reformers' circuit at Spalding, Lincolnshire. Two of these personal letters, written between late December 1852 and early January 1853, revealed a degree of ambivalence on the subject. One theme of the December letter was male headship in marriage, as Catherine reminded William that "the father is, and must be, in every well [-]regulated family[,] the <u>head</u> of his household"[78] [emphasis in original]. Here, she seemed to be advocating a hierarchical marital relationship in which the husband was above the wife. The January letter, however, had a more egalitarian tone.[79] In this epistle Catherine suggested that Christ had restored woman to a position of equality within marriage, thereby reversing the curse of Genesis 3:16, which included wifely subjection to her husband. Christian marriages were to be based upon a "perfect oneness" or union between both spouses. Moreover, Catherine criticized the Victorian educational system for teaching women to accept the notion that they were completely subject to the will of others. In conclusion, she stated that marriages would not be perfect until woman was "valued and <u>educated</u> as man's equal"[80] [emphasis in original]. The substance of this argument was equality rather than submission.

What accounted for the vast difference between these two letters, written just a few days apart? Fortunately, Catherine's subsequent correspondence helps to explain the nature of her ambivalence. Perhaps the best clues to an answer were contained in an April 1855 letter she addressed to William:

> I would not alter woman's domestic position (when indeed it is scriptural) because God has plainly fixed it; *He* has told her to obey her husband.... God *ordained* her subjection as a punishment *for sin,* and *therefore* I submit; but I cannot believe that inferiority was the ground of it.... [Furthermore, Jesus] has taken the bitterest part of her curse "out of the way, nailing it to his cross." ... In *Him* her *equality* with her earthly lord is realised, for "in Him there is neither male nor female," and while the outward semblance of her curse remains, in *Him* it is nullified by love being made the law of marriage.[81] [italics in original]

This highlights the extent to which Catherine's understanding of equality within marriage was primarily spiritual in nature. Besides the obvious fact that she did not wish to challenge the social hierarchy of the home, she also prefaced every reference to equality with the phrase "in Him," thereby placing the concept within the context of spiritual union with Christ. In Catherine's mind, spiritual equality seemed to be separate from a husband's rule in the household. She believed that a partnership on the religious plane could flourish, even though the "outward semblance" of a woman's curse forbade mutuality on the social plane.

The belief, however, that male headship could coexist with spiritual equality was ultimately flawed. Domestic or social servitude did indeed have a direct bearing on a woman's spiritual standing. Catherine suggested as much in her later pamphlet *Female Teaching*. Near the conclusion of this thirty-two-page treatise, she asserted that a woman had a right to preach and teach "except when, as a wife, silence is imposed upon her by her own husband."[82] In other words, a wife's freedom to minister equally alongside men was in the hands of her spouse. As the head of his household, he alone possessed the power to uphold or undermine his wife's equality in the pulpit. While Catherine appeared to be comfortable with this arrangement—William allowed her to preach—it created an ambiguous environment for the overwhelming majority of married female officers who followed in her footsteps. Male headship rarely sanctioned anything other than a modest public role for them in the life of the organization. A woman's responsibilities and rank were derived from those given to her husband. This patriarchal model ensured that public roles and power remained predominantly in the hands of men, thereby placing female ministry upon a precarious foundation. Married women's access to preaching and leadership roles did not constitute an inalienable right, but more of a privilege granted to them by their husbands. Such opportunities were only meaningful insofar as women had husbands who shared their convictions on the subject. It will be recalled from chapters 3 and 4 that not all male officers held liberal views on this subject. Male headship, therefore, functioned to keep a woman's public roles modest and on a tenuous footing.

To claim, as Catherine did in her 1855 letter to William, that wifely submission was governed by the law of love may have sounded somewhat liberating for the Victorian age, but it did not mean very much in daily life. Given what Catherine said in *Female Teaching*, a woman could not appeal to the law of love to legitimize her calling to preach if her husband objected to the practice. This moral stipulation had very little impact upon a husband's authority in this area. Furthermore, it is unclear what purpose it had in any sphere of married life, because Catherine admitted that her tempered version of subjection seldom lasted beyond a couple's courting days.[83] In reality, her appeal to the law of love merely put a benevolent face on patriarchy, and therefore did nothing to challenge the assumption that power rested ultimately with the husband. He was the earthly equivalent of the Father in heaven. Catherine's unwillingness or inability to distance herself from this evangelical and Victorian understanding of marriage worked against her more liberal views concerning a woman's right to preach. Despite her advanced views in the area of female ministry, she believed that a married woman remained dependent upon her spouse. This conviction, which lay at the heart of evangelicalism, would haunt the female Salvationists who sought to follow Catherine's example. Her version of spiritual equality did not alleviate the social subordination of women.[84]

VIEWS ON MOTHERHOOD

Having been raised by an evangelical mother who devoted so much of her time to the spiritual and mental nurture of her offspring, it is not surprising that Catherine Booth held strong views on the maternal role in raising children. In fact, Catherine viewed motherhood as a sacred obligation that was not being taken seriously enough by her Victorian contemporaries. As a young adult in the early 1850s, she criticized the English educational system for failing to prepare women morally and mentally for the responsibilities of motherhood. In her mind, female education was "calculated to render woman anything but a helpmate to man, and a judicious self[-]dependent trainer of children."[85] Then, in 1857, Catherine lamented the fact that working-class girls employed in factories were receiving hardly any training for their future role as mothers: "What pitiable wives and mothers they will make! Mothers! Alas, I should say bearers of children, for we have lamentable evidence that in every thing desirable to the sacred relationship they are awfully deficient."[86] Years later, she continued to believe that maternal duty remained on the decline within Britain, as demonstrated by her addresses to the middle classes of the West End of London. She felt it necessary to remind women themselves of the vocation to which they were called: "[T]he great want of England is mothers—right-minded, able, competent, Christian mothers, who realize their responsibility to God and to their children, and who are resolved at all costs and sacrifices to discharge it."[87] Even as she approached death in October 1890, Catherine continued to see herself as a crusader for motherhood.[88] She urged society in general, and women in particular, to recognize its importance.

Catherine Booth believed that the chief responsibility of mothers was to educate their children entirely at home. She shared her mother's conviction that Victorian schools, even so-called Christian ones, were seedbeds of immorality and impurity.[89] In her book entitled *Popular Christianity*, written in 1887, Catherine warned women not to neglect their God-given capacity and duty to educate their young at home:

> God has given every child a tutor in his mother, and she is the best and only right tutor for the heart. I defy you to fill a proper mother's place for influence over the heart. … God has tied the child to its mother by such peculiar moral and mental links that no other being could possibly possess. I tell you mothers here, that if you are good mothers, you are committing the greatest wrong to send away your child from your homes, and I believe this wretched practice is ruining half our nation today.[90]

At one level this admonition simply reflected an extreme evangelical philosophy of education, but on another level it signalled how much Catherine's thinking was shaped by the nineteenth-century assumption that mothers were suited naturally to the domestic realm as the guardians of their children's moral and intellectual training.

One particular vehicle for promoting these views during the Salvation Army's earliest days as a mission was the mothers' meeting. This type of ministry was quite common in evangelical circles by the mid-1860s, and reflected a belief in "the power of a mother's influence for good or for evil" in the raising of her children.[91] This sentiment was echoed in the Christian Mission, where mothers were reminded: "You should be such a saint, and so impress your children's minds, that away in the years to come, when you are in your grave, they may remember you as an angel of purity and love."[92] William and Catherine Booth's mission work assigned an important place to mothers' meetings at least as early as 1868. Mary Billups, an early Missioner, hoped that through these societies the Mission would be able to reach "struggling mothers" and their homes.[93] The mothers who attended these groups were urged to keep their houses clean and to provide a spiritual and moral environment for their children. Given her convictions in this area, there can be little doubt that Catherine Booth was fully behind this venture. Much of the same thinking and assumptions were held as well by Mary Sumner, an Anglican minister's wife, who established the Mothers' Union in 1876. Sumner, like Catherine Booth and the Christian Mission, was out to raise the standards of mothering in Britain by instructing women on their duties in the home.[94]

Increasing expectations about motherhood in Victorian society placed enormous pressures on evangelical women who wished to combine family duties with female ministry. When, for instance, Catherine Booth agreed in 1860 to take on William's circuit while he recovered from a nervous breakdown, it was difficult for her, as a mother of four young children, to fulfil both ministerial tasks and domestic obligations. A late summertime letter she addressed to William, who was away from home seeking treatment for his illness, revealed how stressful this situation could be: "You see[,] I cannot get rid of the care and management of things at home, and this sadly interferes with the quiet necessary for [sermon] preparation."[95] What Catherine never appreciated, however, was how her own stringent views on motherhood exacerbated an already frustrating set of circumstances. At no time did she allow her public role to be fulfilled at the expense of her maternal duties. Even with the birth of four more children between 1862 and 1867, Catherine Booth sought to balance her maternal obligations with her public ministry. There is little doubt that her ability to cope with such a demanding schedule owed something to her exceptional talents. Perhaps even more significant was the fact that the Booths were able to employ domestic help, especially after Catherine's entry onto the platform.[96] Domestic servants helped her with the household chores, while a governess assisted her with the education of the Booth children. Although Catherine Booth remained intimately involved with the upbringing of her family, this kind of assistance allowed her to enjoy a preaching ministry outside the home.

There is no doubt that this more public aspect of Catherine Booth's life was a significant part of her legacy to female Salvationists. Her example inspired many young women to find a voice and embark upon a preaching career in a male-dominated profession. Yet, the more domestic side of Catherine's legacy to Army women made it difficult for them to nurture this public heritage. According to Catherine Booth, motherhood was a sacred vocation with clearly defined responsibilities within the home. Even with the assistance of a servant in the home—a luxury beyond the means of most Army households—female Salvationists faced family pressures that often curtailed their involvement on the platform.[97] Furthermore, Catherine Booth's adherence to male headship within marriage placed restrictions on a woman's public ministry. Even though Catherine alluded to male privilege in the church as part of the reason why women were excluded from the pulpit, she left the pre-eminent expression of male privilege—headship in the home—largely unchallenged. In so doing, she left the application of Salvationist principles of equality in the hands of men. Male headship and a demanding maternalism would hardly provide Army women with equal opportunities to minister alongside men, or to assume prominent leadership roles in the organization's administration. Unfortunately, Catherine left women with no clear way to resolve the tensions between their private and public lives. Because more and more single women were marrying their male counterparts by the late 1880s, this inequitable arrangement was experienced by an increasing majority of women within the Army.[98]

Catherine Booth's beliefs and teachings were indeed incorporated into the Salvation Army, but most scholars of her life and thought have largely chosen to ignore the more problematic aspects of this institutional legacy. Regardless of the intentions behind this approach, it has led to a less than complete picture of this complex nineteenth-century woman. In particular, those pursuing this one-sided strategy have given the impression that Catherine's evangelical and Victorian background, especially what she learned in the home, had little bearing on the kind of public life she envisioned for herself and other women. Yet, it is clear from the preceding pages that Catherine Booth's evangelical assumptions, especially those concerning self, marriage and motherhood, played a significant role in how she interpreted and lived out her vision of a woman's place within society. Taken together, the public and domestic aspects of her thinking represented an ambiguous legacy. While she did much to attack sexism in the church and to expand the opportunities of women in ministry, she also helped to reinforce theological convictions and cultural mores that identified women with selflessness, submission and domesticity.

The last chapter of this book addresses the extent to which Salvationist women reinforced or challenged the public and domestic paradigm bequeathed by Catherine Booth. Particular attention is focused upon the years from 1890 to 1930, which were formative ones for the Salvation Army in a number of areas. In spite of the dynamism of this foundational era, very little historical energy has been spent upon it. Even less is known about the lives of female Salvationists beyond the early 1900s—how they forged their public and domestic roles in the Army, and what they did to expand or restrict their responsibilities in either realm. Data on women's representation at various levels of the organization's leadership have been available for years, but remain to be tabulated. The next chapter begins such a tabulation, assessing the degree to which these women, married or single, found either the time or the opportunity to pursue a public role in the middle and upper levels of Salvationist leadership and administration. Even a cursory examination of this quantitative evidence points to a much different set of circumstances than has been appreciated by those within and outside the organization.

❖

CHAPTER 6

Public and Domestic Service: The Experiences of Female Officers

WRITING TO FEMALE OFFICERS IN 1913, Florence Booth, the wife of the Salvation Army's second General, suggested that women's equality with men in the ranks depended upon these officers maintaining their feminine identity: "Now, in order that we may take and retain the place prepared for us, we must be true to our womanhood. There is no need for us to abandon this in any sense, even though we take a position of equal authority and influence with men, or use to the full all the opportunities afforded us by The Salvation Army."[1] A similar message was conveyed by Catherine Higgins, another high-ranking Army officer, in 1915. Higgins was convinced that the effectiveness of a female leader in the organization lay in her staying true to the "instincts" of her womanhood.[2] Both women claimed to support the idea of women in positions of authority, but they believed that a female officer's presence in the public offices and roles of the denomination should not come at the expense of her nature. Equality with men was attainable, they asserted, but only if female officers remained faithful to certain notions of femininity. Leadership was to be based upon the complementary traits of men and women.

Arguments of this kind were not uncommon in the nineteenth and early twentieth centuries, and some avowed feminists were known to describe sexual equality in very similar terms. The problem with this model, however, was that it invariably produced gender segregation rather than gender inclusion. In both the secular and the religious contexts of the age, the correlation of sexual difference with equality was confining rather than liberating for both genders. For instance, the association of human qualities like instinct with women made it all too easy to assume that they were ideally suited for certain roles and responsibilities, while men were fitted for others. This was certainly the experience in the early Salvation Army, where images of femininity worked against any widespread application of gender equality. With the odd exception, female officers assumed a womanhood that reflected and reinforced societal and evangelical convictions. Such an approach did not necessarily rule out a public role for female officers, but it seldom led to their promotion beyond the pulpit or the more traditional areas of female ministry. This final chapter pays close attention to the cultural and theological pillars of womanhood that Salvationist women embraced and fortified, but seldom modified in any significant ways.

❖ Women and the Domestic Realm

The Victorian ideology of separate spheres became an increasing reality for many working-class women in Britain between the 1890s and the 1920s.[3] Notwithstanding their involvement in the public arena during the First World War, and a gradual reduction in the size of families, British women faced increasing pressure to remain at home, looking after their husbands and children. By the early 1900s, for instance, alarm over a high infant mortality rate, fuelled by fears of a degenerating imperial race, had a direct bearing upon women. Legislators and middle-class observers came to see motherhood as the key to reviving the British Empire at home and abroad. Perceived neglect in this area, especially within the working classes, led to renewed calls for women to look after the needs of the home and family. One key component of this campaign was domestic science, which included courses to prepare working-class schoolgirls for motherhood and household management. On the economic front, a rising standard of living after 1918 led a growing number of men to discourage their wives from working outside the home. The notion of the male breadwinner, earning enough to support the entire family, became a possibility for more and more working-class households, thereby making a married woman's paid work unnecessary. Marriage bars became increasingly prevalent during this period as well, preventing women from combining motherhood with a career. After having their first child, many women were forced out of a variety of occupations. Taken together, these circumstances helped to strengthen and broaden the Victorian and evangelical belief that a woman's rightful place was in the domestic realm.

Unlike many middle-class women, and a growing number of their working-class peers, female officers in the Salvation Army were not tied exclusively to the home. They generally had some means of public expression in corps life and social work. Furthermore, there were no obvious marriage bars within the organization, since Salvation Army guidelines did not prohibit women with children from undertaking a public ministry. Yet, even here, pervasive cultural and theological assumptions about a woman's place in the home found expression, serving to overshadow official guidelines on sexual equality and shared ministry. An ideology of separate spheres, while sometimes more insidious than its expression within the broader society, was accepted and reinforced by the early Salvation Army. The fact remained that female officers were responsible for the home and children in a way that their menfolk were not. Although there were occasional exceptions to this pattern, this overriding ethos was accepted by most officer women, some of whom even helped to foster domestic science and imperial notions of motherhood within the working classes. The collective beliefs and practices in this area had obvious implications for women's status as officers, given the problems of combining home and family with opportunities for public ministry.

MORALITY, SPIRITUALITY AND THE HOME

Perhaps the clearest indication of the Salvation Army's assumptions about women and the home was the introduction of a "Women's Section" in its weekly periodical *The War Cry* in January 1899. This development bore witness to the growing number of families in the organization, and the need to ensure that mothers attended to their duties in the domestic realm. This feature page appeared without a break for six years, and reappeared on a regular basis in 1921 after wartime paper rationing restrictions were lifted. Among the numerous themes discussed in this section were motherhood, child-raising and religion in the home. Articles throughout the period stressed that only a mother could create a home, establishing within it an atmosphere of love and godliness. As one early article noted: "The management of a Home… is an important field for the woman-Salvationist who realises her opportunities and the value of a holy influence."[4] A central part of this godly responsibility was to train children to love and serve God. Mothers were called upon to ensure that their children received adequate moral and spiritual training to prepare them for an evil and increasingly secular world. The female officers who wrote for this page believed that mothers had a sacred duty to bring the entire family, including husbands, closer to God and moral excellence.[5]

The belief that women were largely responsible for establishing the moral climate within the home was an important theme in the life and work of Florence Booth.[6] This influential woman had grown up in an Anglican upper-middle-class home in Wales, where her father was a medical doctor. In 1876, at the age of fifteen, Florence left home to attend a finishing school run by two of her aunts in London. Four years later, near the end of her studies, she came into contact with Catherine Booth after hearing her preach in London's fashionable West End. Catherine Booth's sermon had a special effect upon Florence, who was beginning to contemplate her future career. Not long after this initial meeting in 1880, Florence joined the Salvation Army. Following a brief period helping one of the Booth daughters to pioneer the organization's work in France, she married the Booths' son Bramwell in October 1882. Upon marriage to Bramwell, who served as William Booth's chief assistant at the time, Florence became involved with the Army's social operations for women, and in this and other capacities she helped to shape the nature and expectations of Salvationist womanhood.

Part of Florence Booth's influence in the early Salvation Army lay in her speeches and writings, a number of which were directed at women. One of her notable publications was *Mothers and the Empire*, essentially a compilation of speeches she had delivered in Britain between 1905 and 1912. Reflecting the Edwardian association between womanhood and imperial concerns, this text explicitly linked the nation's international stature and character with women's involvement in the domestic realm:

> For woman generally, the home offers a wide field; and while she exercises herself to the utmost of her ability, and wields an influence for good in the home, whether as wife, mother, or daughter, she is undoubtedly rendering a service to the nation. For the home represents the nation; and only as far as the homes of its people are pure and good can the nation itself be pure and good, and fitted to take its place in the world.[7]

Like other middle-class commentators on the subject, Florence Booth believed that a woman's "influence" in this sphere was a significant calling. This feminine vocation served to sanctify families and the wider society, ensuring the continuance of the British Empire. Elsewhere in this book, she went on to stress that the home, whether heavenly or earthly, should be marked by love, because "God ha[d] especially entrusted [women] with the power to love!"[8] According to this reasoning, women's unique capacity for love suited them to be the moral guardians of home and empire.

A woman's moral and spiritual imprint upon home life was of such vital concern to Florence Booth that she established a Home League in early 1907.[9] In the creation of this body, she shared the Edwardian and evangelical conviction that the moral and physical impoverishment of British society was directly related to a woman's neglect of the domestic sphere. This kind of assessment was echoed in the Infant Welfare movement, which gained strength during the first two decades of the twentieth century.[10] Governments and middle-class women sought to promote a nurturing and domestic

An Early Home League Meeting. Courtesy of The Salvation Army International Heritage Centre, London.

conception of motherhood among working-class women, even though such an expectation often clashed with a poor mother's need to supplement her husband's wages. Whether realized or not, this ideal was actively championed by many observers and groups during this period, including those with religious convictions on the subject. The Anglican Mothers' Union, which had emerged in 1876, was one notable example. Through its meetings and literature for working-class women, it aimed, like the Home League, to impress upon women a sense of responsibility for the spiritual life of their families and the training of their children. By 1900, there were almost 3,400 branches of the Mothers' Union across Britain.[11]

Florence Booth's Home League also grew to significant proportions, becoming a fixture of all Army corps in Britain and around the world. To some degree, this exclusively female body also had parallels with the organization's earliest mothers' meetings, which were held during the days of the Christian Mission. The objectives of the Home League mirrored those of the mothers' meetings, since both groups were designed to instruct and assist women in the spiritual and domestic concerns of the household. According to one early article on the progress of the Home League, local branches also had thrift and clothing clubs to help the poorest women in attendance.[12] In addition to advice on housekeeping and healthful cooking, the Home League encouraged its female members to assume a pure and godly role in their families, especially among unsaved loved ones who remained outside the Army fold. One early report in *The War Cry* was quick to emphasize the effectiveness of this kind of domestic evangelism: "Numerous instances are on record of women who received their first heart-impressions of religion through the League, and have straightway put the lessons learned into practice at home, with the result that husbands and children have become influenced and led to God."[13] This kind of practical Christianity, with its potential effects on society as a whole, was central to the mission of the Home League.

While providing opportunities for fellowship, Home League meetings were also didactic in nature. Suitable lectures on all aspects of a woman's domestic and spiritual duties were read at weekly meetings, and the best of these presentations were occasionally published in the Salvation Army's periodical *The Officer*. Invariably, these published lectures reinforced the belief that a woman's primary task was to be a moral and spiritual beacon in the domestic realm. One article, for instance, depicted the ideal housewife as a person of "moral power and excellence" who serves her family with an "unselfish womanly spirit" from behind the scenes.[14] A second article, entitled "Husbands and Wives in Unison," conveyed a similar message: "If women cannot be much at the front, they can wield such an influence at home that its mark

Florence Booth. Courtesy of The Salvation Army International Heritage Centre, London.

shall be seen in the world."[15] The author went on to urge Home League members to make the most of this function by encouraging their husbands and children to serve God. Yet another lecture, appearing in the January 1919 issue of *The Officer*, reminded its readers that "woman represents the *heart* of the home"[16] [italics in original]. Consequently, a central female task was to cultivate a pure and tender atmosphere within the home so that the spiritual and moral needs of the family might be met.[17] Because these articles identified godly purity and morality with the traditionally feminine—sacrifice, service, the heart, and work behind the scenes—they strengthened the conviction that a woman's identity was more inward and domestic than outward and public.

Feminine piety was expressed pre-eminently in motherhood, which was considered to be a sacred undertaking. According to women like Florence Booth, it was one of "the holiest and highest vocations" open to a woman.[18] Central to this calling was the supervision of a child's ethical development. Moral training was meant to prepare young people for an outside world that was, for many evangelicals, a place of lurking evils. A mother's role, wrote one married woman, was to alert her children to the "moral dangers" beyond the home, and to instruct them "lovingly and carefully [as to] what their pure eyes will see in [such] surroundings."[19] This sentiment was echoed by Florence Booth, who was convinced that a godly mother sent her children "forewarned and forearmed to meet the evils of the world around [them]."[20] She believed that, if at all possible, children should be educated at home, where the mother could "make her own mark on them for God."[21] Florence felt very strongly about this matter, having educated her own children in this way. Given the state's increasing role in the field of education, especially after 1870, this was a very sectarian viewpoint, and one that Florence had undoubtedly learned from Catherine Booth. Even if one's offspring had to be sent to school, as Beatrice Wallis suggested in a 1916 Home League paper, it remained within the mother's province to prepare her child morally for this new learning environment.[22] A young person's character was dependent on maternal diligence in this area, since Beatrice Wallis believed that ethical principles were learned "almost entirely at home."[23] Or, as another female writer noted, mothers were "responsible for laying the foundations of [their] children's characters."[24] Such commentators clearly believed that the cultivation of virtue during childhood was a female responsibility.

A mother was also expected to be a spiritual counsellor to the young. Her task here, as one early female Salvationist expressed it, was to shape the home environment in such a way that her children would be "led early to Jesus and into the Army Fold."[25] In a similar vein, an early *War Cry* journalist had this

to say about Agnes Lucas, the wife of a Staff-Captain: "As a mother, she feels
the importance of personal example in training her two children … so that
they too shall be warriors for God and the Salvation Army, and from their earliest days be taught to shun evil and love that which is good."[26] This theme
was evident as well in another *War Cry* feature in 1896. After noting a female
officer's numerous accomplishments before marriage, the interviewer concluded by stating: "As a mother, Mrs. [Flora] Lee is fully alive to her responsibilities and she is determined to train up her little ones to become true
soldiers of Jesus Christ in The Salvation Army."[27] Using comparable language
years later, another married female officer emphasized that her maternal
mission was to cultivate the hearts of her offspring so that they would grow
up to live for God.[28] This godly role, which often overlapped with moral concerns, was conventionally feminine. Few, if any, sought to question why
women alone should be left with such a responsibility. However significant
the spiritual nurture of children may have been in the organization, it tied
women to the domestic realm. As spiritual guardians, their role was to train
and to discipline children in the private sphere so that as adults they would
remain faithful to God in a temptation-ridden public world.

There is little question that these Salvationist writers, explicitly or implic-
itly, assumed that the domestic realm was feminine in nature, a place where
women were to train their children to confront—and hopefully change—a
less than virtuous public world. Because the nurturing of a child's moral and
spiritual being was associated with the heart, a conventionally feminine
domain, women appeared to be naturally gifted for these aspects of the
young's education. Moreover, since evangelical religion linked virtue with
self-sacrifice, a woman's traditional propensity for putting the interests of
others before her own made her the obvious choice for teaching the young
about selflessness and service to God. There was, in other words, a congru-
ence between this notion of femininity and certain elements of an evangelical child's development. Not surprisingly, therefore, Army women, rather
than Army men, were held accountable for these things. Although this gender-specific responsibility tied officer mothers to the home in a way not
expected of their husbands, women themselves rarely questioned how this
arrangement infringed upon their right to an equal share with men in the
public life of the Salvation Army.[29]

DOMESTIC LABOURERS

Within the British working classes of the late nineteenth and early twentieth centuries, it was widely assumed that women bore the responsibility

for household chores. The educational system of the day did much to reinforce this conviction, because it required working-class girls to take domestic subjects at school. Whether as domestic servants, wives, mothers or
daughters, women were called upon to concern themselves with the incessant demands of the home: shopping, cooking, cleaning, sewing and washing. The average woman's domestic work after the turn of the century remained
quite similar to that of her Victorian ancestors, and this was especially true
of women who lived in houses constructed prior to 1914. These dwellings
often lacked a hot water supply, making chores like washing and ironing time-
consuming and difficult. A great deal of energy was expended within religious and respectable households in particular, where Sunday clothes had
to be washed and ironed on a weekly basis. Furthermore, since domestic servants were largely a luxury of the middle and upper classes, there was often
very little in the way of reliable, live-in help. A great deal of effort went into
maintaining working-class households, and the Salvation Army's regulations
were especially exacting in this area, impressing upon both officers and
soldiers the need for clean clothes and houses.[30]

Early Salvationist literature, including *The War Cry* pages for women, provided occasional glimpses into the domestic experiences of working-class
officer families. These descriptions, while often brief, revealed the many jobs
to be done in an Army home, and almost always they gave the impression
that such tasks were exclusively female ones. One early picture of home life
was provided in an 1893 article written by Emma Booth-Tucker, a daughter
of William and Catherine Booth. Addressing her married officer peers, she
gave a clear indication of the arduous nature of their household work: "I am
fully aware of your possible weakness of body, of the cares of the little family, of the heat of the kitchen, of the much washing and hard water ... of the
often scanty means, and of the many other things which, as sisters of the one
dear Army family, we more or less share in common with each other."[31] Cooking
and washing were, as Emma Booth-Tucker suggested, essentially female
chores carried out with less than adequate resources. Moreover, the endless
cycle of preparing meals in hot kitchens and washing clothes by hand left
female officers physically exhausted. Put simply, domestic work within the
average Army home was not easy.

References to a woman's labours within the home appeared increasingly
in the years that followed, as more and more female officers married.[32] The
substance of such material not only revealed the many demands on officer
women, but also could highlight a desire to raise expectations about motherhood in the broader society. This was evident in what Marianne Railton, a
senior married officer, wrote on the subject in 1900. In one article, written

early in the year, she lamented that people in Britain were losing sight of the "domestic ideal," and she felt that women should embrace more actively the "small and humble duties" that made houses into homes.[33] It seems, however, that this demanding ideal was being attained in Army circles, for, as Marianne Railton noted in another article a few months later, a woman's greatest challenges came after marriage, when a "wife, mother, laundress, cook, needlewoman, nurse and Field Officer h[ad] all to be united in one poor, tired little woman!"[34] Recognizing that the domestic roles of her married colleagues left them with little time to prepare for a ministry on the platform, Marianne Railton went on to suggest that they could craft sermons while at the washtub.[35] As resourceful as this advice may have been, it underscored the challenges a woman officer faced when trying to combine an exacting domesticity with a public life.

Female responsibilities within the home could be associated with imperialism and domestic science, and justified in terms of a divine calling. As one commentator noted in 1904, clean homes were not only vital to childhood health but crucial to the advancement of an imperial race.[36] The pride and survival of an empire were at stake, so success in the domestic realm required a methodical course of action. As one Army officer reminded her peers in 1916: "The work of a home should be done systematically … [since] there is the washing and ironing, baking and cooking, making and mending of clothes, shopping to the best advantage, cleaning, and the host of other things … which only a mother knows need doing."[37] Or, as another writer explained, a good housekeeper has a "nicely set table" and works to keep the house in good order.[38] In addition to offering this guidance on household routine, Army commentators urged their peers to make the most of their domestic work and not despise the opportunities that lay within this sphere. In fact, this avenue of usefulness was to be embraced with thankfulness to God.[39] By looking after their homes in a prescribed manner, women were glorifying God and serving the interests of the British Empire.

In addition to these ideological justifications for feminine domesticity, female officers were often tied to the home because of meagre financial resources. The modest incomes provided to Salvationists often left little room in household budgets for reliable, long-term domestic assistance.[40] As one writer for *The Salvation Army Year Book* noted, the organization's low salaries permitted "little or no hired help."[41] Even though officers received a house rent-free from the Salvation Army, they were obliged to pay the local expenses of their corps before they could draw a modest living allowance. This stipulation meant that officers, on numerous occasions, received less than their set wages. Faced with these financial constraints, female Salvationists tended to see domestic servants as rare treasures or as exceptions to the norm.[42] At best, an Army household might have one for short periods of time. Even when more favourable conditions prevailed, however, it was not always easy to obtain a responsible helper. Consequently, women who wanted to engage in public ministry had to take their children with them, which was often impractical as a long-term solution. This overall pattern, however, did not prevail in Booth households, where female officers were assigned to help with domestic affairs. For instance, both Emma Booth-Tucker and Florence Booth enjoyed the prolonged support of female assistants in the home.[43] Yet, apart from such privileged exceptions, female officers typically received less than adequate outside or live-in help.

To make matters worse, female officers were seldom fortunate enough to receive domestic assistance from their husbands. Few women shared the experience of Mary Aspinall, who noted that her officer husband helped her with the washing each week.[44] Although most of the housework remained in her hands, this kind of assistance was quite exceptional for the times. Margaret Narraway, another female officer, admitted as much when she alluded to her husband's help with household chores.[45] While emphasizing that this co-operation had enabled her to maintain an equitable role alongside her husband, she went on to acknowledge that too few married men supported their wives in this manner. Male officers, she claimed, were "largely responsible for their wives having sunk the officer in the wife and mother."[46] Even more troubling was the fact that Salvationist regulations did little to address this problem. These policies may have urged senior staff to make allowances for a woman's domestic work when assigning her a public role, but they also made it clear that household responsibilities were the province of the wife. As William Booth noted in his *Orders and Regulations*, a male officer needed "a wife capable of keeping his home, preparing his food, and training up a family to serve God and to help Jesus Christ in the fight."[47] In the end, therefore, Salvationist behaviour and policy largely mirrored the widespread societal belief that domestic work was women's work.

IMPACT OF DOMESTICITY UPON OFFICER STATUS

What was the status of an Army woman's public life, given her roles as moral guardian, religious teacher and manual labourer within the home? Was her public function as an officer given a high or low value in comparison with her domestic responsibilities? Three distinct responses to these questions emerged when female officers weighed the demands of home and ministry. One type of response among women was to seek a balance between the demands of home and public work, paying equal attention to both spheres.

This did not mean that women could have as large a share as men in public life, but it did suggest a commitment to some kind of public ministry. Betty Pagaway illustrated this position well, noting in 1899 that women needed to avoid the extremes of neglecting the home and forsaking public ministry: "Few of us can do as our talented Army Mother did, and do both public and domestic duties perfectly, but we can, at any rate, divide our duties equally."[48] While her remarks underscored the ambiguous legacy that Catherine Booth left to Army women, she implied that the proclamation of salvation to the world was at least as important as the concerns of the home. Another article with a similar message appeared the following year, urging women not to neglect their duties in either sphere, but to strike a balance between the domestic and public sides of their lives.[49] Overall, however, this was not a common viewpoint in the organization's literature.

A second type of response to the challenges of negotiating the public and private realms was occasionally apparent during the earliest years of the Salvation Army. While not addressing female officers directly, Emma Booth-Tucker provided one instance of this perspective in an 1893 article. Explicitly urging her Army sisters to see public witness as their first priority, she asserted that "[t]he *lesser* things of self and home and pleasure fall into their right and secondary places … [when you experience] the joy of blessing and lifting and saving poor sinners"[50] [italics mine]. Emma Booth-Tucker continued to assume that housekeeping was a female undertaking, but she believed that it should not come before female ministry. The cares of the home were to take second place when the salvation of the world was at stake. In fact, she felt that mothers who let their domestic duties get in the way of public witness should have remained single.[51] Perhaps an even clearer illustration of this position was provided by Hettie Hobbs, when she was asked if marriage was a hindrance: "Of course, what I am going to say may shock some people. I do not put my home first. You will always find it clean and fit to come into and kneel down in; but I don't make an idol of it. The Kingdom is first with me."[52] As Hettie Hobbs herself seemed to indicate, however, this was not a common viewpoint. Even so, this was not going to deter another notable married female officer, who was determined "to take a full share of responsibility for everything connected with [her husband's] corps, and to go in for the salvation of souls with just as much zeal … as a single woman."[53] While admitting that it was not easy to live up to such a resolution, especially with the care of children, she went on to state that she had "not once departed from it."[54] Although the women who took this approach did not question their association with the home and child-raising, they were willing to place a greater priority on their public work.

The third, and most pervasive, type of response to domestic and public demands was to put the claims of home and children before the claims of officership. Those holding this viewpoint encouraged female ministry, but not at the expense of home and children. An early article entitled "A Mother's Sphere" made the point succinctly, noting that a woman's children had the "first claim" upon her life.[55] A modest ministry in the corps might remain possible, but it was not to come before her youngsters. Mary Andrews, a married female officer interviewed by *The War Cry* in 1904, captured the essence of this position in reverse fashion: "Though a woman's first duty is her home and children, it is not by any means her last."[56] Although she asserted her right to a public ministry, it clearly remained a secondary responsibility. Kate Hodder, a leading British officer, also supported a public role for women, but went on to exclaim that "it was not right for a woman to neglect home duty to attend meetings [at the corps]."[57] Another female writer, while praising women's public role in the Army, reiterated the theme that such opportunities should be pursued "without neglecting home duties."[58] Equally illuminating were the remarks of a senior officer, Elsie Shaw, in 1929. She rejected the notion that married women should abandon public ministry for the sake of their families, but remained convinced that her peers "should [never] take up so large an amount of work outside as to cause neglect to [their] duties, temporal or spiritual, at home."[59] Because a number of these writers associated the word "neglect" solely with the domestic realm, they left the impression that a woman's absence from the home was more of a transgression than her absence from the public life of the Army. Put simply, according to this viewpoint the foremost obligation of a woman was to meet the needs of her household.

The home ultimately represented a female officer's highest calling because she bore the primary responsibility for raising her children to follow God. This was a divine obligation, thereby making it highly inappropriate for a woman to put public ministry and leadership ahead of the needs of her children. When faced with a possible conflict between the public and private demands of their lives, most female officers were clear about what duties came first. One writer, addressing other mothers in the organization, expressed this conviction in a straightforward and candid manner:

> God has entrusted our children to us as very precious gifts, to be brought up in His fear and love and *trained for His Service*, and should not this part of our duty stand first when it comes to deciding between the claims of the Corps and our responsibility to God for developing the character and spiritual life of our children? We are responsible for our own children in a sense in which we cannot be responsible for those of others.[60] [italics in original]

Catherine Higgins *Courtesy of The Salvation Army National Archives, Alexandria, Virginia*

According to this reasoning, a married woman's accountability to God for her children surpassed any commitment she had to the corps. Unlike her husband, she had parental obligations that restricted her freedom to minister publicly.

There was always the danger, however, that the claims of home and children could force a female officer largely to abandon public ministry after marriage. According to one early observer, this was indeed a problem. After describing the case of an officer wife who had given up all interests beyond the home, this commentator went on to state that it was "a pity to confine life's horizon within such narrow bounds."[61] While admitting that women had more to do in the home than men, this writer urged female officers to pursue some kind of modest public role in the organization.[62] Such advice was clearly needed, judging from the comments of another early Salvationist. From the perspective of this woman, a mid-ranking officer, it was not easy "to combat the idea—far too prevalent—that because an Officer becomes a wife and mother she in any sense loses her identity as an Officer."[63] Noting the same kind of problem among her fellow officers, another woman wrote: "The novelty of having her own home and the extra house duties claim her attention, and there is a tendency to feel that *that* is her share of the work"[64] [italics in original]. Even women higher up in the ranks found that the burdens of domestic life kept them tied primarily to the home. One early *War Cry* feature on a mid-ranking officer, Robert Hoggard, concluded by noting that his wife was "forced to devote herself almost completely to her children and the home."[65] This passing reference, while not soliciting any particular judgement, pointed to the tremendous burdens placed upon female officers. Their domestic work often compromised their public roles.

Some female officers may have been powerful preachers in corps settings prior to marriage, but, as Florence Thomas noted, many of them were now "content merely to give out the second song."[66] One married female officer being interviewed by *The War Cry* in 1895 suggested as much when she stated quite simply: "I don't do many meetings."[67] She preferred a ministry of encouragement among female soldiers to a preaching role on the platform. Margaret Fitzgerald, writing in 1922, also did little to inspire her peers to greater public service, since she believed that the home was a woman's "natural" sphere.[68] This was not a message that female officers needed to hear, as domestic roles often came close to supplanting their public calling. Even Catherine Higgins, a woman who believed that a good deal of female work should be done behind the scenes, expressed some concern here. She feared that her peers might "permit their [public] opportunities to slip by, excusing [them] on the ground of the burdens and anxieties of home life."[69] Judging from the comments of another female officer, such fears were justified. Reflecting upon the place of her officer sisters in the English-speaking Army world, she sadly noted that they no longer took as "active a part in Army service as they formerly did, but seem[ed] satisfied to have their husbands 'fill the whole bill.'"[70] For an increasing number of women, any kind of public work, however modest, was jeopardized by the duties of marriage and motherhood.

Throughout the period under review, Salvationist women, with the odd exception, viewed their roles in ways that were more domestic than public. In keeping with the cultural and theological assumptions of the day, they fulfilled clearly defined spiritual and temporal tasks within the home. These responsibilities, however important they may have been, did not leave women with the time or the energy to pursue the ministerial and leadership opportunities available to their husbands. Theoretically, female officers had as much right to a public life as their male counterparts, but the reality was much different. At the corps level, it was not unusual for a married woman to conclude that her "strength must be used in other things besides the purely active work of a corps."[71] At the administrative levels of the Army, it was likewise taken for granted that the "claims of home and family prevent[ed] her [from] undertaking any large responsibility."[72] In the end, domestic demands helped to ensure that most female officers would enjoy little more than a modest role in the public ministry of the Salvation Army.

✤ **Women and the Public Realm**

The demands of housework and child-raising placed obvious and significant restrictions upon a woman's public role in the Salvation Army. Most Salvationist men and women placed a high premium upon these domestic duties, the nature of which had the potential to jeopardize a female officer's public ministry altogether. Army regulations did little to help women in this area, because men were rarely exhorted to help with chores in the home.[73] Male officers, in particular, were simply urged to take a woman's special burdens into account when assigning her a public role. The cares of home and family, however, were not the only obstacles that female officers faced when considering opportunities outside the home. A number of related theological and cultural beliefs also helped to produce a problematic public environment for women, whether married or single. These assumptions often conveyed troubling messages about female ministry and leadership, leaving the impression that a woman's femininity suited her to stereotypical, subordinate and less than visible public roles.

SEXUAL DIFFERENCE AND SACRIFICE

Self-improvement was, according to an early Army manual, necessary for success in ministry and promotion through the ranks.[74] Personal betterment, however, required time for study and a desire to succeed. The former condition was obviously difficult for married women, because the concerns of the home filled up so much of their lives. Yet, for women as a whole, the latter requirement was also in short supply. Reflecting on the absence of women, single or married, from the front ranks of the organization, one early observer noted: "Many are not fired with that determined ambition, which enables them to take hold of themselves with a desperate resolution to develop and cultivate their powers, and become all that is essential to securing their highest and truest success as officers."[75] This writer urged her peers to make a more determined effort to cultivate solid qualifications for ministry and leadership.[76] Women clearly needed to possess this kind of drive if they were to rise in the ranks, but such initiative was at odds with the Victorian image of sacrificial, unselfish femininity. The typical girl was taught at a young age to put the interests of others ahead of her own, whether at home or in the wider society.[77] More often than not this meant subordinating her dreams and desires to those of the opposite sex. Throughout her life she usually faced religious and cultural pressure to abandon her own needs for the more important needs of her male counterparts. Since ambition was associated with self-interest and selfishness, it was hardly compatible with the expectations of female gender.

For the message of self-improvement to be heard unambiguously by Salvationist women, the underlying assumptions about selfless femininity had to be redefined. Yet, this did not happen. Occasional references to personal betterment were overshadowed by deep-seated convictions about womanhood. Nowhere was this more apparent than in the thinking of Florence Booth. Certain of her thoughts gave the impression that women had to be assertive and ambitious if they were to move ahead in the organization. In 1906, she exclaimed: "[Women] will never hold the position that is offered to them in The Salvation Army unless they are individually worthy of it."[78] A few years later she boasted that female officers had unlimited opportunities for leadership in the organization, provided that they qualified themselves for such roles.[79] These remarks, however, were difficult to reconcile with Florence Booth's overall depiction of womanhood. She portrayed the ideal woman as a person who based her life on self-denial rather than on "competition with the other sex."[80] Not only did this perception of womanhood imply that women's opportunities for leadership were more restricted than those of men, but it also gave the impression that ambition was an unfeminine trait. The validity of this inference was only strengthened by Florence Booth's belief that godly, heroic women were those who "relinquished comfort and position ... to toil behind the scenes for the salvation of precious souls."[81] In her mind, the door of feminine self-sacrifice was one that "should be opened as widely as possible" within the Salvation Army.[82] All things considered, a woman's humble calling to serve others was more in keeping with her gender than any competition with men for senior positions in this religious body.

The image of selfless womanhood remained dominant throughout the period in question. Early pioneers of female ministry were often remembered more for their self-denial than for their assertiveness. Tributes to Catherine Booth, for example, emphasized her self-sacrifice much more than her arguments for women's right to preach.[83] Emma Booth-Tucker, who died in a railway accident in 1903, was memorialized as a woman "in whom the principle of self was lost in a passion of love to God and [humanity]."[84] These legacies of selflessness did not encourage female Salvationists, especially mothers, to pursue leading roles in the organization's hierarchy. It was evident throughout this era that a godly mother was expected to devote herself to her children, exemplifying "unselfish courage" and sacrificial love as she prepared them for life beyond the home.[85] The female mission was one of sacrifice and devotion, and it overshadowed the more unconventional aspects of a woman's public ministry, such as preaching.

Female self-denial was equally apparent in the Salvation Army's emerging social ministries. Officer women were increasingly involved in this avenue of service, which began in 1884 with the opening of a home for rescued prostitutes and unwed mothers.[86] Florence Booth was soon appointed to head this ministry to the "fallen," which sought to redeem young women through loving maternal influences and godly discipline. Great care was taken to ensure that these facilities were home-like in appearance and function. According to the Army's *Orders and Regulations for the Rescue Work,* these homes were ideally situated in residential areas and accommodated no more than about twenty girls at a time.[87] As Leonore Davidoff has noted, this kind of Victorian rescue work, with a matron exerting a moral and spiritual influence over the girls who were her responsibility, was particularly suited to a woman's stereotypical nature.[88] Whether single or married, evangelical women were believed to be naturally fitted for roles requiring maternal and spiritual guidance. Furthermore, even though the Salvation Army was highly critical of the male vice associated with prostitution, it sought to transform "fallen" women into pious and productive examples of conventional femininity. Coupled with its efforts to save these women, Army Rescue homes taught them the skills they would need for domestic service and later married life. By the 1900s, the organization was establishing numerous homes in Britain and overseas.

Another significant field for female service was work in the slums, which also began in 1884 when "Cellar, Gutter and Garret" brigades were established.[89] The key figure behind this particular venture was Emma Booth, who, prior to marriage, was in charge of the Salvation Army's London Training Home for women. Emma Booth was aware of the desperate needs of the London poor, whose plight had been exposed in graphic detail a few months earlier in Andrew Mearns's pamphlet *The Bitter Cry of Outcast London*. After conducting a systematic survey of the worst areas surrounding the Training Home, she organized a small band of her female students to live and work among the poor. To meet the growing demands of this undertaking, Emma Booth was assisted by her sister Eva in 1885.[90]

The work that these two Booth women helped to organize was part of a broader Victorian trend towards addressing the needs of the less fortunate.[91] As early as 1857, Ellen Ranyard, an evangelical Anglican, was employing working-class women to help their impoverished neighbours. While these women initially visited the poor in order to sell them cheap editions of the Bible, they later began to offer nursing and domestic assistance to those in desperate straits. Further interest in the plight of slum inhabitants took root in the 1880s and 1890s, when Anglicans and Wesleyans established settlements in areas like the East End of London. Often staffed by university graduates who wished to engage in social work before embarking upon their chosen professions, these centres sought to educate the poor and discover the sources of poverty. In many respects, therefore, these settlements had more abstract objectives than those of the Salvation Army. Salvationists attached to slum posts were motivated by more practical and evangelical aims when they ministered to the poor in their midst. Moreover, Army officers engaged in "slumming" were expected to view their work as a lifelong calling rather than as an interlude between college and career.

Although the occasional married couple was appointed to slum posts during the earliest days of the Salvation Army, this avenue of ministry was staffed primarily by single female Salvationists. The gendered nature of this work was not lost on the wider public, who spoke admiringly of the Army's "slum sisters" and "slum angels."[92] William Booth himself did much to foster this gender-specific association, because his *Orders and Regulations for Field Officers* stressed that women were the best candidates for slum brigades.[93] This policy remained in place when Booth issued his *Orders and Regulations* for social officers in 1898.[94] To ensure that this area of service remained a female province, it was placed under the Salvation Army's Women's Social

Salvation Army work at a slum post. Courtesy of The Salvation Army International Heritage Centre, London.

Work Department by the early twentieth century. In 1906, there were forty-five slum posts in large British cities, and by the mid-1920s there were approximately 600 female officers employed in numerous slum locations at home and overseas.[95]

These female Salvationists embodied the essence of Victorian morality and religion: purity and selfless service. By cooking meals, nursing sick babies, protecting the abused and witnessing to the spiritually lost, these female officers were models of Christlike love, sacrifice and devotion. In fact, the self-lessness of these women was so in evidence that they were not paid regular salaries, since they were known to quickly give away anything they received.[96] Working and residing in overcrowded areas like Whitechapel, Bethnal Green and Seven Dials, where violence was a part of working-class culture, female slum officers put their lives in constant danger. Whether protecting wives from the blows of their abusive husbands or challenging irate, drunken men to become sober and responsible breadwinners, these "ministering angels" exemplified complete abandonment to the needs of others.[97] Rarely did these social officers stop to contemplate the risks that they faced in such confrontations. Although this expression of Army work was a powerful display of Christian love, it was admittedly, in the words of one female officer, "somewhat behind the scenes."[98] Commentary of this nature pointed to the fact that these positions were less than visible to those within the denomination, and the women appointed to slum posts found themselves far from the Army's centres of leadership and power.

Even women higher up in the ranks felt pressure to put sacrificial service ahead of any aspirations for leadership roles in the Salvation Army. When, for example, the wives of senior officers were left without official appointments, they were reminded by one commentator that there was no shortage of "humble and unobtrusive work" for them to do.[99] This included, among other things, ministry to other women, the sick and the young. While acknowledging that it was "desirable" for a woman to have her own position, this writer felt that it was incumbent upon a female officer to "make the most of the lesser task, [and] to accept whatever service offers itself behind the scenes."[100] The use of the word "desirable" underscored the double standard in the organization: it was taken for granted that a man had a right to an appointment, but it was merely advantageous for a woman to have one. In the face of such inequality a female Salvationist was expected to display self-effacement rather than self-interest.

An environment of self-abnegation was, in the final analysis, hardly conducive to the promotion of sexual equality within the Salvation Army. H. Rider Haggard, an early student of the organization's social work in Britain, unwittingly suggested as much when he described the attitude he discovered among female social officers:

> In truth, a study of the female Officers of the Salvation Army is calculated to convert the observer not only to the belief in the right of women to the suffrage, but also to that of their fitness to rule among, or even over[,] men. Only I never heard that any of these ladies ever

> sought such privileges; moreover, few of the sex would care to win
> them at the price of the training, self-denial, and stern experience
> which it is their lot to undergo.[101]

Having been socialized to live for others, these women lacked the motivation to pursue a more ambitious place within the organization. Notwithstanding their obvious potential for leadership, early female officers lived and breathed within an atmosphere of self-denial, which did little to equip them with the determination necessary to develop their capabilities and skills in nontraditional ways. Army regulations may have given women the right to leadership roles alongside or even over men—this was not, as Haggard believed, a right yet to be won—but the implementation of this principle in any meaningful way was hampered by the persistence of the Victorian belief that women were suited best for selfless activities.

SEXUAL DIFFERENCE AND OPPORTUNITIES FOR WOMEN

Selfless femininity was one aspect of the Victorian belief that men and women possessed largely opposite natures. The contrast between the "giving female" and the "acquisitive male" was taken for granted in the nineteenth century, and persisted well into the twentieth century. Sexual difference, however, was not simply confined to the moral and spiritual realms. The average person of this period—following the lead of social commentators, clergymen and scientists—believed that there were other significant gender differences as well.[102] It was assumed, for example, that men were powerful and independent whereas women were weak and dependent. Consequently, chivalry was the prescribed male behaviour, submission to men the expected female behaviour. Once married, a woman's divinely ordained role was that of a "helpmeet" to her spouse; her marital identity was defined in terms of subordination to male authority. Gender division was also maintained by the widespread conviction that men were rational while women were emotional. In symbolic language man represented the head, woman the heart. Furthermore, women continued to be identified with the home even when they assumed a role in public life. Throughout the period under review, these stereotypes were reinforced by the ideology of separate spheres. Whether in the home or in the workplace, women and men generally performed jobs suited to their natures.

First and foremost, female ministry was depicted as an extension of the domestic realm rather than as a rejection of it. It will be recalled from chapters 3 and 4 that this perspective was mirrored in the views of William Booth and George Scott Railton. This line of reasoning was notably apparent in an article written by Vitty Ward in the Army's monthly magazine *All the World*, which she helped to edit. She argued that the Salvation Army had done a great deal for women, and went on to list a handful of female pioneering leaders, a number of whom were members of the Booths' extended family. Even more interesting, however, was the way in which she conceived their public work. Vitty Ward went out of her way to place the achievements of these women within the context of the home: "[The Army] has brought the home, or rather those characteristics of home for which we are indebted to woman, into the Church."[103] Her attention was also focused upon Catherine Booth, who had died in 1890. She placed Catherine's numerous contributions to the Army in a domestic context, and likened her to the "mother of a home [who] is called away."[104] These domestic images revealed the extent to which an Army woman's ministry was dependent upon her traditional work in the private sphere. Victorian womanhood might be manipulated to allow a female Salvationist to assume a presence outside the home, but her source of identity and justification for such public service continued to be based upon restrictive associations and expectations. She had to embody domestic feminine virtues in order to maintain a visible position. Her public role was tied to the home in a way that a man's was not.

Added to the intimate association of women with domesticity was the assumption that weakness was a characteristically feminine trait. Florence Booth, the most influential female Army officer in Britain after 1890, described this aspect of womanhood in her book *Mothers and the Empire:* "Women and children represent the weaker portion of the community; weaker, that is, both in their powers of self-preservation and in their means of expressing need or danger."[105] She felt, therefore, that women should be protected by men. This kind of medieval chivalry had become a key component of middle-class gender relations by the mid- to late nineteenth century, having been revived by the Crimean War, the Indian Mutiny and threats of a French invasion.[106] Like other respectable men and women of her age, Florence Booth worked within this framework, believing that such an atmosphere was to be encouraged within the Army's ranks: "We want this spirit in The Salvation Army as well as in the knights of old—this spirit of protection."[107] Although Florence did not suggest that women were the weaker sex intellectually, she portrayed them as helpless individuals, resembling children more than men. This image hardly portrayed women as ideal candidates for leadership in the Army.

In addition to equating womanhood with helplessness, Salvationists generally assumed that women were, physically speaking, less fit than men for the burdens of public life. Clara Case, while herself a notable leader in India, admitted that a woman's physical frame was poorly adapted for the pressures

of senior administration: "The leadership of women naturally has its difficulties. It is acknowledged that women are not so physically strong as men...
therefore a life of public service presses more hardly upon them."[108] A vari-
ation of this theme was offered by Agnes Povlsen, a social work officer, in
1930: "As for the single women officers it is often said that their health is not
equal to the strain and stress of the work and responsibilities connected with
[the Army's] leading positions."[109] Povlsen was hesitant to subscribe unre-
servedly to this argument. Poor health, she claimed, was no more a sign of
unfitness in a female leader than in a male leader. Nevertheless, her reference to the issue underscored the widespread acceptance of this sentiment
within the organization. This general viewpoint was also apparent at the lower
levels of the organizational hierarchy. Explaining why a man should take the
more active role in a corps, one female officer stated that "the physical frame
of a woman is not built to stand the same kind of strain as a man's [body]."[110]
Those advancing this position never explained how public life required more
physical energy than a woman's more traditional labours in the home, but in
the end they left the impression that physical weakness put leadership beyond
the reach of the average female officer.

What also put authoritative roles out of reach of most female officers was
the notion that the husband was the head of his family. Male headship ensured
that a wife remained dependent upon her husband, even when she performed
tasks outside the home. This patriarchal arrangement was especially hard on
women who had been commanding officers before marriage. One early officer, perhaps reflecting on her own experience, remarked that a newly married woman was "almost certain to find it a little difficult at first to subordinate
her ideas of how things should be managed to those of her husband."[111]
Nevertheless, a woman gradually learned the rules of this marital system.
Decision-making, for example, remained a male preserve. A wife might discuss corps matters with her husband, but she gave him the "casting vote."[112]
The successful officer wife recognized that "where a command [had] to be
given or a decision arrived at, her husband's voice should be heard, and not
hers."[113] Her overall function in the corps was ultimately secondary to that of
her husband. A female ensign, describing her past experience in corps work,
unwittingly revealed the extent to which this was true: "I looked well after
the minor details of the corps, and helped my husband by sharing his councils and plans for meetings."[114] The words "minor" and "his" betrayed the subordinate status of female ministry in the Salvation Army. Much the same held
true for the wife of a senior officer, because a large part of her task was "to be
an inspiration of her husband's work"[115] [italics in original]. As each of these
cases suggested, married women lived out a role that was largely dependent
on, and in the shadow of, their spouses.

The perception of women as weak and dependent determined what Army positions were unlikely to be filled by female officers, but the corresponding assumption about feminine emotion suggested where women might be utilized. One of their characteristic tasks, as outlined by official regulations, was to deal with sinners who came to the church services at a local corps:

> The power of the sympathetic and emotional nature of women is of immense service in this respect. After the powerful talk of a man, who may have convinced every sinner in the house that he is wrong, and that unless he alters his course he will die in despair, and lie down amongst everlasting burnings, some gentle, tender, appeal from a woman's loving heart will break up every stubborn nature present, and some will be brought over the bar into the harbour of Salvation by this wave of feeling.[116]

While a woman's emotional appeal to sinners might be public in nature, it ideally followed the rational discourse of a man. Her modest preaching role was justified more in terms of what she elicited than in what she said. Emotion obviously had a place within a religious setting, but in the Salvation Army this human trait was equated largely with femininity. Women failed to be appreciated for their reason, while men were assumed to possess a more "manly" rational authority.

When women themselves occasionally described their responsibility towards sinners, they likewise highlighted the emotional component of their ministry. Maud Booth, a daughter-in-law of the founders, conveyed the emotional power of women among unsaved men when she wrote: "Men who would resent any sympathy or interest expressed by a fellow man will listen quietly to a woman ... [because of] the tenderness of [her] words and touch."[117] A similar sentiment was expressed by Marianne Railton a few years later: "[The] Captain may be a very wonderful officer, but he cannot do what a woman can. [Her] touch on some hardened sinner's shoulder will draw where his would irritate."[118] While this feminine work of convicting hearts figured prominently in corps settings or in "open-airs" on the streets, it also had a place in Army social centres. In such settings, a married female officer might not have an official appointment or an authoritative position, but she did have a special part to play in the conversion of the destitute, especially alcoholics, who came to the Army for help. Her role was to care for a poor man's soul by offering him a "heartening word" and a "smiling welcome."[119] By making a "kindly inquiry" into his circumstances, and demonstrating gentleness and a "mother-touch," she might bring him into the Kingdom of God.[120] In any event, a female officer's evangelistic endeavours, public or otherwise, were viewed in terms of emotion rather than reason.

Since preaching in the early Salvation Army was often directed towards an emotional end—the conviction of the heart—female officers retained a modest role on the platform. At the same time, however, the identification of women with passion also placed them in more conventional fields of service. One such area was the Home League, which, as noted earlier, was a group designed exclusively for women. This corps ministry was a logical extension of passionate femininity, because it was believed that a woman had "a special capacity for loving her own sex."[121] Not surprisingly, therefore, Army regulations of the period stipulated that, when an officer couple entered a corps, the wife was to oversee this program.[122] Moreover, the Home League activities in a given region or country were typically put under the jurisdiction of the wives of administrative officers.[123] These characteristically female roles quickly became institutionalized within the Salvation Army: in Britain alone the Home League had nearly 300 branches and more than 12,000 members by 1915.[124] This success continued in the years ahead, and by 1927 the Home League had been established in almost every corps in the United Kingdom, and could claim a total membership of 81,000 women.[125] The substance of this ministry came to be seen as an important vehicle "for the exercise of all a woman's best gifts [in the Army]."[126]

Youth ministry was another area of corps life where a female officer, especially after marriage, had a unique role. Although a married woman did not have to run activities for the young, since Sunday school programs were operated by the local soldiers of a corps, she was expected, unlike her husband, to attend these events on a regular basis.[127] This somewhat supervisory function was ultimately an expansion of her spiritual influence in the home, and consistent with her "natural love and tenderness" for the young.[128] It became a distinctive part of a woman's public work in the Army in Britain. Furthermore, British officers serving overseas helped to institutionalize this female responsibility in other places as well. Describing the nature of her accomplishments in America at the turn of the century, Emma Booth-Tucker noted: "[W]ith few exceptions all our married women have separate and definite work apart from that of their husbands, such as the oversight of the Juniors' War in their various commands."[129] Public involvement with children became, in time, an essential aspect of the ideal officer wife's identity; such a woman went out of her way to have an influence on the young people of the corps.[130]

A final sphere consistent with a woman's emotional nature was the care of the sick and the suffering. Addressing the subject of women's place in the Salvation Army in 1914, Florence Booth drew a clear connection between feminine emotion and service to the suffering: "God is graciously using the streams of love and sympathy and tenderness flowing from the hearts of Salvation Army women, all round the world, for … the sick and for the brokenhearted and the suffering everywhere."[131] Whether within or outside the corps, a female officer had opportunities to engage in this work of the heart. The visitation of sick corps members was one such task, because, as one officer expressed it, they "generally need the cheer, counsel, and help of a sympathetic and tender woman."[132] Higher up in the ranks a woman also had occasion to minister to those in distress. The staff wife, for instance, was called upon to counsel the troubled female officers who came under her husband's command. Writing of this particular responsibility, one senior officer told her peers that their "advice and sympathy may often help a younger officer to strike an even balance when reviewing her difficulties and may help her over a rough passage in her experience."[133] Because ministry to the sick and the suffering depended more on emotion and the heart than on reason and the mind, it seemed fitting for Salvationist women to undertake such caregiving roles.

Despite the fact that official regulations stated and leading figures in the Salvation Army claimed that all positions in the organization were open to both women and men, an underlying adherence to the idea of sexual difference seriously jeopardized any principle of gender equality. Sexual difference led, in turn, to separate spheres for male and female officers in the public, not to mention the private, life of the denomination. In one of her more candid moments, Florence Booth acknowledged that the two sexes had different public functions in the Army: "Her part is not the same part as the man's part, although their positions may be interchangeable. A woman's work in the corps is not exactly the same as a man's work. A woman's work in the division is not the same as a man's work. And so throughout all its departments, the visiting, the praying, the speaking, the writing, the governing."[134] The words "may be interchangeable" suggested that occasionally a woman might be able to fill a traditionally masculine role, such as having authority over others, but ideally her ministry was in keeping with Victorian notions of womanhood. As indicated previously, suitable female tasks included ministry to the unsaved, other women, children and the sick.

UNDER-REPRESENTATION OF WOMEN IN LEADERSHIP

Gender assumptions of the foregoing variety, coupled with the very similar views held by male Salvationists, help to explain why women were poorly represented in the leadership ranks of the Salvation Army. As table 6.1 indicates, the organization's top administrative positions were held almost exclusively by men.[135] Between 1906 and 1930, the Salvation Army's senior commands nearly doubled as it expanded around the world, but the number of female

TABLE 6.1
Gender and senior leadership worldwide between 1906 and 1930

Year	Total Leadership	Total Men	Total Women	(%) Men	(%) Women
1906	47	40	7	85.1	14.9
1910	54	47	7	87	13
1914	62	55	7	88.7	11.3
1918	65	59	6	91	9
1922	81	77	4	95.1	4.9
1926	84	77	7	91.7	8.3
1930	87	83	4	95.4	4.6

Source: *The Salvation Army Year Books* for the years cited.

leaders remained remarkably low throughout this entire period. Women filled, on average, only six or seven of these postings at any given time. The low absolute numbers were indicative of the Army's acceptance of the notions of male headship and sexual difference. First of all, the few women in international leadership roles were, apart from Florence Booth, single or widowed. Married women generally did not receive authoritative positions, but were included in their husbands' appointments. This sexist practice effectively excluded the majority of women—those who were married—from leadership roles. Second, Salvationist views on gender were at odds with any substantial movement of single female officers into the higher offices. Women were believed to possess a sacrificial and emotional nature, making them the ideal candidates for a caregiving ministry in the Army's spiritual and social work. Positions of real power were left essentially to men, who were identified with authority, assertiveness and reason.

The notions of male headship and sexual difference also help to explain why the overall percentage of women leaders declined between 1906 and 1930. During the period in question an increasing number of women married, thereby leaving a smaller pool of potential female leaders.[136] The proportion of women to men within the leadership ranks, while always very low, dropped even lower as the Salvation Army filled its burgeoning international bureaucracy with married men. Furthermore, the organization's social ministries continued to expand rapidly in the early twentieth century, due in large measure to William Booth's 1890 social commentary *In Darkest England and the Way Out*. The Army built institutions around the world to help the destitute, delinquent and homeless children, expectant and unwed mothers, the sick and the aged. Between 1906 and 1916 alone, the number of these social institutions grew from just under 700 to over 1,200.[137] Single female officers, given their traditional association with selflessness and love, were found increasingly in this area of Army ministry. While social work among destitute men remained the preserve of male officers, most of whom were married, the Salvation Army's slum posts, rescue homes, maternity hospitals, children's homes and residences for the elderly became "natural" places for single female officers.[138]

Among the few women who held positions in the upper ranks of the organization, members of the Booth family figured most prominently: William and Catherine's daughters Eva and Lucy, and Bramwell's wife Florence and daughters Catherine and Mary all held significant commands at various times throughout this period. At any given time between 1906 and 1930, these women occupied two or three of the senior female postings. In 1930, Booth women were even more conspicuous, holding three of the four female positions available. More often than not they were also given commands in developed regions—such as North America and Europe—whereas their peers were confined exclusively to positions in missionary countries like India and in the Women's Social Work Department in Britain.

Whether sexual equality had anything to do with the high visibility of Booth women is difficult to know, but there is evidence to suggest that nepotism was one significant factor behind their appointments. William and Bramwell Booth, the generals of the period, were ultimately responsible for the promotion of key personnel, and they clearly used this power to benefit their family members.[139] Both men gave their families and relatives important positions, elevating them rapidly through the ranks.[140] Eva Booth, for instance, was quickly promoted from the rank of captain to the very senior rank of commissioner, bypassing the intermediate ranks altogether. Notwithstanding their capabilities, Booth children were placed in positions of considerable authority at very young ages, often replacing more seasoned officers in the process. This blatant kind of favouritism was the source of resentment among some officers, especially after Bramwell Booth took office in 1912. He was always quick to promote the interests of his family, ensuring that they received key appointments and prominent mention in Army periodicals. Favouritism of this nature did not necessarily explain why few women held positions in the upper ranks of the Army, since there was nothing stopping the Booths from promoting their family members and a significant number of other women, but it did constitute one reason for the disproportionate number of Booth women in senior leadership positions.

The marginalization of women was even more pronounced at the mid-levels of Army leadership within Britain. This was made strikingly apparent on the front page of *The War Cry* as early as the spring of 1893. Under the caption "The Twelve New Provincial 'Apostles'" was a group sketch of freshly minted British leaders, all of whom were men. This reference signalled the establishment of another level of leadership to provide closer supervision of the Army's rapidly growing field operations. These provincial officers were charged with the responsibility for large regions in the United Kingdom known as provincial commands. For the next sixteen years these prestigious commands, which fluctuated in number, were held almost exclusively by men. The one woman assuming a provincial post during the mid-1890s was Eva Booth. In 1896, however, she was transferred to Canada, and it took until 1905 for the only other female officer, Minnie (Mary) Reid, another single woman, to be appointed as the head of a provincial command.[141] Given the rarity of a woman being assigned to this leadership position, Reid's appointment was seen as "an interesting development" in the British field. Interesting or not, however, she was not in this position for long, since she relinquished it when she became a married officer in June 1906. Incidentally, the 1906 yearbook came out before the month of June, so Reid is listed among the provincial commanders for that year in table 6.2. In any case, female officers were profoundly under-represented in this area.

TABLE 6.2

Gender and provincial leadership in the United Kingdom between 1893 and 1908

Year	Total Provinces	Total Men	Total Women	(%) Men	(%) Women
1893	12	12	0	100	0
1895	12	11	1	91.7	8.3
1899	13	13	0	100	0
1901	8	8	0	100	0
1906	10	9	1	90	10
1908	10	10	0	100	0

Sources: "The Twelve New Provincial 'Apostles,'" *The War Cry* (April 29, 1893): 1; "Results of Self-Denial Week, 1895," *The War Cry* (October 26, 1895): 7; "The British Provincial Officers," *All the World* 20, 8 (August 1899): 412-13; "The New Provincial Commanders of the United Kingdom," *The War Cry* (December 28, 1901): 16; *The Salvation Army Year Book for 1906* (London: The Salvation Army Book Department, 1906), 10; and *The Salvation Army Year Book for 1908* (London: The Salvation Army Book Department, 1908), 17-18.

Below the provincial commands, which were phased out before 1910, were smaller regions called divisions. The most senior officer in a division, known as either a divisional officer or a divisional commander, was in charge of Army operations in a small region, city or section of a city. This position had been created in 1880, as William Booth sought to keep control of the growing

TABLE 6.3

**Gender and divisional leadership in Britain and Ireland
between 1880 and 1930**

Year	Total Divisions	Total Men	Total Women	(%) Men	(%) Women
1880	7	6	1	85.7	14.3
1884	13	13	0	100	0
1890	38	35	3	92.1	7.9
1894	30	29	1	96.7	3.3
1901	41	41	0	100	0
1906	36	36	0	100	0
1910	25	25	0	100	0
1914	29	29	0	100	0
1918	30	30	0	100	0
1922	35	32	3	91.4	8.6
1926	39	37	2	94.9	5.1
1930	37	36	1	97.3	2.7

Sources: "Important. Formation of The Army into Divisions," *The War Cry* (September 18, 1880): 2; *The Advance of The Salvation Army: 1880* (London: The Salvation Army Headquarters, 1880), ii; "Divisions in Competition," *The War Cry* (April 30, 1884): 4; "England's First Lass D.O.," *The War Cry* (March 8, 1890): 9-10; [George] Jolliffe, "Lasses Again," *The War Cry* (May 17, 1890): 9; "The Christmas 'War Cry' and 'Young Soldier' Competition List," *The War Cry* (January 11, 1890): 15; "An Interview with the General," *The War Cry* (March 31, 1894): 9; "Advances," *The War Cry* (September 7, 1901): 9; *The Salvation Army Year Books* for the years cited between 1906 and 1930; Robert Sandall, *The History of The Salvation Army*, Vol. 2 (1950; reprint, New York: The Salvation Army, 1979), 16-19; and Arch Wiggins, *The History of The Salvation Army*, Vol. 4 (1964; reprint, New York: The Salvation Army, 1979), 195-96.

Salvation Army. As table 6.3 demonstrates, this mid-level of authority was largely male-dominated between 1880 and 1930.[142] The first female officer to assume command of a division was Caroline Reynolds, a widow, who started the Army's work in Northern Ireland in 1880. Although she had left the scene by 1884, three women were appointed as divisional officers in 1890, the year that Catherine Booth died. Undoubtedly, Catherine Booth had had something to do with the promotion of these women, all of whom were also single. It appears that only one married female officer, Harriet Lawley, ever took command of a division during the early days of the Salvation Army. In 1894, she was briefly in charge of the organization's work in the Channel Islands, but she soon had to give up this position because of her family responsibilities.[143] Her husband, incidentally, was seldom home, since he accompanied

William Booth on many of his campaigns in Britain and overseas. So, even this one exception to the rule did not last, revealing once again the demands that married women faced in the home. All the other women in divisional commands were single or widowed, denoting a pattern consistent with the Army's beliefs about male headship and female gender. The typical arrangement saw married men appointed as divisional commanders, while their wives filled subordinate roles. One expected avenue of female service here was supervision of the numerous divisional Home League groups.

Table 6.3 also reveals the influence of Florence Booth, who was responsible for the appointment of the three women reflected in the statistics for 1922. In early 1919, Florence Booth became the British territorial commander, and she held this post during the period when single and widowed women re-entered divisional leadership positions.[144] Her senior position gave her the power to appoint divisional commanders, and she clearly used this authority to promote the five women who held divisional leadership positions between 1922 and 1930. While this showed some willingness on Florence's part to place single women in leadership roles, two of the five female appointees were her own daughters, Mary and Olive Booth. It should be noted as well that Florence Booth herself had been appointed by her husband Bramwell, who was General at the time. Such examples showed yet again that familial connections had a good deal to do with the few women in Army leadership positions. By 1930, Mary and Olive Booth had moved into the upper ranks, thereby leaving only one female divisional commander in office. With these Booth women factored out of the calculation, the actual percentage of female leaders in the divisional ranks was negligible. While the number of male divisional commanders climbed between 1880 and 1930, the numerical strength of their female counterparts during the same period never exceeded three.

Officially, the Salvation Army gave no indication of the glaring inconsistency between its theory and its practice of sexual equality. In fact, its public statements on the subject left the opposite impression. In 1927, for example, the organization's publication *Outlines of Salvation Army History*, issued under the authority of General Bramwell Booth, suggested that equality had been "held and consolidated" within its ranks.[145] This kind of claim may not have been a deliberate attempt to mislead the public, but it underscored the denomination's failure to think critically about the roles given to its women. Only rarely did the issue of women's marginalization surface in Salvation Army literature. Perhaps the only reference ever to this issue in *The War Cry* appeared in 1899, where it was noted that women were not receiving "either the courtesy or the recognition they and their work [were] entitled to from the men officers and soldiers."[146] This brief commentary went on to argue that, if women were to enjoy better postings in the organization, male Salvationists needed to adhere to regulations on equality. The irony, however, was that this article appeared on a page designed for women, underscoring the fact that the implementation of sexual equality was indeed a problem. Literature intended for officers alone was only marginally better in addressing this concern, because it rarely examined the issue of gender discrimination in any serious fashion. On the one occasion when the topic was discussed candidly, it was confined to *The Staff Review*, a journal designed exclusively for senior officers. Given the opportunity in 1930 to discuss the question "Are Equal Standards for Men and Women Officers Maintained?," the three female respondents answered largely in the negative.[147] Pointing to the scarcity of women in leadership roles, they stressed that Salvationist practice was decidedly out of step with its professed principle of equality. An acknowledgement of the problem was a necessary first step if the Salvation Army hoped to confront sexual discrimination within its ranks, but such complaints never received the exposure or attention they deserved.

The imbalance between men and women in the middle to upper ranks of Salvationist leadership, whether criticized or largely ignored, owed a great deal to the cultural and theological foundations upon which the organization was established. Reflecting views that were similar to those of their male counterparts, most Army women espoused beliefs and accepted roles that were incompatible with a principle of sexual equality. A female officer's moral and spiritual functions in the home, combined with her other domestic tasks, either called into question or placed restrictions upon her public ministry. Furthermore, within the public realm, a married or single female officer was usually confined to responsibilities consistent with the notion of sexual difference. She was encouraged to possess a femininity defined in terms of self-sacrifice, weakness, dependency and emotion. This construction of womanhood allowed women to challenge sinners publicly from the platform or engage in social work, but their overall ministry remained a modest one. A conventional vocation of service to other women, children and the suffering was most reflective of the average female Salvationist's life. Her ideal role was one of service and submission rather than leadership and authority.

❖

Epilogue

THE SALVATION ARMY EMERGED as a notable product of late Victorian Protestant revivalism. Located initially in the East End of London, its goal was to convert the impoverished masses. This overall purpose remained in place as the organization expanded throughout England and the world. To attract those beyond the reach of organized religion, the Army made use of many unconventional methods. Female preaching in the streets and on the platform was one of its most successful measures, and Hallelujah Lasses played a role in the denomination's efforts to save the world from sin. The Salvation Army's evangelical roots required all devoted Christians, men and women, to engage in the work of the gospel. In seeking to be faithful to this theological mandate, female Salvationists challenged the nineteenth- and early twentieth-century belief that preaching was the province of male clergy. Female preaching was exceptional for the period in question, and put female Army officers ahead of their sisters in other religious bodies. A few women in Unitarian and Congregationalist circles, which were known for their liberal and progressive views, would begin to enjoy pastoral responsibilities only in the early twentieth century, long after female Salvationists had stepped onto the platform.[1] The public nature of this expression of ministry in the Army helped to undermine the conviction that women belonged exclusively in the home.

Catherine Booth, the cofounder of the Salvation Army, had a great deal to do with the preaching opportunities afforded to the young women in the organization. Her revivalist campaigns throughout Britain inspired them to seek an active role in the church. Catherine Booth's comprehensive justification for female preaching, which she had formulated earlier in her life, served as a forceful answer to critics who viewed the Army's female preachers as unbiblical and unconventional. Catherine's scriptural arguments in this area were not unique, but they were framed in such a manner as to give the practice a sound theological foundation. Furthermore, her contention that women had a *right* to preach the gospel was significant for her age, going beyond the rationale of other defenders of female ministry. Importantly, this language of rights found its way into the Christian Mission, which became the Salvation Army in 1878.

Women belonging to this religious body possessed the right to hold any office in the hierarchy, from that of a soldier to that of General. Claiming that St. Paul's words in Galatians 3:28 referred to the eradication of gender barriers within the church, early Salvationist publications stated that Army leadership positions were equally available to both sexes. Such documents suggested that gender was not a determining factor in a person's promotion through the ranks of the organization. In many respects, this principle of equality was remarkable for the late nineteenth and early twentieth centuries. Given prominent exposure in numerous regulatory and doctrinal manuals, not to mention its promotional literature, this tenet appeared to have solid roots in the denomination. Certain comments by the Army's leading figures seemed to support this conclusion. Given this rhetoric, the average person of the day, unfamiliar with the internal dynamics of this religious group, would have largely accepted Florence Booth's boast that the Salvation Army was the "latest act" of God in "the emancipation of woman."[2] To the uncritical observer, this was an egalitarian religious body that gave its female officers unparalleled opportunities to work in every area of its institutional life.

Behind such pronouncements, however, was a more troubling reality. Although the Salvation Army provided women with opportunities to preach alongside men, it largely failed to implement sexual equality beyond the pulpit. This had much to do with the organization's cultural and evangelical assumptions about femininity. Salvationists cultivated beliefs about womanhood that were at cross-purposes with any notion of male and female partnership. Feminine gender was constructed along very conservative lines, which served more to restrict women than to liberate them for public ministry and leadership. Catherine Booth and her husband William, and most of the officers in the ranks, accepted, and indeed perpetuated, a theological and Victorian understanding of sexual difference. Masculinity was centred around reason and authority, whereas femininity was associated with passion, persuasion and sacrificial service. Apart from preaching, where reason and emotion could coexist, the roles assigned to officers were determined primarily on the basis of gender. The only notable exception to this rule occurred in the Booth family, where blood or relational ties seemed to take precedence over gender. Yet, for the vast majority of Salvationists, opportunities for advancement depended on their gender rather than on their abilities. This helped to create a pervasive culture of separate spheres: men assumed commanding and decision-making responsibilities at the corps and administrative levels, while women largely looked after the needs of other women, young people, slum inhabitants and the sick.

Even though the Salvation Army's evangelical heritage, with its emphasis upon salvation, encouraged female preaching, it did not promote an egalitarian sharing of roles by women and men. In fact, this theological framework legitimized male rule over women in the Army. The evangelical notion of male headship was a case in point. The relative freedom that single female officers experienced during the 1870s and early 1880s was generally lost once they were married, because it was believed that a husband was the final authority within the family. This patriarchal arrangement was apparent in the areas of appointments, duties, salaries and promotion through the ranks. The identification of men with power and authority was reinforced as well by the Salvation Army's language for the deity. Given its conservative evangelical tendency towards a literalistic reading of scripture, Salvationist theology depicted God exclusively in terms of a ruling male or father. When placed within the context of the Army's hierarchy, the fatherly roles of William and Bramwell Booth bore a striking resemblance to the fatherly role in the divine realm. A belief in the masculine nature of God made male leadership in the Army appear normal and appropriate. Female leadership, therefore, became exceptional at best. These evangelical motifs, whether operative within the domestic, public or cosmic realms, resulted in women's subordination to men.

Any meaningful promotion of sexual equality within the Salvation Army was hampered as well by its evangelical interpretation of the human condition. Sin, for example, was cast almost solely in terms of male experience. Selfishness, pride and self-interest were equated with sin and ungodliness, a definition that held troubling implications for female officers. Having been taught from birth to put the interests of others ahead of their own, these women faced temptations of a different nature. What they needed to guard against was self-abnegation and diminished agency—a failure to value and assert the self. Self-denial may have been a message heard by Army men and women, but women were invariably the ones called upon to practise it at every level of the organization. Because the early Army demonized the self and deified self-denial, it encouraged women to question their abilities and remain behind the scenes. Male officers did very little to discourage this, believing that God had given women special burdens and particular responsibilities towards others.

The organization's Methodist doctrine of holiness, which emphasized the crucifixion rather than the actualization of the self, simply added to this troubling environment. While an evangelical woman moved by the Holy Spirit might speak in public, she tended to do so out of self-denial and submission rather than as expressions of self-assertion and sexual equality. Even exceptional women like Catherine Booth, who appealed to a woman's right to preach, often placed their own ministries within the context of submission to a masculine Holy Spirit. To some degree, this may have been a clever ploy to avoid unnecessary criticism, given the fact that assertive women were frowned upon in Victorian society. Yet, even if this were so, the fact remains that such a strategy was hardly conducive to the long-term maintenance and expansion of women's initial gains within the organization. The doctrine of holiness advocated by evangelicalism might have allowed women to justify their place on the platform, but it lacked the power to keep them there. Moreover, when wed to a patriarchal and authoritarian structure, such as that found in the Salvation Army, the doctrine of holiness functioned more to keep people in their place than to emancipate them from sexist attitudes and practices.

Given that the Salvation Army continues to situate itself within the evangelical tradition of holiness, these kinds of theological issues remain problematic for its female officers. It would be fair to say that the theological sources of women's inequality within the organization have yet to be fully appreciated by Salvationists.[3] At the same time, however, there are some signs that the Army's administration is beginning to address some of the inequitable arrangements outlined in this book. An important step in this direction was taken in the early 1990s, with the formation of a Commission on the Ministry of Women Officers. This fifteen-member body, which grew out of a 1991 conference of international Salvation Army leaders, sought to re-examine a female officer's role and function in the life of the organization.[4] In May 1994, the commission issued a thirty-nine-page final report, with a number of recommendations regarding female ministry. These proposals affirmed the equality of women with men, and asserted that there was no theological barrier preventing female officers from assuming any role in the organization.[5] More specifically, this document recommended that leadership and administrative roles be distributed more equitably between the sexes, that married women be given appointments and ranks in their own right, and that domestic support be given to women whose family duties conflicted with their public ministry.

To the Salvation Army's credit, the second recommendation has already been implemented with some success. A recent revision to the Army's *Orders*

and Regulations for Officers includes the directive that a married female officer should be recognized by her rank and full name.[6] A further amendment
to this manual states that the administration will consider the gifts and abilities of both spouses when making appointments, which will be issued to
both husbands and wives.[7] The other recommendations will prove more
challenging to implement, especially the call to distribute authoritative roles
in a more equitable fashion. Despite the resolutions of the 1994 commission,
women continue to hold very few international, national or regional positions of command. According to a recent Salvation Army yearbook, women
account for only 9.5 percent of the most senior positions, and all the Army's
eighteen divisions in Britain and Ireland are overseen by men.[8] Moreover,
since the women in senior leadership positions are predominantly single,
there remains an urgent need to implement the third recommendation outlined above. Inequality is sure to persist, particularly for married women, if
domestic responsibilities prevent them from having the same public opportunities afforded to men. If anything, the third proposal highlighted above
does not go far enough, because it does not address the part that men should
play in the home. Real inequities remain in place when housework and child-
raising are not shared equally by both spouses.

   If the history of the early Salvation Army teaches us anything, it is the fact
that recommendations and principles, however well-intentioned, are not
enough to ensure equality between the sexes. Although Salvationists made
numerous pronouncements on the subject of sexual equality between 1870
and 1930, they failed to address the deep-seated assumptions and the discriminatory practices that worked against the possibility of an egalitarian
environment. Undoubtedly, as one historian has suggested, sexual equality
became the early Salvation Army's "proudest boast,"[9] but it was one that rang
hollow. Preoccupied with appearances, the members of the organization,
especially those in leadership, found little time to deal seriously with the issue
of gender and equality in the ranks. Over the years, scholars with an interest
in the Army have been equally uncritical in this area, since they have often
been too quick to accept the egalitarian image put forward by Salvationist
literature. History from a feminist perspective, with its hermeneutics of suspicion, has much to teach us here. Such an approach prods us to go beneath
the surface, and to question the claims that are made by the sources we
encounter. In the end, this is the essence of all historical investigation.

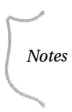

Notes

❖ **A Note on the Notes**

Although the notes are largely self-explanatory, a couple of issues deserve brief clarification. First, Salvation Army publications usually provided the first names of its male and single female authors, but often failed to do so for its married female writers. Wherever possible, I have attempted to address this concern by finding and citing the full names of married female officers (e.g., [Catherine] Higgins). If, however, the first name of a married female author appears in the preface or foreword of a book, I have avoided the use of brackets. Moreover, for the sake of aesthetics, brackets have not been incorporated into the bibliography that follows these notes. Second, early Salvationist publications always capitalized the definite article in the organization's name (i.e., *The* Salvation Army), which reflected the way the name was recorded in the Army's founding deed. In company with a number of other scholars and writers, I have preserved this practice in the notes and the bibliography for the sake of accuracy.

❖ **Notes**

<u>PREFACE</u>

1 William Booth, *Orders and Regulations for The Salvation Army* (London: The Salvation Army Headquarters, 1878), iii. As early as 1870 the organization gave women the right to preach, hold any office and participate in its annual conferences. The substance of these rights is reproduced in Glenn K. Horridge, *The Salvation Army: Origins and Early Days, 1865-1900* (Godalming, Surrey, UK: Ammonite Books, 1993), 255-57. See also William Booth, *Orders and Regulations for Field Officers of The Salvation Army* (London: International Headquarters of The Salvation Army, 1886), iv; William Booth, *Orders and Regulations for*

Field Officers of The Salvation Army (London: Headquarters of The Salvation Army, 1901), 294-95; William Booth, *Orders and Regulations for Staff Officers of The Salvation Army* (London: International Headquarters of The Salvation Army, 1904), 8-9; Bramwell Booth, *Orders and Regulations for Officers of the Men's Social Work of The Salvation Army* (London: The Salvation Army Book Department, 1915), 21; *Orders and Regulations for Field Officers of The Salvation Army* (London: The Salvation Army Book Department, 1917), 309; Bramwell Booth, *Orders and Regulations for Territorial Commanders and Chief Secretaries of The Salvation Army* (London: International Headquarters of The Salvation Army, 1920), 100; and *Orders and Regulations for Officers of The Salvation Army* (London: International Headquarters of The Salvation Army, 1925), 51-52.

2   See, for example, *Orders and Regulations for Officers of The Salvation Army* (London: International Headquarters of The Salvation Army, 1936), 50-51; and *Orders and Regulations for Officers of The Salvation Army* (London: International Headquarters of The Salvation Army, 1946), 50-51.

3   For popular examples of this viewpoint, see Bernard Watson, *A Hundred Years' War: The Salvation Army, 1865-1965* (London: Hodder and Stoughton, 1965), 28-29; Frederick Coutts, *No Discharge in This War: A One Volume History of The Salvation Army* (London: Hodder and Stoughton, 1974), 27; Cyril Barnes, *God's Army* (Berkhamsted, Herts, UK: Lion Publishing, 1978), 28; and Henry Gariepy, *Christianity in Action: The Salvation Army in the U.S.A. Today* (Wheaton, IL: Victor Books, 1990), 24-25. Academic works that convey this message include Donald W. Dayton, *Discovering an Evangelical Heritage* (1976; reprint, Peabody, MA: Hendrickson Publishers, 1994), 94-95; Douglas Clarke, "Female Ministry in the Salvation Army," *The Expository Times* 95, 8 (May 1984): 232-35; Lynne Sorrel Marks, "The 'Hallelujah Lasses': Working-Class Women in the Salvation Army in English Canada, 1882-1892," in *Gender Conflicts: New Essays in Women's History*, ed. Franca Iacovetta and Mariana Valverde (Toronto, ON: University of Toronto Press, 1992), 67-117; Roger J. Green, "Settled Views: Catherine Booth and Female Ministry," *Methodist History* 31, 3 (April 1993): 131-47; Diane Winston, *Red-Hot and Righteous: The Urban Religion of The Salvation Army* (Cambridge, MA: Harvard University Press, 1999), 44-95; Lillian Taiz, *Hallelujah Lads and Lasses: Remaking the Salvation Army in America, 1880-1930* (Chapel Hill, NC: University of North Carolina Press, 2001), 9-71; and Pamela J. Walker, *Pulling the Devil's Kingdom Down: The Salvation Army in Victorian Britain* (Berkeley, CA: University of California Press, 2001), 8-40, 94-174. One exception to this dominant viewpoint can be found in the work of Laura Lauer, who begins to offer a more sobering perspective on female equality within the early Salvation Army in Britain. She argues that the organization's egalitarian beginnings foundered as female officers were funnelled into the Army's emerging social programs, and domestic expectations began to relegate wives and mothers to the home. There is a good deal of merit to Lauer's explanation, but it needs to be broadened and deepened. Beyond the fact that she engages with only limited primary sources, her work fails to address the ambiguities that existed

within the organization from its inception, including the problematic view-points espoused by its founding fathers and mothers. Furthermore, Lauer's theological analysis rarely extends beyond the doctrine of holiness, thereby leaving unexamined the important areas of sin, sacrifice, male headship and God-language. Related matters, such as leadership statistics, are left out of her research as well. See Laura E. Lauer, "Soul-saving Partnerships and Pacifist Soldiers: The Ideal of Masculinity in the Salvation Army," in *Masculinity and Spirituality in Victorian Culture*, ed. Andrew Bradstock et al. (London: Macmillan, 2000), 194-208; which is based upon her dissertation, "Women in British Nonconformity, circa 1880-1920, with Special Reference to the Society of Friends, Baptist Union and Salvation Army" (Ph.D. thesis, University of Oxford, 1998), 228-93. See also Andrew Mark Eason, "Gender and Equality in God's Army: An Examination of Women's Public and Domestic Roles in the Salvation Army, British Origins to 1930" (M.A. thesis, University of Windsor, Windsor, ON, 1998), where part of my argument parallels that of Lauer. We arrived at such conclusions independent of each other.

4 See, for example, Dayton, *Discovering an Evangelical Heritage*, 94; Elizabeth K. Helsinger et al., *The Woman Question: Society and Literature in Britain and America, 1837-1883*, Vol. 2 (London: Garland, 1983), 183; and Roger J. Green, *Catherine Booth: A Biography of the Cofounder of The Salvation Army* (Grand Rapids, MI: Baker Books, 1996), 124.

CHAPTER 1

1 J.J. Mueller, *What Are They Saying about Theological Method?* (New York: Paulist Press, 1984), 1.

2 *All about The Salvation Army* (London: S.W. Partridge and Co., 1882), 9-10. The desire to justify sensational tactics was apparent from the Salvation Army's earliest days as a mission in the East End of London. See George Scott Railton, "About Sensationalism," *The Christian Mission Magazine* (July 1874): 177-81.

3 Although Christian feminists are typically eclectic when it comes to the conceptual tools they employ, they generally agree upon a process of deconstruction and reconstruction. The deconstructive task is one of uncovering the oppressive and liberating features of women's existence in the past. This largely historical step addresses the ways in which Christian and cultural concepts, images and roles have functioned either to subvert or to legitimize women's subordination to men. Reconstruction takes the positive aspects of this critique and combines them with contemporary women's experiences to create a liberating, inclusive environment for both sexes in the present. Since the reconstructive project is one that must involve contemporary women themselves, it falls outside the scope of this investigation of early Salvationist women. For further information on this model, see Lisa Isherwood and Dorothea McEwan, *Introducing Feminist Theology*, 2nd ed. (Sheffield, UK: Sheffield

Academic Press, 2001), 13-22, 74-106; Pamela Dickey Young, *Feminist Theology/ Christian Theology: In Search of Method* (Minneapolis, MN: Fortress Press, 1990), esp. 1-13; and Anne-Louise Eriksson, *The Meaning of Gender in Theology: Problems and Possibilities* (Uppsala, Sweden: Uppsala University Press, 1995), 11.

4 For good overviews of the relationship between gender and religion, see Randi R. Warne, "Gender and the Study of Religion," *Method and Theory in the Study of Religion* 13, 2 (2001): 141-52; Elizabeth A. Clark, "Women, Gender, and the Study of Christian History," *Church History* 70, 3 (September 2001): 395-426; Elaine L. Graham, *Making the Difference: Gender, Personhood and Theology* (Minneapolis, MN: Fortress Press, 1996), 35-56, 214-31; and Ursula King, ed., *Religion and Gender* (Oxford: Blackwell, 1995).

5 Two helpful introductions to the study of gender are Hilary M. Lips, *Sex and Gender: An Introduction*, 3rd ed. (Mountain View, CA: Mayfield, 1997); and Rhoda Unger and Mary Crawford, *Women and Gender: A Feminist Psychology* (New York: McGraw-Hill, 1992).

6 One of the first scholars to draw attention to this human propensity was the anthropologist Gayle Rubin. See her groundbreaking article, "The Traffic in Women: Notes on the 'Political Economy' of Sex," in *Toward an Anthropology of Women*, ed. Rayna Reiter (New York: Monthly Review Press, 1975), 157-210.

7 For a lucid account of role development, see Peter L. Berger, *Invitation to Sociology: A Humanistic Perspective* (Garden City, NY: Anchor Books, 1963), 93-121. See also Graham, *Making the Difference*, 219-20. Graham argues that gender is a performative reality that arises within a culture.

8 See, for example, Gerda Lerner, *The Creation of Feminist Consciousness: From the Middle Ages to Eighteen-Seventy* (New York: Oxford University Press, 1993), and her companion volume, *The Creation of Patriarchy* (New York: Oxford University Press, 1986); M.E. Hawkesworth, *Beyond Oppression: Feminist Theory and Political Strategy* (New York: Continuum, 1990); Lips, *Sex and Gender*, 5-15; and Mary Daly, *The Church and the Second Sex* (1968; reprint, Boston, MA: Beacon Press, 1985).

9 For excellent discussions of bipolarity and gender roles, see Rosemary Radford Ruether, "Christian Understandings of Human Nature and Gender," in *Religion, Feminism, and the Family*, ed. Anne E. Carr and Mary Stewart Van Leeuwen (Louisville, KY: Westminster John Knox Press, 1996), 95-110; Graham, *Making the Difference*, 59-76; and Nancy Jay, "Gender and Dichotomy," *Feminist Studies* 7, 1 (Spring 1981): 38-56.

10 The classic articulation of this phenomenon is by Sherry B. Ortner, "Is Female to Male as Nature Is to Culture?" in *Women, Culture and Society*, ed. Michelle Z. Rosaldo and Louise Lamphere (Stanford, CA: Stanford University Press, 1974), 67-87. In this article, Ortner provides convincing reasons for the claim that women are universally devalued by being seen as closer to nature, whereas men are identified with culture—a superior association because of culture's ability to transform and socialize nature. For more on the problems associated with gender complementarity, see Graham, *Making the Difference*, 47-49.

11 For an understanding of how reality—and thus gender—is socially constructed, see Peter L. Berger and Thomas Luckmann, *The Social Construction of Reality: A Treatise in the Sociology of Knowledge* (1966; reprint, Garden City, NY: Doubleday, 1989), esp. 47-183.

12 Joan W. Scott, "Gender: A Useful Category of Historical Analysis," *American Historical Review* 91, 5 (December 1986): 1053-75. For some indication of the influence that Scott's insights have had on subsequent historians, see Joy Parr, "Gender History and Historical Practice," *The Canadian Historical Review* 76, 3 (September 1995): 354-76; and Anna Green and Kathleen Troup, *The Houses of History: A Critical Reader in Twentieth-Century History and Theory* (Washington Square, NY: New York University Press, 1999), 253-62.

13 Lerner, *The Creation of Patriarchy*, 228.

14 Anne E. Carr, *Transforming Grace: Christian Tradition and Women's Experience* (San Francisco: HarperCollins, 1988), 76-84; Judith M. Bennett, "Feminism and History," *Gender and History* 1, 3 (Autumn 1989): 258.

15 June O'Connor, "The Epistemological Significance of Feminist Research in Religion," in King, ed., *Religion and Gender*, 58.

16 A brief but helpful discussion of gender and stratification is provided by Meredith B. McGuire, *Religion: The Social Context*, 4th ed. (Belmont, CA: Wadsworth, 1997), 120-30, 231. The inclusion of gender in definitions of social stratification represents a trend towards addressing the ways in which masculinity and femininity are correlated with power and status in a society. One of the earliest attempts to explore this relationship is Rosemary Crompton and Michael Mann, eds., *Gender and Stratification* (Cambridge, MA: Polity Press, 1986).

17 For some indication of the strength of these criticisms, see R.G. Moyles, *The Salvation Army and the Public: Historical and Descriptive Essays* (Edmonton, AB: AGM Publications, 2000), 1-21, 181-205.

18 In addition to the various *Orders and Regulations* issued by the Army, all of which will be cited in the chapters ahead, there were numerous editions of *The Why and Wherefore of The Salvation Army Regulations* (London: The Salvation Army, 1904). Such material was standard fare in the organization's training programs for officers.

19 I prefer the word "derived" to the word "ascribed." While both terms refer to status that may bear little relationship to a person's ability, the use of the word "derived" is better suited to a critique of patriarchy. Given the fact that, within patriarchal societies, women often receive their status through men, to look for the presence or absence of derived status is one good indicator of a group's sexist assumptions. Moreover, this concept is better equipped to identify the extent to which gender is a variable in social stratification.

20 King, "Introduction: Gender and the Study of Religion," in King, ed., *Religion and Gender*, 2-4.

21 See Elizabeth A. Johnson, *She Who Is: The Mystery of God in Feminist Theological Discourse* (New York: Crossroad, 1992), esp. 3-57. Johnson's work represents

one of the most detailed and erudite critiques of conventional language for the Godhead. The continued importance of God-language within feminist theology is outlined in Isherwood and McEwan, *Introducing Feminist Theology*, 107-122.

22 This type of theological inquiry was pioneered by Valerie Saiving Goldstein, "The Human Situation: A Feminine View," *The Journal of Religion* 40 (1960): 100-12. For more recent discussions of this issue, see Isherwood and McEwan, *Introducing Feminist Theology*, 26-48; Anne E. Carr and Douglas J. Schuurman, "Religion and Feminism: A Reformist Christian Analysis," in Carr and Van Leeuwen, eds., *Religion, Feminism, and the Family*, 11-32; Sally Purvis, "A Common Love: Christian Feminist Ethics and the Family," in Carr and Van Leeuwen, eds., *Religion, Feminism, and the Family*, 111-24; Lucy Tatman, "Sin," in *An A to Z of Feminist Theology*, ed. Lisa Isherwood and Dorothea McEwan (Sheffield, UK: Sheffield Academic Press, 1996), 217-18; and Joann Wolski Conn, "Toward Spiritual Maturity," in *Freeing Theology: The Essentials of Theology in Feminist Perspective*, ed. Catherine Mowry LaCugna (San Francisco: HarperCollins, 1993), 235-59.

23 Rosemary Radford Ruether, *Sexism and God-Talk: Toward a Feminist Theology* (Boston, MA: Beacon Press, 1983), 18-19.

24 Ibid., 19.

25 See Clifford Geertz, "Religion as a Cultural System," in *Anthropological Approaches to the Study of Religion*, ed. Michael Banton (London: Tavistock Publications, 1966), 1-46.

26 For more on this approach, see Melissa Raphael, "Hermeneutics from a Feminist Perspective," in Isherwood and McEwan, eds., *An A to Z of Feminist Theology*, 99-102.

❖

CHAPTER 2

1 "In Doubt?" *The War Cry* (June 6, 1903): 2. Other instances of this tendency include *Orders and Regulations for Field Officers of The Salvation Army* (London: The Salvation Army Book Department, 1917), 35; Bramwell Booth, "The Salvation Army," in *Modern Evangelistic Movements*, ed. Two University Men (London: Thomson and Cowan, 1924), 21; and Albert Orsborn, "Foreword," in Robert Sandall, *The History of The Salvation Army*, Vol. 1 (1947; reprint, New York: The Salvation Army, 1979), vii-viii.

2 Walter L. Arnstein, *Britain Yesterday and Today: 1830 to the Present*, 7th ed. (Toronto, ON: D.C. Heath and Co., 1996), 27-29. See also E.K. Hunt, *Property and Prophets: The Evolution of Economic Institutions and Ideologies*, 5th ed. (New York: Harper and Row, 1986), 48-52; and Chris Cook, *The Longman Companion to Britain in the Nineteenth Century 1815-1914* (London: Longman, 1999), 119-20.

3 Samuel Smiles, *Self-Help* (1859; reprint, London: John Murray, 1958), 35.

4   See Andrew Mearns, *The Bitter Cry of Outcast London*, Edited with an Introduction by Anthony S. Wohl (1883; reprint, Leicester, UK: Leicester University Press, 1970), esp. 58-68.

5   See William Booth, *In Darkest England and the Way Out* (1890; reprint, Atlanta, GA: The Salvation Army, 1984); Robert Sandall, *The History of The Salvation Army*, Vol. 3 (1955; reprint, New York: The Salvation Army, 1979), 62-97; and Frederick Coutts, *Bread for My Neighbour: The Social Influence of William Booth* (1978; reprint, London: Hodder and Stoughton, 1982), 73-162. For more on the numerous other responses to urban poverty during this period, see Gerald Parsons, "Social Control to Social Gospel: Victorian Christian Social Attitudes," in *Religion in Victorian Britain*, Vol. 2, ed. Gerald Parsons (Manchester: Manchester University Press, 1988), 39-62.

6   Cook, *The Longman Companion to Britain in the Nineteenth Century 1815-1914*, 111; Arnstein, *Britain Yesterday and Today*, 18; Hugh McLeod, *Religion and Society in England, 1850-1914* (London: Macmillan, 1996), 27; and David Hempton, "Religious Life in Industrial Britain, 1830-1914," in *A History of Religion in Britain: Practice and Belief from Pre-Roman Times to the Present*, ed. Sheridan Gilley and W.J. Sheils (Oxford: Blackwell, 1994), 307-308.

7   "The Poor in the East of London," *The Revival* (April 14, 1864): 232.

8   "Irregular Religious Agencies," *The Nonconformist* (April 10, 1867): 289-90.

9   *All about The Salvation Army* (London: S.W. Partridge and Co., 1882), 4. See also *All about The Salvation Army* (London: International Headquarters of The Salvation Army, 1888), 4-5.

10 William Booth offered guidelines on how to conduct a "free and easy" in his *Orders and Regulations for Field Officers of The Salvation Army* (London: International Headquarters of The Salvation Army, 1886), 322-24. For an excellent treatment of the Victorian Music Hall, see Peter Bailey, *Popular Culture and Performance in the Victorian City* (Cambridge: Cambridge University Press, 1998), 80-150.

11 For an intriguing discussion of Salvation Army working-class conversion stories, see Pamela J. Walker, *Pulling the Devil's Kingdom Down: The Salvation Army in Victorian Britain* (Berkeley, CA: University of California Press, 2001), 64-93.

12 Janet Wolff, "The Culture of Separate Spheres: The Role of Culture in Nineteenth-Century Public and Private Life," in *The Culture of Capital: Art, Power and the Nineteenth-Century Middle Class*, ed. Janet Wolff and John Seed (Manchester: Manchester University Press, 1988), 118-19; Barbara Ehrenreich and Deirdre English, *For Her Own Good: 150 Years of the Experts' Advice to Women* (Garden City, NY: Anchor Press, 1978), 9-17. Even when business and domestic life continued to take place under one roof, there was a growing distinction between home and work. See Leonore Davidoff and Catherine Hall, *Family Fortunes: Men and Women of the English Middle Class, 1780-1850* (Chicago: University of Chicago Press, 1987), 364-69.

13 Ellen Jordan, *The Women's Movement and Women's Employment in Nineteenth-Century Britain* (London: Routledge, 1999), 23-41; Sally Mitchell, *Daily Life in Victorian England* (Westport, CT: Greenwood Press, 1996), 50; Sally Alexander, *Becoming a Woman and Other Essays in Nineteenth and Twentieth Century Feminist History* (London: Virago Press, 1994), 6; and Philippa Levine, *Victorian Feminism: 1850-1900* (London: Hutchinson, 1987), 106.

14 See Anna Clark, *The Struggle for the Breeches: Gender and the Making of the British Working Class* (Berkeley, CA: University of California Press, 1995), 197-271; and Jutta Schwarzkopf, *Women in the Chartist Movement* (London: Macmillan, 1991), esp. 41-51, 265-85.

15 Good overviews of these political developments are found in John Wolffe, *God and Greater Britain: Religion and National Life in Britain and Ireland, 1843-1945* (London: Routledge, 1994), 38-42, 130-40; Edward Norman, "Church and State since 1800," in Gilley and Sheils, eds., *A History of Religion in Britain,* 277-90; Cook, *The Longman Companion to Britain in the Nineteenth Century 1815-1914,* 56-64, 154-56; Gerald Parsons, "From Dissenters to Free Churchmen: The Transitions of Victorian Nonconformity," in *Religion in Victorian Britain,* Vol. 1, ed. Gerald Parsons (Manchester: Manchester University Press, 1988), 67-116; and Hugh McLeod, *Religion and the Working Class in Nineteenth-Century Britain* (London: Macmillan, 1984), 18-19.

16 "Nonconformists Will Help Us in Self-Denial Week," *The War Cry* (September 28, 1895): 4.

17 For more on the Salvation Army's efforts to raise the age of sexual consent, see "The Recent Revelations," *The War Cry* (July 29, 1885): 1; "The Horrible Immorality of London," *The War Cry* (August 1, 1885): 1; "The General's Letter," *The War Cry* (August 8, 1885): 1-2; Coutts, *Bread for My Neighbour,* 45-62; and R.G. Moyles, *The Salvation Army and the Public: Historical and Descriptive Essays* (Edmonton, AB: AGM Publications, 2000), 47-69.

18 *All about The Salvation Army* (1882), 26. See also *All about The Salvation Army* (1888), 31; "The Church of England Should Uphold Us in Self-Denial Week," *The War Cry* (September 28, 1895): 4; and "Light on Questions that Perplex Some People," *All the World* 17, 8 (August 1896): 345.

19 Catherine Booth, *The Salvation Army in Relation to the Church and State, and Other Addresses* (London: S.W. Partridge and Co., 1883), 1-26.

20 See, for example, "Apostolic Warfare," *The War Cry* (January 4, 1890): 6; and "Fifty Years' Salvation Service: Some of Its Lessons and Results. Interview with The General," *All the World* 14, 1 (July 1894): 2.

21 See Barbara Caine, *Victorian Feminists* (Oxford: Oxford University Press, 1993), 1-17; Jane Lewis, *Women in England, 1870-1950: Sexual Divisions and Social Change* (Bloomington, IN: Indiana University Press, 1984), 88-89; and Olive Banks, *Faces of Feminism: A Study of Feminism as a Social Movement* (Oxford: Martin Robertson, 1981), 29-42.

22 John Stuart Mill, *The Subjection of Women* (1869; reprint, Mineola, NY: Dover Publications, 1997), 1.

23 For more on the Contagious Diseases Acts, see Trevor Fisher, *Scandal: The Sexual Politics of Late Victorian Britain* (Cornwall, UK: Alan Sutton, 1995); and Judith R. Walkowitz, *Prostitution and Victorian Society: Women, Class and the State* (Cambridge: Cambridge University Press, 1980).

24 John Bowle, *The English Experience: A Survey of English History from Early to Modern Times* (New York: G.P. Putnam's Sons, 1971), 433.

25 For some indication of the rationalist strain in Britain and Western Europe, see Edward Royle, "Secularists and Rationalists, 1800-1940," in Gilley and Sheils, eds., *A History of Religion in Britain*, 406-22; and Hugh McLeod, *Religion and the People of Western Europe 1789-1989* (Oxford: Oxford University Press, 1997), 44-47.

26 See Herbert Schlossberg, *The Silent Revolution and the Making of Victorian England* (Columbus, OH: Ohio State University Press, 2000), 135-55; and James C. Livingston, *Modern Christian Thought: From the Enlightenment to Vatican II* (New York: Macmillan, 1971), 80-114.

27 See John R. Rhemick, *A New People of God: A Study in Salvationism* (Des Plaines, IL: The Salvation Army, 1993), 129-224.

28 Ibid. See also Walker, *Pulling the Devil's Kingdom Down*, 180-87.

29 G. Kitson Clark, *The Making of Victorian England* (New York: Atheneum, 1967), 189.

30 Gerald Parsons, "Victorian Religion: Paradox and Variety," in Parsons, ed., *Religion in Victorian Britain*, Vol. 1, 5. See also McLeod, *Religion and Society in England, 1850-1914*, 71-224.

31 Cited in McLeod, *Religion and the People of Western Europe 1789-1989*, 106. For more on the importance of church and chapel life within the Victorian middle class, see Simon Gunn, *The Public Culture of the Victorian Middle Class: Ritual and Authority and the English Industrial City, 1840-1914* (Manchester: Manchester University Press, 2000), 106-133.

32 The standard survey of British evangelicalism thus far is David W. Bebbington, *Evangelicalism in Modern Britain: A History from the 1730s to the 1980s* (1989; reprint, Grand Rapids, MI: Baker Book House, 1992). See also Boyd Hilton, *The Age of Atonement: The Influence of Evangelicalism on Social and Economic Thought, 1795-1865* (Oxford: Clarendon Press, 1988); John Kent, *Holding the Fort: Studies in Victorian Revivalism* (London: Epworth Press, 1978); Richard Carwardine, *Transatlantic Revivalism: Popular Evangelicalism in Britain and America, 1790-1865* (Westport, CT: Greenwood Press, 1978); and Ian Bradley, *The Call to Seriousness: The Evangelical Impact on the Victorians* (New York: Macmillan, 1976).

33 Good treatments of this aspect of evangelicalism include Gerald Parsons, "A Question of Meaning: Religion and Working-Class Life," in Parsons, ed., *Religion in Victorian Britain*, Vol. 2, 63-87; and Donald M. Lewis, *Lighten Their Darkness: The Evangelical Mission to Working-Class London, 1828-1860* (Westport, CT: Greenwood Press, 1986).

34   A recent detailed analysis of this census is provided in K.D.M. Snell and Paul S. Ell, *Rival Jerusalems: The Geography of Victorian Religion* (Cambridge: Cambridge University Press, 2000). A helpful overview of the 1851 census, as well as other patterns of church and chapel membership, can be found in McLeod, *Religion and Society in England, 1850-1914*, 11-70.

35   Religious observers like Horace Mann often underestimated the strength of upper-working-class religious participation and too easily equated church attendance with religiosity. Although the poor may not have been regular churchgoers, they combined popular religious beliefs with certain orthodox rites of passage. This blending of unofficial and official religion enabled lower-working-class individuals to take sacred matters on their own terms, showing up at the local church or chapel when they felt it was necessary. Since the work of Jeffrey Cox, historians have increasingly demonstrated that the working classes were not indifferent to religion. See Jeffrey Cox, *The English Churches in a Secular Society: Lambeth, 1870-1930* (Oxford: Oxford University Press, 1982); Callum Brown, *Religion and Society in Scotland since 1707* (Edinburgh: Edinburgh University Press, 1997); Sarah Williams, *Religious Belief and Popular Culture in Southwark, c. 1880-1939* (Oxford: Oxford University Press, 1999); and Dorothy Entwistle, "'Hope, Colour and Comradeship': Loyalty and Opportunism in Early Twentieth-Century Church Attendance among the Working Class in North-West England," *The Journal of Religious History* 25,1 (February 2001): 20-38.

36   For more on the reasons outlined here, see David Hempton, *Religion and Political Culture in Britain and Ireland: From the Glorious Revolution to the Decline of Empire* (Cambridge: Cambridge University Press, 1996), 122-23; McLeod, *Religion and the Working Class in Nineteenth-Century Britain*, 15-17; and Clark, *The Making of Victorian England*, 147-49, 163.

37   Those who have highlighted the ambiguity surrounding women in evangelicalism include Clark, *The Struggle for the Breeches*, 92-118; Susan Juster, *Disorderly Women: Sexual Politics and Evangelicalism in Revolutionary New England* (Ithaca, NY: Cornell University Press, 1994), 1-13; Davidoff and Hall, *Family Fortunes*, 107-48; Jane Rendall, *The Origins of Modern Feminism: Women in Britain, France and the United States, 1780-1860* (London: Macmillan, 1985), 73-107; and Carol Dyhouse, *Girls Growing Up in Late Victorian and Edwardian England* (London: Routledge and Kegan Paul, 1981), 28-30.

38   Bebbington, *Evangelicalism in Modern Britain*, 1-17. A similar summary of evangelical beliefs can be found in R.T. France and Alister E. McGrath, "Introduction," in *Evangelical Anglicans: Their Role and Influence in the Church Today*, ed. R.T. France and Alister E. McGrath (London: SPCK, 1993), 3; George A. Rawlyk and Mark A. Noll, "Introduction," in *Amazing Grace: Evangelicalism in Australia, Britain, Canada, and the United States*, ed. George A. Rawlyk and Mark A. Noll (Grand Rapids, MI: Baker Books, 1993), 17-18; and George Marsden, *Understanding Fundamentalism and Evangelicalism* (Grand Rapids, MI: Eerdmans, 1991), 4-5. These theological beliefs remain normative for most evangelicals today.

39 Helpful overviews of female activism within religious circles can be found in F.K. Prochaska, *Women and Philanthropy in Nineteenth-Century England* (Oxford: Clarendon Press, 1980); Frances Knight, "'Male and Female He Created Them': Men, Women and the Question of Gender," in *Religion in Victorian Britain*, Vol. 5, ed. John Wolffe (Manchester: Manchester University Press, 1997), esp. 47-53; Sean Gill, *Women and the Church of England: From the Eighteenth Century to the Present* (London: SPCK, 1994), 131-72; and McLeod, *Religion and Society in England, 1850-1914*, 160-68.

40 McLeod, *Religion and Society in England, 1850-1914*, 165.

41 *The Works of John Wesley*, Vol. 12 (Grand Rapids, MI: Zondervan, 1958), 355.

42 Ibid., 356. For a more detailed account of the female preachers within early Methodism, and John Wesley's influence on their work, see Paul Wesley Chilcote, *John Wesley and the Women Preachers of Early Methodism* (Metuchen, NJ: Scarecrow Press, 1991); Deborah M. Valenze, *Prophetic Sons and Daughters: Female Preaching and Popular Religion in Industrial England* (Princeton, NJ: Princeton University Press, 1985); Earl Kent Brown, *Women of Mr. Wesley's Methodism* (New York: Edwin Mellen Press, 1983); Leslie F. Church, *More about the Early Methodist People* (London: Epworth Press, 1949), esp. 136-76; and John C. English, "'Dear Sister': John Wesley and the Women of Early Methodism," *Methodist History* 33, 1 (October 1994): 26-33.

43 Brown, *Women of Mr. Wesley's Methodism*, 92-99; Chilcote, *John Wesley and the Women Preachers of Early Methodism*, 171.

44 Chilcote, *John Wesley and the Women Preachers of Early Methodism*, 235-36.

45 For more on the origins of Primitive Methodism, see Hugh Bourne, *History of the Primitive Methodists. Giving an Account of Their Rise and Progress Up to the Year 1823* (Bemersley Near Tunstall, UK: Primitive Methodist Connexion, 1835); and Julia Stewart Werner, *The Primitive Methodist Connexion: Its Background and Early History* (Madison, WI: University of Wisconsin Press, 1984).

46 This pamphlet is reproduced in its entirety in John Walford, *Memoirs of the Life and Labours of the Late Venerable Hugh Bourne* (1856; reprint, Totton, UK: Berith Publications, 1999), Vol. 1, 184-89.

47 Werner, *The Primitive Methodist Connexion*, 142.

48 Ibid., 140-44.

49 Bourne, *History of the Primitive Methodists*, 48-49. Bourne only devoted *one* paragraph to the women who preached in the connexion.

50 See David Shorney, "'Women May Preach but Men Must Govern': Gender Roles in the Growth and Development of the Bible Christian Denomination," in *Gender and Christian Religion*, ed. Robert N. Swanson (Woodbridge, Suffolk, UK: Boydell Press, 1998), 317-18.

51 See the notes accompanying 1 Corinthians 11: 5-9;14:34-35; and 1 Timothy 2:9-15 in Adam Clarke, *The Holy Bible, Containing the Old and New Testament: Including the Marginal Readings and Parallel Texts, with a Commentary and Critical Notes*, Vol. 6 (1800; reprint, London: Ward, Lock and Co., n.d.). This edition is not paginated.

52   See F.W. Bourne, *The Bible Christians: Their Origin and History (1815-1900)* (London: Bible Christian Book Room, 1905), 79-81, 97, 126, 165-81.

53   Shorney, "'Women May Preach but Men Must Govern'," 318-22; Michael J.L. Wickes, *The Westcountry Preachers: A New History of the Bible Christian Church (1815-1907)* (Bideford, Devon, UK: Jamaica Press, 1987), 30-34; Richard Pyke, *The Early Bible Christians* (London: Epworth Press, 1941), 26-30.

54   Bourne, *The Bible Christians*, 293.

55   Olive Anderson, "Women Preachers in Mid-Victorian Britain: Some Reflections on Feminism, Popular Religion and Social Change," *The Historical Journal* 12, 3 (1969): 467-84.

56   See "Miss Hooper at Luton," *The Revival* (April 19, 1866): 220; "Miss Hooper at Dunstable," *The Revival* (May 17, 1866): 272; "Miss Hooper at Leighton Buzzard," *The Revival* (June 28, 1866): 357; and "Miss Hooper in Bedfordshire," *The Revival* (August 9, 1866): 82.

57   For some indication of the long struggle behind the expansion of women's roles in the Anglican communion, see Brian Heeney, *The Women's Movement in the Church of England 1850-1930* (Oxford: Clarendon Press, 1988); and Gill, *Women and the Church of England*, 206-59. A brief overview of women's opportunities in some other denominations can be found in Elaine Kaye, "A Turning-Point in the Ministry of Women: The Ordination of the First Woman to the Christian Ministry in England in September 1917," in *Women in the Church*, ed. W.J. Sheils and Diana Wood (Oxford: Basil Blackwell, 1990), 505-12; and McLeod, *Religion and Society in England, 1850-1914*, 161-68.

58   Nancy A. Hardesty, *Women Called to Witness: Evangelical Feminism in the Nineteenth Century*, 2nd ed. (Knoxville, TN: University of Tennessee Press, 1999), 53. For one early indication of the Bible's importance within the Salvation Army, see William Booth, "The Salvation Army, the Bible, and Sunday Schools," *The War Cry* (December 8, 1881): 2

59   Phoebe Palmer, *Promise of the Father; or, A Neglected Speciality of the Last Days* (Boston, MA: Henry V. Degen, 1859), esp. 68, 87, 171-72, 231, 246, 320, 324, 338, 358, 366. Here, in particular, Palmer echoed a central argument used to support female ministry during the earliest days of sectarian Methodism. See "On the Rise of Female Preachers in the Connexion which Originated in Cornwall," *The Primitive Methodist Magazine* (July 1821): 161-67.

60   Catherine Booth, *Female Teaching: Or, the Rev. A.A. Rees versus Mrs. Palmer, Being a Reply to a Pamphlet by the Above Gentleman on the Sunderland Revival* (London: G.J. Stevenson, 1861), 7-12; and Antoinette L. Brown, "Exegesis of 1 Corinthians, XIV., 34, 35; and 1 Timothy, II., 11, 12," *The Oberlin Quarterly Review* (January 1849): 358-73.

61   For more on the evangelical exegesis of scripture, see Janette Hassey, *No Time for Silence: Evangelical Women in Public Ministry around the Turn of the Century* (Grand Rapids, MI: Zondervan, 1986), 95-121. In contrast, the largely liberal thrust of Elizabeth Cady Stanton's biblical hermeneutics led her to disregard the authority and legitimacy of passages that were often used to justify women's

subordination to men. See Elizabeth Cady Stanton, *The Woman's Bible* (1898; reprint, Amherst, NY: Prometheus Books, 1999).

62 Henry Venn, *The Complete Duty of Man: Or, A System of Doctrinal and Practical Christianity* (1763; reprint, London: The Religious Tract Society, 1799), 221.

63 See Phoebe Palmer, *Faith and Its Effects: Or, Fragments from My Portfolio* (1848; reprint, Toronto, ON: G.R. Sanderson, 1856), 304-05; Booth, *Female Teaching*, 6, 22, 30; and Letha Dawson Scanzoni and Susan Setta, "Women in Evangelical, Holiness, and Pentecostal Traditions," in *Women and Religion in America. Volume 3: 1900-1968*, ed. Rosemary Radford Ruether and Rosemary S. Keller (San Francisco: Harper and Row, 1986), 226-29.

64 For more on the theme of dependence, see Davidoff and Hall, *Family Fortunes*, 107-15; and Elizabeth K. Helsinger et al., *The Woman Question: Society and Literature in Britain and America, 1837-1883*, Vol. 2 (London: Garland, 1983), 165-68.

65 See Brown, "Exegesis of 1 Corinthians, XIV., 34, 35; and 1 Timothy, II., 11, 12," 371-72; Palmer, *Promise of the Father*, 7-9, 48; and Booth, *Female Teaching*, 10-12.

66 Palmer, *Faith and Its Effects*, 269.

67 Catherine Booth, *Papers on Godliness* (1881; reprint, London: International Headquarters of The Salvation Army, 1890), 93-94. See also Catherine Booth, *Aggressive Christianity* (1880; reprint, Toronto, ON: William Briggs, 1883), 128.

68 Jordan, *The Women's Movement and Women's Employment in Nineteenth-Century Britain*, 48-54; Davidoff and Hall, *Family Fortunes*, 114-16, 149-92, 319-94; and Rendall, *The Origins of Modern Feminism*, 73.

69 For more on religious women in the home, see Linda Wilson "'She Succeeds with Cloudless Brow ...': How Active Was the Spirituality of Nonconformist Women in the Home during the Period 1825-75?" in Swanson, ed., *Gender and Christian Religion*, 347-59; Knight, "'Male and Female He Created Them,'" in Wolffe, ed., *Religion in Victorian Britain*, Vol. 5, 25-30; Leonore Davidoff, *Worlds Between: Historical Perspectives on Gender and Class* (New York: Routledge, 1995), 51-55; and Joan N. Burstyn, *Victorian Education and the Ideal of Womanhood* (New Brunswick, NJ: Rutgers University Press, 1984), 30-31, 129-31.

70 One recent volume that addresses the domestic and public sides of this image is *Women of Faith in Victorian Culture: Reassessing the Angel in the House*, ed. Anne Hogan and Andrew Bradstock (London: Macmillan, 1998).

71 [Maud] Ballington Booth, "The New Woman," *All the World* 16, 3 (September 1895): 145-47.

CHAPTER 3

1 The best sources for William Booth's early life are St. John Ervine, *God's Soldier: General William Booth*, Vol. 1 (1934; reprint, New York: Macmillan, 1935), 3-11, 28-42; Harold Begbie, *The Life of General William Booth: The Founder of The*

Salvation Army, Vol. 1 (New York: Macmillan, 1920), 1-98; and Roy Hattersley, *Blood and Fire: William and Catherine Booth and Their Salvation Army* (New York: Doubleday, 2000), 11-29.

2 See Daniel Wise, ed., *Methodism in Earnest: Being the History of a Great Revival in Great Britain, in Which Twenty Thousand Souls Were Justified, and Ten Thousand Sanctified, in about Six Years, through the Instrumentality of Rev. James Caughey* (Boston, MA: Charles H. Peirce, 1850), esp. 13-41, 423, and 426. A good overview of James Caughey's work in England can be found in Richard Carwardine, *Transatlantic Revivalism: Popular Evangelicalism in Britain and America, 1790-1865* (Westport, CT: Greenwood Press, 1978), 102-33.

3 According to Hugh Bourne, Primitive Methodism's work in Nottingham was quite extensive by the early 1820s. See Hugh Bourne, *History of the Primitive Methodists. Giving an Account of Their Rise and Progress Up to the Year 1823* (Bemersley Near Tunstall, UK: Primitive Methodist Connexion, 1835), 51, 56-57, 65. See also Julia Stewart Werner, *The Primitive Methodist Connexion: Its Background and Early History* (Madison, WI: University of Wisconsin Press, 1984), 84-116. For more on female cottage preaching, see Deborah M. Valenze, *Prophetic Sons and Daughters: Female Preaching and Popular Religion in Industrial England* (Princeton, NJ: Princeton University Press, 1985).

4 Cited in Frederick Booth-Tucker, *The Life of Catherine Booth: The Mother of The Salvation Army*, Vol. 1 (London: International Headquarters of The Salvation Army, 1892), 87.

5 For more on this period, see Walter L. Arnstein, *Britain Yesterday and Today: 1830 to the Present*, 7th ed. (Toronto, ON: D.C. Heath and Co., 1996), 30-58; and F.M.L. Thompson, *The Rise of Respectable Society: A Social History of Victorian Britain, 1830-1900* (London: Fontana Press, 1988), 30-50.

6 See William Booth, "How We Began," in George Scott Railton, *Twenty-One Years' Salvation Army* (1886; reprint, London: International Headquarters of The Salvation Army, 1891), 10.

7 See Ervine, *God's Soldier*, Vol. 1, 47-50; Begbie, *The Life of General William Booth*, Vol. 1, 99-115; and Hattersley, *Blood and Fire*, 36-50.

8 For more on this controversy, see Gerald Parsons, "From Dissenters to Free Churchmen: The Transitions of Victorian Nonconformity," in *Religion in Victorian Britain*, Vol. 1, ed. Gerald Parsons (Manchester: Manchester University Press, 1988), 82-85; David Hempton, *Methodism and Politics in British Society 1750-1850* (Stanford, CA: Stanford University Press, 1984), 197-202; and "The Recent Disciplinary Decisions of the Wesleyan Conference," *The Wesleyan Methodist Magazine* (October 1849): 1062-71.

9 William T. Stead, *General Booth: A Biographical Sketch* (1891; reprint, Oakville, ON: Triumph Press, n.d.), 36; Begbie, *The Life of General William Booth*, Vol. 1, 107.

10 Booth-Tucker, *The Life of Catherine Booth*, Vol. 1, 87-88. For a brief overview of the preaching career of Miss Buck, see William Barker, "The Women-Preachers

of Early Methodism," *The Primitive Methodist Quarterly Review* 20 (April 1898): 276.

11 Begbie, *The Life of General William Booth*, Vol. 1, 114-25; Ervine, *God's Soldier*, Vol. 1, 48-57.

12 Ervine, *God's Soldier*, Vol. 1, 61.

13 Begbie, *The Life of General William Booth*, Vol. 1, 126.

14 For more on this important religious body, see Kenneth D. Brown, *A Social History of the Nonconformist Ministry in England and Wales, 1800-1930* (Oxford: Clarendon Press, 1988); and Michael R. Watts, *The Dissenters*, Vol. 2 (Oxford: Clarendon Press, 1995).

15 Begbie, *The Life of General William Booth*, Vol. 1, 131-36; Ervine, *God's Soldier*, Vol. 1, 63-70; Hattersley, *Blood and Fire*, 50-55.

16 Ervine, *God's Soldier*, Vol. 1, 70-94; Hattersley, *Blood and Fire*, 55-66.

17 Booth-Tucker, *The Life of Catherine Booth*, Vol. 1, 82.

18 For more on the gender ideology of the period, see Anthony Fletcher, "Introduction," in *Gender and Christian Religion*, ed. Robert N. Swanson (Woodbridge, Suffolk, UK: Boydell Press, 1998), xvii-xxii; Leonore Davidoff and Catherine Hall, *Family Fortunes: Men and Women of the English Middle Class, 1780-1850* (Chicago: University of Chicago Press, 1987); and Carol Christ, "Victorian Masculinity and the Angel in the House," in *A Widening Sphere: Changing Roles of Victorian Women*, ed. Martha Vicinus (Bloomington, IN: Indiana University Press, 1977), 146-62.

19 Ervine, *God's Soldier*, Vol. 1, 94-122; Hattersley, *Blood and Fire*, 66-73.

20 Booth Papers, British Library, Add. Mss. 64802, letter dated April 9, 1855. The Booth Papers consist mainly of letters that Catherine wrote to William and to her parents during the 1850s and the early 1860s. The vast majority of this correspondence has found its way into the various biographies of William and Catherine Booth, albeit in somewhat edited form. It is worth noting as well that the Booth Papers are incomplete, and therefore need to be consulted alongside the published correspondence. The April 9th letter is reproduced, among other places, in Catherine Bramwell-Booth, *Catherine Booth: The Story of Her Loves* (London: Hodder and Stoughton, 1970), 138-42.

21 Begbie, *The Life of General William Booth*, Vol. 1, 236.

22 Ibid.

23 Bramwell-Booth, *Catherine Booth*, 180-87. See also the Booth Papers, British Library, Add. Mss. 64805, letter from Catherine to her parents, dated December 25, 1859. In this correspondence, Catherine tells her parents of William's eager support of her written defence of female ministry.

24 For perceptive insights into the revivalism of the period, see John Kent, *Holding the Fort: Studies in Victorian Revivalism* (London: Epworth Press, 1978); David W. Bebbington, *Evangelicalism in Modern Britain: A History from the 1730s to the 1980s* (1989; reprint, Grand Rapids, MI: Baker Book House, 1992), 114-18; and Gerald Parsons, "Emotion and Piety: Revivalism and Ritualism in Victorian Christianity," in Parsons, ed., *Religion in Victorian Britain*, Vol. 1, 213-34.

25 Ervine, *God's Soldier*, Vol. 1, 235-71; Hattersley, *Blood and Fire*, 115-46.

26 See "Mrs. Booth at Rotherhithe," *The Revival* (March 16, 1865): 166; Ervine, *God's Soldier*, Vol. 1, 275-86; and Hattersley, *Blood and Fire*, 146-59.

27 See C.M.S.L., "'Want as an Armed Man,' in the East of London," *The Revival* (December 22, 1864): 387-88; "Irregular Religious Agencies," *The Nonconformist* (April 10, 1867): 289-90; and Robert Sandall, *The History of The Salvation Army*, Vol. 1 (1947; reprint, New York: The Salvation Army, 1979), 28-36.

28 For more on the Christian Community, see James Atkinson, "Tent Preaching," *The Revival* (July 20, 1865): 43-44; James Atkinson, "Christian Community," *The Revival* (August 31, 1865): 143; x., "The Christian Community," *The Revival* (March 22, 1866): 166; and "The Christian Community," *The Revival* (May 10, 1866): 259. For the first references to William Booth's work in the East End, see W.J. Hayden, "East-End Services," *The Revival* (July 13, 1865): 27; and S[amuel] C[hase], "The Rev. W. Booth in Whitechapel," *The Revival* (July 27, 1865): 59-60. Chase and Morgan were the editors of *The Revival*, which changed its name to *The Christian* in 1870.

29 Booth, "How We Began," 19.

30 Sandall, *The History of The Salvation Army*, Vol. 1, 37-42.

31 See William Booth, "East of London Revival Effort," *The Revival* (August 17, 1865): 106-107; "Mr. and Mrs. Booth," *The Revival* (September 14, 1865): 163; William Booth, "Evangelistic Work in the East of London," *The Revival* (September 21, 1865): 180-81; and Sandall, *The History of The Salvation Army*, Vol. 1, 46-98.

32 Booth, "How We Began," 22. See also Booth, "East of London Revival Effort," 107; and William Booth, "Evangelistic Work in the East of London," *The Revival* (September 6, 1866): 138.

33 Sandall, *The History of The Salvation Army*, Vol. 1, 99-143. It is interesting to note that *The Christian* continued to refer to Booth's mission as the "East London Christian Mission" throughout 1870, which suggests that it took some time for the new name to be recognized by some Christian observers. See Jane Short, "East London Christian Mission," *The Christian* (March 31, 1870): 15; "The East London Christian Mission," *The Christian* (August 4, 1870): 11; Richard Eason, "East London Christian Mission," *The Christian* (August 18, 1870): 12; and Jane Short, "East London Christian Mission," *The Christian* (December 29, 1870): 9. Obviously Short and Eason, who were themselves Mission members, did not notice the incorrect captions being attached to their submissions.

34 *Christian Mission Minutes*, 1st Conference, June 15-16, 18, 1870, section 12.

35 See Robert Sandall, *The History of The Salvation Army*, Vol. 2 (1950; reprint, New York: The Salvation Army, 1979), 304-05.

36 Sandall, *The History of The Salvation Army*, Vol. 1, 86, 108, 174, 177, 271.

37 There were twenty-nine men and six women at the 1870 conference, and 106 men and thirty-six women at the 1878 conference. See *Christian Mission Minutes*, 1st Conference; and *Christian Mission Minutes*, 8th Conference, August 5-7, 1878.

38 William Booth, "The Opening Address," *The Christian Mission Magazine* (July 1877): 178.

39 William Booth, "The Past of the War," *The Christian Mission Magazine* (September 1878): 236.

40 See Elijah Cadman, "Whitby," *The Christian Mission Magazine* (December 1877): 318; and Elijah Cadman, "Whitby," *The Christian Mission Magazine* (January 1878): 14. For more on Cadman's colourful life in the Salvation Army, see Eileen Douglas, "From Chimney Sweep to Colonel," *The War Cry* (December 25, 1888): 1, 3; and Humphrey Wallis, *The Happy Warrior: The Life-Story of Commissioner Elijah Cadman* (London: Salvationist Publishing and Supplies, 1928).

41 Sandall, *The History of The Salvation Army*, Vol. 1, 228-30.

42 See Olive Anderson, "The Growth of Christian Militarism in Mid-Victorian Britain," *The English Historical Review* 86, 338 (January 1971) : 64- 72; and John Wolffe, *God and Greater Britain: Religion and National Life in Britain and Ireland, 1843-1945* (London: Routledge, 1994), 213-36.

43 Sandall, *The History of The Salvation Army*, Vol. 1, 287-92.

44 Douglas Clarke, "Female Ministry in the Salvation Army," *The Expository Times* 95, 8 (May 1984): 233.

45 William Booth cites these rights in a number of places. For one of the earliest references, see his *Orders and Regulations for Staff Officers of The Salvation Army in the United Kingdom* (London: International Headquarters of The Salvation Army, 1895), 16.

46 William Booth, *Orders and Regulations for The Salvation Army* (London: The Salvation Army Headquarters, 1878), iii. This manual, and the numerous ones that would follow, was not a legal document, and could be modified by any General. In contrast, changes to the Salvation Army's constitution needed parliamentary approval. Obviously, a woman continued to have ministerial rights within the organization, but such rights were no longer legally recognized.

47 Cited in Sandall, *The History of The Salvation Army*, Vol. 1, 215-16.

48 William Booth, "The General's Address at the Wesleyan Conference," *The War Cry* (August 14, 1880): 1.

49 Norman H. Murdoch, *Origins of the Salvation Army* (Knoxville, TN: University of Tennessee Press, 1994), 113-45. Murdoch's broader claim that "by 1886, the Salvation Army's growth had come to a halt in England" (113) is much less clear. In 1886 alone, the British operations of the Army increased by 491 officers and 237 corps. See *The Advance of The Salvation Army: 1886* (London: International Headquarters of The Salvation Army, 1886), 9. Moreover, by mid-June 1888 the Army's British territory had opened 278 new corps and had gained an additional 956 officers. See *All about The Salvation Army* (London: International Headquarters of The Salvation Army, 1888), 7. These figures hardly suggest that the organization was entering into a period of stagnation by 1886. Even more importantly, Murdoch fails to adequately deal with the fact that this growth occurred at the same time as the Army was sending British officers all over the

world to open new corps. As *The War Cry* noted in 1894, England had given at least 1,000 of its officers to other countries since 1880. See "The Army's May Meeting," *The War Cry* (June 2, 1894): 11; and "Jubilee!" *The War Cry* (July 14, 1894): 2. In spite of tight resources at home, the Salvation Army still managed to expand. Murdoch's argument may have weight when applied to a later period, but it seems less applicable to the earliest days of the Army.

50 See *The Advance of The Salvation Army: 1886,* 9; and *The Present Position of The Salvation Army* (London: International Headquarters of The Salvation Army, 1888), 2.

51 Numerous articles and booklets were written criticizing Army methods. See, for example, C. Raleigh Chichester, "The Salvation Army," *The Month* 44, 214 (April 1882): 467-83; Randall T. Davidson, "The Methods of The Salvation Army," *The Contemporary Review* 42 (1882): 189-99; "The Salvation Army," *The Saturday Review* (October 6, 1883): 431-32; Andrew Wilson, *The Salvation Army: Its Government, Principles, and Practices* (Toronto, ON: James Bain and Son, 1884); and C.A. Stork, "The Salvation Army: Its Methods and Lessons," *The Lutheran Quarterly* 12 (October 1882): 548-70. For more on the criticisms surrounding the Salvation Army's activities, see R.G. Moyles, *The Salvation Army and the Public: Historical and Descriptive Essays* (Edmonton, AB: AGM Publications, 2000), 1-46.

52 See Pamela J. Walker, *Pulling the Devil's Kingdom Down: The Salvation Army in Victorian Britain* (Berkeley, CA: University of California Press, 2001), 130-74, 196-98.

53 Sandall, *The History of The Salvation Army,* Vol. 2, 174-83, 193-97; Victor Bailey, "Salvation Army Riots, the 'Skeleton Army' and Legal Authority in the Provincial Town," in *Social Control in Nineteenth-Century Britain,* ed. A.P. Donajgrodzki (Totowa, NJ: Rowman and Littlefield, 1977), 231-42.

54 See "Important. Formation of The Army into Divisions," *The War Cry* (September 18, 1880): 2.

55 For more on this early training program, see Mrs. Charles Garnett, "A Visit to the Training Home of The Salvation Army," *Sunday Magazine* (1884): 638-44; [William] Oliphant, "A History of the Training Homes," *All the World* 6, 8 (August 1890): 386-89; *A School of the Prophets: A Sketch of Training Home Life* (London: The Salvation Army Book Department, 1901); and Sandall, *The History of The Salvation Army,* Vol. 2, 66-70.

56 See "On the War-Path," *All the Year Round* (January 3, 1891): 12-17.

57 For the striking parallels between Salvationist, Methodist and evangelical doctrines, see Murdoch, *Origins of the Salvation Army,* 173-75, and his article "Evangelical Sources of Salvation Army Doctrine," *The Evangelical Quarterly* 59 (July 1987): 235-44. See also David Guy et al., *Salvation Story: Salvationist Handbook of Doctrine* (London: International Headquarters of The Salvation Army, 1998), 130-32.

58 William Booth, *The Doctrines and Discipline of The Salvation Army* (London: The Salvation Army Headquarters, 1881), 109-10.

59 Ibid., 110.

60 Walker, *Pulling the Devil's Kingdom Down*, 117-19.

61 See Catherine Booth, *Popular Christianity* (1887; reprint, London: The Salvation Army Book Department, n.d.), 42-49. See also Sandall, *The History of The Salvation Army*, Vol. 2, 129-35; and R. David Rightmire, *Sacraments and the Salvation Army: Pneumatological Foundations* (Metuchen, NJ: Scarecrow Press, 1990). For some indication of the liturgical battles that were fought in the Victorian Age, see Gerald Parsons, "Reform, Revival and Realignment: The Experience of Victorian Anglicanism," in Parsons, ed., *Religion in Victorian Britain*, Vol. 1, 47-56.

62 Ervine, *God's Soldier*, Vol. 1, 607-14; Sandall, *The History of The Salvation Army*, Vol. 2, 146-53; Roger J. Green, *Catherine Booth: A Biography of the Cofounder of The Salvation Army* (Grand Rapids, MI: Baker Books, 1996), 232-36. For a good overview of this incident, see Stuart Mews, "The General and the Bishops: Alternative Responses to Dechristianisation," in *Later Victorian Britain, 1867-1900*, ed. T.R. Gourvish and Alan O'Day (New York: St. Martin's Press, 1988), 209-28.

63 For more on this role in the Victorian Anglican Church, see Sean Gill, *Women and the Church of England: From the Eighteenth Century to the Present* (London: SPCK, 1994), 163-68; and Brian Heeney, *The Women's Movement in the Church of England 1850-1930* (Oxford: Clarendon Press, 1988), 66-74. The evangelical wing of the Anglican Church was largely responsible for sponsoring the deaconess movement.

64 William Booth, *Orders and Regulations for Field Officers of The Salvation Army* (London: International Headquarters of The Salvation Army, 1886), iv. See also 270-71.

65 Francis Peek, "The Salvationists," *The Contemporary Review* 49 (January 1886): 57; Leopold Katscher, "Some Aspects of The Salvation Army," *The National Review* (1885): 73; Abner Sumner, *The New Papacy: Behind the Scenes in The Salvation Army* (Toronto, ON: Albert Britnell, 1889), 61; and *Orders and Regulations for Corps Officers of The Salvation Army* (London: International Headquarters of The Salvation Army, 1925), 318-19. See also Glenn K. Horridge, *The Salvation Army: Origins and Early Days, 1865-1900* (Godalming, Surrey, UK: Ammonite Books, 1993), 80-81; Glenn K. Horridge, "William Booth's Officers," *Christian History* 9, 2 (1990): 15-16; and John Coutts, *The Salvationists* (Oxford: Mowbrays, 1977), 30. Women were also paid less than men in both the Primitive Methodist Connexion and the Bible Christian sect. See Werner, *The Primitive Methodist Connexion*, 141; and F.W. Bourne, *The Bible Christians: Their Origin and History (1815-1900)* (London: Bible Christian Book Room, 1905), 241.

66 William Booth, "The May Meeting Addresses: Summary of the Year's History," *The War Cry* (May 12, 1888): 10.

67 The Salvation Army's marriage requirements are laid out in Booth, *Orders and Regulations for Field Officers* (1886), 52-55.

68 William Booth, "Home at Last: To the Officers and Soldiers of The Salvation Army," *The War Cry* (October 11, 1890): 1. See also Booth's comments in his *Orders and Regulations for Field Officers of The Salvation Army* (London: The Salvation Army Headquarters, 1891), 127-28; and his citation in Robert Sandall, *The History of The Salvation Army*, Vol. 3 (1955; reprint, New York: The Salvation Army, 1979), 50.

69 William Booth, *In Darkest England and the Way Out* (1890; reprint, Atlanta, GA: The Salvation Army, 1984), 54.

70 Joan N. Burstyn, *Victorian Education and the Ideal of Womanhood* (New Brunswick, NJ: Rutgers University Press, 1984), 111. For an in-depth treatment of Victorian prostitution, see Judith R. Walkowitz, *Prostitution and Victorian Society: Women, Class, and the State* (Cambridge: Cambridge University Press, 1980); Karl Beckson, *London in the 1890s: A Cultural History* (New York: W.W. Norton and Co., 1992), 110-28; and Amanda Anderson, *Tainted Souls and Painted Faces: The Rhetoric of Fallenness in Victorian Culture* (Ithaca, NY: Cornell University Press, 1993).

71 For more on the Salvation Army's rescue work, see Ann R. Higginbotham, "Respectable Sinners: Salvation Army Rescue Work with Unmarried Mothers, 1884-1914," in *Religion in the Lives of English Women, 1760-1930*, ed. Gail Malmgreen (Bloomington, IN: Indiana University Press, 1986), 216-33; Frederick Coutts, *Bread for My Neighbour: The Social Influence of William Booth* (1978; reprint, London: Hodder and Stoughton, 1982), 142-49; and my discussion of the subject in chapter 6.

72 See Booth, *In Darkest England and the Way Out*, 71-84.

73 Ibid., 243.

74 William Booth, "Mrs. Booth as a Woman and a Wife," *All the World* 31, 10 (October 1910): 511-12. See also "The Army Mother: An Interview with The General," *The War Cry* (October 8, 1910): 9.

75 Booth, "Mrs. Booth as a Woman and a Wife," 510. See also William Booth, *Religion for Every Day* (London: The Salvation Army Book Department, 1902), 292; and William Booth, "A Husband's Responsibilities," *The War Cry* (September 2, 1905): 2.

76 See, for example, Sandall, *The History of The Salvation Army*, Vol. 2, 161; William T. Stead, *Mrs. Booth of The Salvation Army* (1900; reprint, Oakville, ON: Triumph Press, 1979), 92; Ervine, *God's Soldier*, Vol. 1, 125; Richard Collier, *The General Next to God: The Story of William Booth and the Salvation Army* (1965; reprint, London: Fontana Collins, 1983), 30; Lucille Sider Dayton and Donald W. Dayton, "'Your Daughters Shall Prophesy': Feminism in the Holiness Movement," *Methodist History* 14 (January 1976): 75; Elizabeth K. Helsinger et al., *The Woman Question: Society and Literature in Britain and America, 1837-1883*, Vol. 2 (London: Garland, 1983), 183; Roger J. Green, "Settled Views: Catherine Booth and Female Ministry," *Methodist History* 31, 3 (April 1993): 131-47; Green, *Catherine Booth: A Biography*, 124, 171; and Hattersley, *Blood and Fire*, 4.

77 "Fifty Years' Salvation Service: Some of Its Lessons and Results. Interview with
    The General," *All the World* 14, 1 (July 1894): 2. See also Betty McCaughey, ed.,
    William and Catherine, with Love (Oakville, ON: Triumph Press, 1989), 289,
    328; and *All about The Salvation Army* (London: S.W. Partridge and Co., 1882),
    23.

78 "Fifty Years' Salvation Service," 2. See also William Booth, *A Letter from the
    General to the Officers of The Salvation Army throughout the World on the
    Occasion of His Eightieth Birthday* (London: The Salvation Army, 1909), 33.

79 I broached this issue as well in my 1998 thesis on Salvationist women. See
    Andrew Mark Eason, "Gender and Equality in God's Army: An Examination of
    Women's Public and Domestic Roles in the Salvation Army, British Origins to
    1930" (M.A. thesis, University of Windsor, Windsor, ON, 1998), 92-93. See also
    Laura E. Lauer, "Women in British Nonconformity, circa 1880-1920, with Special
    Reference to the Society of Friends, Baptist Union and Salvation Army" (Ph.D.
    thesis, University of Oxford, 1998), 272-73.

80 William Booth, "Common Snares of Officers," *The Officer* 4, 10 (December 1896):
    306.

81 Ibid., 304-07. See also William Booth, *Orders and Regulations for Field Officers
    of The Salvation Army* (London: The Salvation Army Publishing Department,
    1908), 55.

82 William Booth, *Orders and Regulations for Territorial Commissioners and
    Chief Secretaries of The Salvation Army* (London: International Headquarters
    of The Salvation Army, 1899), 10-13, 143-44.

83 Ibid., 144.

84 William Booth, "On Salvation Women," *The Field Officer* 9, 9 (September 1901):
    422-24.

85 Ibid., 423.

86 William Booth, "More about Women's Rights," *The Field Officer* 9, 11 (November 1901): 514.

87 Ibid.

88 Booth, *Religion for Every Day*, 290, 292. See also 249-57.

89 Ibid., 285-86. See also 286-96, 314-16. Those who have turned their attention
    briefly to male and female Salvationist relationships have largely ignored the
    significance of male headship. See, for example, Walker, *Pulling the Devil's
    Kingdom Down*, 123-27; Lillian Taiz, *Hallelujah Lads and Lasses: Remaking
    the Salvation Army in America, 1880-1930* (Chapel Hill, NC: University of
    North Carolina Press, 2001), 49-71; Diane Winston, *Red-Hot and Righteous: The
    Urban Religion of The Salvation Army* (Cambridge, MA: Harvard University
    Press, 1999), 44-95, 154-64; and Laura E. Lauer, "Soul-saving Partnerships and
    Pacifist Soldiers: The Ideal of Masculinity in the Salvation Army," in *Masculinity
    and Spirituality in Victorian Culture*, ed. Andrew Bradstock et al. (London:
    Macmillan, 2000), 194-208.

90 Norman H. Murdoch, "Female Ministry in the Thought and Work of Catherine
    Booth," *Church History* 53, 3 (September 1984): 359.

91 *The Supplemental Deed of Constitution (1904)*, High Council Schedule, clause 5. A copy of this Deed can be found at the Salvation Army George Scott Railton Heritage Centre, Toronto.

92 See William Booth, *Orders and Regulations for Staff Officers of The Salvation Army* (London: International Headquarters of The Salvation Army, 1904), 8-10.

93 William Booth, *The Founder's Messages to Soldiers during Years 1907-8* (London: The Salvation Army Book Department, 1921), 189-90.

94 Ibid., 178-79. See also Booth, *Religion for Every Day*, 279-80, 292, 312.

95 Booth, *The Founder's Messages to Soldiers*, 180.

96 Ibid., 180-87.

97 Ibid., 190.

98 See Booth, "Mrs. Booth as a Woman and a Wife," 510; and his similar comments in "On Salvation Women," 424; and *Religion for Every Day*, 290, 316-17.

❖

CHAPTER 4

1 For more on these developments, see Carol Dyhouse, *Feminism and the Family in England 1880-1939* (Oxford: Basil Blackwell, 1989), 54-58, 98-104; Deirdre Beddoe, *Back to Home and Duty: Women between the Wars, 1918-1939* (London: Pandora Press, 1989), 1-10, 134; Susan Kingsley Kent, "The Politics of Sexual Difference: World War I and the Demise of British Feminism," *Journal of British Studies* 27, 3 (July 1988): 232-53; and Olive Banks, *Faces of Feminism: A Study of Feminism as a Social Movement* (Oxford: Martin Robertson, 1981), 163-64.

2 See Joan Perkin, *Victorian Women* (London: John Murray, 1993), 186-201; Beddoe, *Back to Home and Duty*, 32-38; Jane Lewis, *Women in England 1870-1950: Sexual Divisions and Social Change* (Bloomington, IN: Indiana University Press, 1984), 3, 31-39, 102-103; and Carol Dyhouse, *Girls Growing Up in Late Victorian and Edwardian England* (London: Routledge and Kegan Paul, 1981), 95-98, 170.

3 William Booth, *Orders and Regulations for The Salvation Army* (London: The Salvation Army Headquarters, 1878), iii; William Booth, *Orders and Regulations for Field Officers of The Salvation Army* (London: International Headquarters of The Salvation Army, 1886), iv; William Booth, *Orders and Regulations for Staff Officers of The Salvation Army in the United Kingdom* (London: International Headquarters of The Salvation Army, 1895), 16-17; William Booth, *Orders and Regulations for the Social Officers of The Salvation Army* (London: International Headquarters of The Salvation Army, 1898), 39-41; and William Booth, *Orders and Regulations for Staff Officers of The Salvation Army* (London: International Headquarters of The Salvation Army, 1904), 8-9. These principles were reiterated by various Army writers throughout the period in question. See, for example, "The Army and Woman," in *The Salvation Army Year Book for 1910* (London: The Salvation Army Book Department, 1910), 55-56; Bramwell

Booth, *Orders and Regulations for Officers of the Men's Social Work of The Salvation Army* (London: The Salvation Army Book Department, 1915), 21; "The Position of Woman in The Salvation Army," in *Some Aspects of the Woman's Movement*, ed. Zoë Fairfield (London: SCM Press, 1915), 229-31; "Women and The Army," in *The Salvation Army Year Book for 1917* (London: The Salvation Army Book Department, 1917), 17; *The Salvation Army: Its Principles and Government* (London: The Salvation Army, 1920), 5; Bramwell Booth, *Orders and Regulations for Territorial Commanders and Chief Secretaries of The Salvation Army* (London: International Headquarters of The Salvation Army, 1920), 100; *Orders and Regulations for Officers of The Salvation Army* (London: International Headquarters of The Salvation Army, 1925), 51-52; *Outlines of Salvation Army History* (1927; reprint, London: Salvationist Publishing and Supplies, 1928), 26; Ruth Tracy, "The Salvation Army and the Emancipation of Women," in *The Salvation Army Year Book: 1928* (London: Salvationist Publishing and Supplies, 1928), 15-17; and "Woman's Position in The Army," in *The Salvation Army Year Book: 1930* (London: Salvationist Publishing and Supplies, 1930), 13-14.

4 See Bernard Watson, *Soldier Saint: George Scott Railton* (1970; reprint, New York: The Salvation Army, 1977); and Eileen Douglas and Mildred Duff, *Commissioner Railton* (London: Salvationist Publishing and Supplies, 1920). Watson's biography is the more critical, and provides greater insight into the disagreements that created tensions between Railton and the Booth leadership. See also George Scott Railton, "Ten First Recollections of the Christian Mission," *The War Cry* (August 6, 1892): 5; and Bramwell Booth, "Death of Commr. Railton," *The War Cry* (July 26, 1913): 9.

5 Douglas and Duff, *Commissioner Railton*, 68, 78; Bramwell Booth, *Echoes and Memories* (1925; reprint, London: Hodder and Stoughton, 1977), 178; Robert Sandall, *The History of The Salvation Army*, Vol. 1 (1947; reprint, New York: The Salvation Army, 1979), 177; Watson, *Soldier Saint*, 13, 31, 60; Edward H. McKinley, *Marching to Glory: The History of the Salvation Army in the United States, 1880-1992*, 2nd ed. (Grand Rapids, MI: Eerdmans, 1995), 11; Roger J. Green, *Catherine Booth: A Biography of the Cofounder of The Salvation Army* (Grand Rapids, MI: Baker Books, 1996), 171-72; Norman H. Murdoch, *Origins of the Salvation Army* (Knoxville, TN: University of Tennessee Press, 1994), 165-66.

6 Watson, *Soldier Saint*, 13.

7 See Watson, *Soldier Saint*, 22; and John D. Waldron, ed., *G.S.R.: Selections from Published and Unpublished Writings of George Scott Railton* (Oakville, ON: Triumph Press, 1981), 66. For more on the Bible Christians, see F.W. Bourne, *The Bible Christians: Their Origin and History (1815-1900)* (London: Bible Christian Book Room, 1905); and David Shorney, "'Women May Preach but Men Must Govern': Gender Roles in the Growth and Development of the Bible Christian Denomination," in *Gender and Christian Religion*, ed. Robert N. Swanson (Woodbridge, Suffolk, UK: Boydell Press, 1998), 309-22.

8 See Charles Finney, *Lectures on Revivals of Religion* (1835; reprint, Cambridge, MA: Belknap Press, 1960). For more on the transatlantic connections of evan-

gelical revivalism, see Richard Carwardine, *Transatlantic Revivalism: Popular Evangelicalism in Britain and America, 1790-1865* (Westport, CT: Greenwood Press, 1978); and Mark A. Noll, David W. Bebbington and George A. Rawlyk, eds., *Evangelicalism: Comparative Studies of Popular Protestantism in North America, the British Isles, and Beyond, 1700-1990* (Oxford: Oxford University Press, 1994).

9   For more on the connection between revivalism and female ministry, see Nancy A. Hardesty, *Women Called to Witness: Evangelical Feminism in the Nineteenth Century*, 2nd ed. (Knoxville, TN: University of Tennessee Press, 1999).

10 See George Scott Railton, "About Sensationalism," *The Christian Mission Magazine* (July 1874): 177-81.

11 Green, *Catherine Booth: A Biography*, 171.

12 George Scott Railton, *Heathen England*, 5th ed. (London: International Headquarters of The Salvation Army, 1889), 117.

13 Pamela J. Walker, *Pulling the Devil's Kingdom Down: The Salvation Army in Victorian Britain* (Berkeley, CA: University of California Press, 2001), 118.

14 Railton, *Heathen England*, 124-25. See also 121-23.

15 See Waldron, ed., *G.S.R.*, 66; and Railton, *Heathen England*, 120. John R. Rhemick has noted the lower-working-class proclivity towards emotive religion in *A New People of God: A Study in Salvationism* (Des Plaines, IL: The Salvation Army, 1993), 133-49. For more on the subject of sexual difference, see Leonore Davidoff and Catherine Hall, *Family Fortunes: Men and Women of the English Middle Class, 1780-1850* (Chicago: University of Chicago Press, 1987), 149-92; Anthony Fletcher, "Introduction," in Swanson, ed., *Gender and Christian Religion*, xvii-xxii; and F. Knight, "'Male and Female He Created Them': Men, Women and the Question of Gender," in *Religion in Victorian Britain*, Vol. 5, ed. John Wolffe (Manchester: Manchester University Press, 1997), 23-57. Among the earliest indications of the evangelical propensity to associate women with an emotional and spiritual nature are William Wilberforce, *A Practical View of the Prevailing Religious System of Professed Christians, in the Higher and Middle Classes in This Country, Contrasted with Real Christianity* (London: T. Cadell and W. Davies, 1797), 434-36; and Hannah More, "On the Importance of Religion to the Female Character," in *The Works of Hannah More*, Vol. 2 (New York: Harper and Brothers, 1835), 569-71.

16 George Scott Railton, *Twenty-One Years' Salvation Army* (1886; reprint, London: International Headquarters of The Salvation Army, 1891), 110-11. See also 105.

17 Railton, *Heathen England*, 117.

18 George Scott Railton, *The Authoritative Life of General William Booth: Founder of The Salvation Army* (London: Hodder and Stoughton, 1912), 145.

19 Cited in Waldron, ed., *G.S.R.*, 97.

20 Ibid.

21 Ibid., 97-101.

22 Cited in Watson, *Soldier Saint*, 33.

23   See Watson, *Soldier Saint*, 11, 28, 80-81, 121-22, 128-30, 160, 191-96.

24   Railton, *Twenty-One Years' Salvation Army*, 103-04.

25   George Scott Railton, "The Woman's Liberator," *The Deliverer* (October 1912): 146.

26   Railton, *Twenty-One Years' Salvation Army*, 95.

27   Railton, *Heathen England*, 124.

28   Ibid., 123-24.

29   Railton, "The Woman's Liberator," 146. See also Railton, *Heathen England*, 119, 123.

30   See Douglas and Duff, *Commissioner Railton*, 210-11.

31   George Scott Railton, "The Empty Chair," *All the World* 6, 11 (November 1890): 537.

32   These images are discussed by Elizabeth K. Helsinger et al. in *The Woman Question: Society and Literature in Britain and America, 1837-1883*, Vol. 2 (London: Garland, 1983), xv. The image of "the Angel out of the House" grew out of the notion of "the Angel in the House," and serves to remind us that a woman's stereotypical traits could be used to justify a public role in Victorian society. For more on the complexity of this feminine construction, see Anne Hogan and Andrew Bradstock, "Introduction," in *Women of Faith in Victorian Culture: Reassessing the Angel in the House*, ed. Anne Hogan and Andrew Bradstock (London: Macmillan, 1998), 1-5.

33   For more on these themes, see Julia Bush, *Edwardian Ladies and Imperial Power* (London: Leicester University Press, 2000), esp. 72-83; George Robb, "Race Motherhood: Moral Eugenics *vs* Progressive Eugenics, 1880-1920," in *Maternal Instincts: Visions of Motherhood and Sexuality in Britain, 1875-1925*, ed. Claudia Nelson and Ann Sumner Holmes (London: Macmillan, 1997), 58-74; and Patrick Brantlinger, *Rule of Darkness: British Literature and Imperialism, 1830-1914* (Ithaca, NY: Cornell University Press, 1988), 227-53.

34   J[ames] B[arker], "Should Married Women with Families Go Out to Work?" *The Social Gazette* 344 (January 27, 1900): 1. See also 3. For more on the subject of female employment, see Ellen Jordan, *The Women's Movement and Women's Employment in Nineteenth-Century Britain* (London: Routledge, 1999); and Elizabeth Roberts, *Women's Work 1840-1940* (London: Macmillan, 1988).

35   See "Should Mothers Work?" *The War Cry* (September 19, 1903): 4.

36   "Wanted, a Wife," *The War Cry* (November 21, 1903): 12.

37   William R. Gilks, "How a Working Man's Wife Should Treat Her Husband," *The Officer* 24, 12 (December 1916): 837-39.

38   "What I Like My Wife to Be," *The War Cry* (September 16, 1922): 9.

39   William Booth, *Orders and Regulations for Field Officers of The Salvation Army* (1886), 56. This viewpoint was reiterated in subsequent editions. See *Orders and Regulations for Field Officers of The Salvation Army* (London: The Salvation Army Book Department, 1917), 62; and *Orders and Regulations for Officers of The Salvation Army* (1925), 116.

40 I.E. Leonard, "Woman's Life Behind The Scenes," *The Officer* 39, 1 (July 1924): 29.

41 Ibid., 30. The same kind of argument is evident in "Unemployed Staff Wives," *The Staff Review* 1 (1922): 111.

42 James Hay, *The Fiery Cross: An Appeal to Salvationists and Others* (Auckland, NZ: Whitcombe and Tombs, 1929), 101-102. For more on the theme of motherhood, see William Clements, "The Power of Woman in the Home," *The Officer* 31, 5 (November 1920): 494-95.

43 Hay, *The Fiery Cross*, 101.

44 Edward J. Higgins, "Women as Leaders of The Salvation Army," *The Officer* 22, 9 (September 1914): 585-88. Interestingly enough, when Edward Higgins returned to Britain in 1905 from an appointment in America, his wife Catherine was given little in the way of public work. William Harris, the biographer of Edward Higgins, notes that this was quite an adjustment for Catherine Higgins, since she had been active in women's work in the United States. See William G. Harris, *Storm Pilot: The Story of the Life and Leadership of General Edward J. Higgins* (London: Salvationist Publishing and Supplies, 1981), 38.

45 For more on the association between women and religion, see Anthony Fletcher, "Beyond the Church: Women's Spiritual Experience at Home and in the Community 1600-1900," in Swanson, ed., *Gender and Christian Religion*, 187-203; and Barbara Taylor, *Eve and the New Jerusalem: Socialism and Feminism in the Nineteenth Century* (London: Virago, 1983), 123-30.

46 Higgins, "Women as Leaders of The Salvation Army," 587.

47 A[madeo] Salvany, "Mothers—A Great Need," *The Officer* 34, 1 (January 1922): 70. See also James Hay, "Domestic Difficulties: A Word with Single Men-Officers," *The Field Officer* 10, 1 (January 1902): 5.

48 Salvany, "Mothers—A Great Need," 71.

49 This kind of feminism is discussed by Martha Vicinus in "Introduction," in *A Widening Sphere: Changing Roles of Victorian Women*, ed. Martha Vicinus (Bloomington, IN: Indiana University Press, 1977), ix-xix; and Barbara Caine, *Victorian Feminists* (Oxford: Oxford University Press, 1993), 37-53.

50 [Frederick] Booth-Tucker, "Looking Backward: Some International Congress Reflections," *The Officer* 22, 8 (August 1914): 517-18.

51 See William Booth, *Orders and Regulations for Field Officers of The Salvation Army* (London: Headquarters of The Salvation Army, 1901), 608; and *Orders and Regulations for Officers of The Salvation Army* (1925), 340.

52 A[lex] M. N[icol], "Word Portraits of Field Officers: The Married Woman-Officer," *The Field Officer* 16, 6 (June 1908): 205.

53 Ibid., 206-07.

54 "Army Wives and Mothers: A Tribute by a Mere Man!" *The Field Officer* 18, 10 (October 1910): 377-78.

55 For more on the subject of self-sacrifice and gender, see Anne E. Carr and Douglas J. Schuurman, "Religion and Feminism: A Reformist Christian Analysis,"

in *Religion, Feminism, and the Family*, ed. Anne E. Carr and Mary Stewart Van Leeuwen (Louisville, KY: Westminster John Knox Press, 1996), 27.

56 Bramwell Booth, *Servants of All: A Brief Review of the Call, Character, and Labours of Officers of The Salvation Army*, 4th ed. (London: The Salvation Army Book Department, 1914), 133-34.

57 Bramwell Booth's daughter Catherine argues that her father was always concerned about the role of female officers, but the evidence I have presented here and in chapter 6 indicates that he was never concerned enough to address the issues related to gender and equality. See Catherine Bramwell-Booth, *Bramwell Booth* (London: Rich and Cowan, 1933), 196-98.

58 Bramwell Booth, "Mrs. Booth and Her Army Family," *All the World* 6, 12 (December 1890): 595. See also Bramwell Booth, "Catherine Booth: After Ten Years," *All the World* 21, 10 (October 1900): 563-69.

59 Bramwell Booth, *These Fifty Years* (London: Cassell, 1929), 25.

60 Booth, *Orders and Regulations for Staff Officers of The Salvation Army* (1904), 8.

61 For more on the hymns of the period, see John Wolffe, "'Praise to the Holiest in the Height': Hymns and Church Music," in Wolffe, ed., *Religion in Victorian Britain*, Vol. 5, 59-99; and J.R. Watson, "Quiet Angels: Some Women Hymn Writers," in Hogan and Bradstock, eds., *Women of Faith in Victorian Culture*, 128-44.

62 See Elizabeth Cady Stanton, *The Woman's Bible* (1898; reprint, Amherst, NY: Prometheus Books, 1999), esp. 14-19. See also Helsinger et al., *The Woman Question*, Vol. 2 , 201-10.

63 See William Booth, *The Doctrines of The Salvation Army, Prepared for the Training Homes* (Toronto, ON: The Salvation Army, 1892), esp. 1-8, 36-39; and *Handbook of Salvation Army Doctrine* (London: International Headquarters of The Salvation Army, 1923), 6-9, 30-33, 41-43, 58, 81-89, 105-06, 126. The title page of the latter book indicates that it was "prepared under the personal supervision and issued by authority of the General [i.e., Bramwell Booth]." According to John Coutts, Alfred Cunningham, a senior officer, helped to prepare this volume. See John Coutts, *The Salvationists* (Oxford: Mowbrays, 1977), 13. The evangelical propensity to consider God as literally and exclusively male was only cautiously addressed by evangelical feminists in the early 1970s. See, for example, Letha Scanzoni and Nancy Hardesty, *All We're Meant to Be: A Biblical Approach to Women's Liberation* (1974; reprint, Waco, TX: Word Books, 1976), 20-21.

64 After the turn of the twentieth century, evangelicals in Britain became divided over issues like biblical criticism. The Salvation Army, however, remained on the conservative side of this controversy. For more on these trends in evangelicalism, see David W. Bebbington, *Evangelicalism in Modern Britain: A History from the 1730s to the 1980s* (1989; reprint, Grand Rapids, MI: Baker Book House, 1992), 181-228. Some indication of the Salvation Army's opposition to biblical criticism and related matters is given in "'The Ascent of Man,'" *The*

War Cry (June 23, 1894): 8; Bramwell Booth, "The Higher Criticism," *The War Cry* (May 6, 1905): 8; and "Man, Monkey, and—Moonshine!" *The War Cry* (September 10, 1927): 6.

65 *Handbook of Salvation Army Doctrine*, 32-33.

66 Booth, "Mrs. Booth and Her Army Family," 594.

67 *The Why and Wherefore of Salvation Army Orders and Regulations* (London: Salvationist Publishing and Supplies, 1924), 3. See also *The Why and Wherefore of The Salvation Army Regulations* (London: The Salvation Army, 1904), 3. I am indebted to Elizabeth A. Johnson for my understanding of how God-language has practical consequences for women and men. See her book *She Who Is: The Mystery of God in Feminist Theological Discourse* (New York: Crossroad, 1992).

68 *Handbook of Salvation Army Doctrine*, 58. See also 50, 124, 137. A similar understanding of sin is evident in Booth, *The Doctrines of The Salvation Army*, 9-13.

69 Bramwell Booth, *Our Master: Thoughts for Salvationists about Their Lord* (1908; reprint, London: Salvationist Publishing and Supplies, n.d.), 141. See also 124-25.

70 For the single, brief references to the sin of omission, see Booth, *The Doctrines of The Salvation Army*, 56; and *Handbook of Salvation Army Doctrine*, 53.

71 For more on the issue of sin and gender, see Valerie Saiving Goldstein, "The Human Situation: A Feminine View," *The Journal of Religion* 40 (1960): 100-12; Lucy Tatman, "Sin," in *An A to Z of Feminist Theology*, ed. Lisa Isherwood and Dorothea McEwan (Sheffield, UK: Sheffield Academic Press, 1996), 217-18; and my more extensive notes on this subject in chapter 1. It is worth noting that Stanton also addressed this issue to some degree in *The Woman's Bible*, 125, 131.

72 See, for example, William Booth, *The Founder's Messages to Soldiers during Years 1907-8* (London: The Salvation Army Book Department, 1921), 192; and Edward J. Higgins, "Some Passing Reflections on Board Ship," *The Staff Review* 10, 4 (October 1930): 309.

73 For more on the subject of holiness, see David W. Bebbington, *Holiness in Nineteenth-Century England* (Carlisle, UK: Paternoster Press, 2000); John Cobb, *Grace and Responsibility: A Wesleyan Theology for Today* (Nashville, TN: Abingdon Press, 1995), 100-14; and Melvin E. Dieter et al., *Five Views on Sanctification* (Grand Rapids, MI: Zondervan, 1987).

74 See Booth, *The Doctrines of The Salvation Army*, 56-85.

75 See, for instance, Lucille Sider Dayton and Donald W. Dayton, "'Your Daughters Shall Prophesy': Feminism in the Holiness Movement," *Methodist History* 14 (January 1976): 91; Janette Hassey, *No Time for Silence: Evangelical Women in Public Ministry around the Turn of the Century* (Grand Rapids, MI: Zondervan, 1986), 125-26; Letha Dawson Scanzoni and Susan Setta, "Women in Evangelical, Holiness, and Pentecostal Traditions," in *Women and Religion in America. Volume 3: 1900-1968*, ed. Rosemary Radford Ruether and Rosemary S. Keller (San Francisco: Harper and Row, 1986), 226; Nancy A. Hardesty, *Your Daughters Shall Prophesy: Revivalism and Feminism in the Age of Finney* (Brooklyn, NY: Carlson, 1991), 39-45, 56-59; Margaret McFadden, "The Ironies of Pentecost:

Phoebe Palmer, World Evangelism, and Female Networks," *Methodist History* 31, 2 (January 1993): 63-75; and Hardesty, *Women Called to Witness*, 44-52.

76 See Finney, *Lectures on Revivals of Religion*, esp. 107-39. Charles Finney believed that men and women should exercise their gifts in mixed assemblies.

77 See Phoebe Palmer, *Faith and Its Effects: Or, Fragments from My Portfolio* (1848; reprint, Toronto, ON: G.R. Sanderson, 1856), 83-84.

78 Catherine Booth, *The Holy Ghost, An Address* (Toronto, ON: The Salvation Army, [1885?]), esp. 6-16. This sermon can also be found in Catherine Booth, *Aggressive Christianity* (1880; reprint, Toronto, ON: William Briggs, 1883), 161-74.

79 Booth, *The Doctrines of The Salvation Army*, 84; *Handbook of Salvation Army Doctrine*, 145. Of course, as I noted in chapter 3, the Salvation Army had a more explicit understanding of female ministry as well.

80 See also Walker, *Pulling the Devil's Kingdom Down*, 54-56, 130; and Laura E. Lauer, "Women in British Nonconformity, circa 1880-1920, with Special Reference to the Society of Friends, Baptist Union and Salvation Army" (Ph.D. thesis, University of Oxford, 1998), 84-85, 235, 242-43.

81 *Handbook of Salvation Army Doctrine*, 124-37. Many of the same themes are evident as well in T. Henry Howard, *Standards of Life and Service* (London: The Salvation Army Book Department, 1909), 47, 132-40.

82 *Handbook of Salvation Army Doctrine*, 146. See also 112-13; and Railton, *Twenty-One Years' Salvation Army*, 181. I drew attention to the association between the doctrine of holiness and social control in my earlier work. See Andrew Mark Eason, "Gender and Equality in God's Army: An Examination of Women's Public and Domestic Roles in the Salvation Army, British Origins to 1930" (M.A. thesis, University of Windsor, Windsor, ON, 1998), 51, 139-40. See also Lauer, "Women in British Nonconformity," 272-73.

83 See Leopold Katscher, "Some Aspects of The Salvation Army," *The National Review* 5 (1885): 73; Francis Peek, "The Salvationists," *The Contemporary Review* 49 (January 1886): 57; Glenn K. Horridge, *The Salvation Army: Origins and Early Days, 1865-1900* (Godalming, Surrey, UK: Ammonite Books, 1993), 81; Glenn K. Horridge, "William Booth's Officers," *Christian History* 9, 2 (1990): 15; and *Orders and Regulations for Corps Officers of The Salvation Army* (London: International Headquarters of The Salvation Army, 1925), 318-19. For a wider societal view, see Roberts, *Women's Work 1840-1940*, 24.

84 For the pay disparity between male and female preachers within nineteenth-century branches of Methodism, see Bourne, *The Bible Christians*, 241; and Julia Stewart Werner, *The Primitive Methodist Connexion: Its Background and Early History* (Madison, WI: University of Wisconsin Press, 1984), 141.

85 *Orders and Regulations for Corps Officers of The Salvation Army*, 144-45.

86 "Important and Interesting Appointments at I.H.Q.," *The War Cry* (July 26, 1913): 9. See also "Important Changes," *The War Cry* (January 29, 1898): 4; "The Bond of Service and Fellowship: Officer Wives of the International Headquarters," *The Officer* 25, 6 (July 1917): 395; "Unemployed Staff Wives," 110-11; [Elsie] Shaw,

"The Opportunity and Influence of a Staff Wife," *The Staff Review* 8, 4 (October 1928): 461; Mary MacFarlane et al., "Are Equal Standards for Men and Women Officers Maintained?" *The Staff Review* 10, 4 (October 1930): 339, 345; and Harris, *Storm Pilot*, 38. For evidence of the same discriminatory practices in recent times, see Flora Larsson, *My Best Men Are Women* (London: Hodder and Stoughton, 1974), 202-03; and Coutts, *The Salvationists*, 30.

87 "Important and Interesting Appointments at I.H.Q.," 9.

88 "The Position of Woman in The Salvation Army," 231.

89 See Booth, *Orders and Regulations for Territorial Commanders and Chief Secretaries of The Salvation Army*, 200; Arch Wiggins, *The History of The Salvation Army*, Vol. 4 (1964; reprint, New York: The Salvation Army, 1979), 82, 86, 118-19, 366; Arch Wiggins, *The History of The Salvation Army*, Vol. 5 (1968; reprint, New York: The Salvation Army, 1979), 279; Frederick Coutts, *The History of The Salvation Army: The Better Fight*, Vol. 6 (1973; reprint, New York: The Salvation Army, 1979), 41; and Norman H. Murdoch, "Female Ministry in the Thought and Work of Catherine Booth," *Church History* 53, 3 (September 1984): 359.

90 For the argument that female officers retained their commission after marriage, see Booth, *Servants of All*, 133; "The Position of Woman in The Salvation Army," 231; and "The Wife of a Salvation Army Officer," in *The Salvation Army Year Book: 1924* (London: Salvationist Publishing and Supplies, 1924), 23.

91 See Dwight Cuff, "The Two Shall Become One: An Examination of the Impact of a One Flesh Theology on the Salvation Army Officer-Wife" (Paper presented at the Catherine Booth Bible College [now known as the William and Catherine Booth College] Symposium, Winnipeg, MB, 1989), 18. The Salvation Army George Scott Railton Heritage Centre in Toronto has a copy of this paper. See also Lawrence Fellows, *A Gentle War: The Story of The Salvation Army* (New York: Macmillan, 1979), 68. This discriminatory patriarchal practice stopped only in 1995. See *The Salvation Army Year Book: 1997* (London: International Headquarters of The Salvation Army, 1996), 31; and Minute IA/20 from the Salvation Army International Headquarters, dated July 7, 1995.

92 See, for example, William Booth, *Orders and Regulations for Field Officers of The Salvation Army* (London: The Salvation Army Publishing Department, 1908), 55; "Our Officers: The Adjutant's Wife," *The Field Officer* 16, 12 (December 1908): 471-72; "An Officer's Wife," *The Field Officer* 17, 5 (May 1909): 190-91; *Orders and Regulations for Corps Officers of The Salvation Army*, 144-45; and "Woman's Position in The Army," in *The Salvation Army Year Book: 1930*, 14.

93 Booth, *Orders and Regulations for Officers of the Men's Social Work of The Salvation Army*, 21. This view continued to be espoused in the 1920s. See Booth, *Orders and Regulations for Territorial Commanders and Chief Secretaries of The Salvation Army*, 100-101; and *Orders and Regulations for Officers of The Salvation Army* (1925), 51. It will be recalled that this perspective originated with William Booth, *Orders and Regulations for Staff Officers of The Salvation Army in the United Kingdom*, 16.

94 Booth, *Orders and Regulations for Officers of the Men's Social Work of The Salvation Army*, 21.

❖

CHAPTER 5

1   Minnie L. Carpenter, *Women of the Flag* (London: Salvationist Publishing and Supplies, 1945), 5.

2   See, for instance, Pamela J. Walker, *Pulling the Devil's Kingdom Down: The Salvation Army in Victorian Britain* (Berkeley, CA: University of California Press, 2001), 8-40; Roger J. Green, *Catherine Booth: A Biography of the Cofounder of The Salvation Army* (Grand Rapids, MI: Baker Books, 1996); and David J. Sears, "An Overview of the Thought of Catherine Booth" (S.T.M. thesis, University of Winnipeg, 1995).

3   This is especially apparent in the work of John R. Rhemick, *A New People of God: A Study in Salvationism* (Des Plaines, IL: The Salvation Army, 1993), 9; and Raymond Caddy, "Co-Founder: Catherine Booth and The Salvation Army," in *Catherine Booth: Her Continuing Relevance*, ed. Clifford W. Kew (London: International Headquarters of The Salvation Army, 1990), 114-37. See also the much earlier work of Salvationist historian Bernard Watson, *A Hundred Years' War: The Salvation Army, 1865-1965* (London: Hodder and Stoughton, 1965), 29-32.

4   Carpenter, *Women of the Flag*, 6.

5   Prior to the 1980s, most works on Catherine Booth largely ignored the Victorian and evangelical context of her life. See, for example, Frederick Booth-Tucker, *The Life of Catherine Booth: The Mother of The Salvation Army.* 2 vols. (London: International Headquarters of The Salvation Army, 1892); William T. Stead, *Mrs. Booth of The Salvation Army* (1900; reprint, Oakville, ON: Triumph Press, 1979); Mildred Duff, *Catherine Booth: A Sketch* (1901; reprint, London: The Salvation Army Book Department, 1914); Joan Metcalf, *God Used a Woman: Catherine Booth* (London: Challenge Books, 1967); and Catherine Bramwell-Booth, *Catherine Booth: The Story of Her Loves* (London: Hodder and Stoughton, 1970). In the last two decades or so, scholars have begun to address this omission, although some have done so more than others. Norman Murdoch begins to add historical context in his 1984 article on Catherine Booth; see Norman H. Murdoch, "Female Ministry in the Thought and Work of Catherine Booth," *Church History* 53, 3 (September 1984): 348-62. Roger Green's *Catherine Booth: A Biography* is by far the best treatment of Catherine Booth to date, but even so it fails at times to provide enough historical background. Green acknowledges this weakness, however, in the introduction to the book (see p. 15). The same can be said about his earlier article on Catherine Booth, "Settled Views: Catherine Booth and Female Ministry," *Methodist History* 31, 3 (April 1993): 131-47. Perhaps the best attempts thus far to relate Victorian studies to Catherine Booth are Pamela Walker's *Pulling the Devil's Kingdom Down*, and Laura E. Lauer's "Women in British Nonconformity, circa 1880-1920, with Special Reference to the Society of Friends, Baptist Union and Salvation Army" (Ph.D. thesis, University of Oxford, 1998), 228-93. In spite of these more recent works,

much more remains to be gained from studies of Catherine Booth within her Victorian environment and in relation to her evangelical convictions.

6   For more on the early life of Catherine Booth, see Booth-Tucker, *The Life of Catherine Booth*, Vol. 1, 10-50; and Green, *Catherine Booth: A Biography*, 17-37.

7   See John Walford, *Memoirs of the Life and Labours of the Late Venerable Hugh Bourne* (1856; reprint, Totton, UK: Berith Publications, 1999), Vol. 1, 276-83, 337-42, 379-86, and Vol. 2, 326; Hugh Bourne, *History of the Primitive Methodists. Giving an Account of Their Rise and Progress Up to the Year 1823* (Bemersley Near Tunstall, UK: Primitive Methodist Connexion, 1835), 47; and Julia Stewart Werner, *The Primitive Methodist Connexion: Its Background and Early History* (Madison, WI: University of Wisconsin Press, 1984), 84-116. Pamela Walker, citing the work of Deborah Valenze, notes that there were at least six female preachers in the Derbyshire area in the 1820s. See Walker, *Pulling the Devil's Kingdom Down*, 12.

8   Bramwell-Booth, *Catherine Booth*, 176.

9   Puritanism was one stream flowing into Methodism, helping to shape its attitude towards the surrounding culture. See David W. Bebbington, *Evangelicalism in Modern Britain: A History from the 1730s to the 1980s* (1989; reprint, Grand Rapids, MI: Baker Book House, 1992), 18, 34-36. For a detailed examination of the broader relationship between evangelicalism and culture, see Doreen M. Rosman, *Evangelicals and Culture* (London: Croom Helm, 1984). Also helpful is Sheridan Gilley, "Official Religion," in *The British: Their Religious Beliefs and Practices 1800-1986*, ed. Terence Thomas (London: Routledge, 1988), 19-47.

10   Frank M. Turner describes this expectation concisely in his essay "The Victorian Crisis of Faith and the Faith That Was Lost," in *Victorian Faith in Crisis: Essays on Continuity and Change in Nineteenth-Century Religious Belief*, ed. Richard J. Helmstadter and Bernard Lightman (London: Macmillan, 1990), 20-21.

11   William Wilberforce, *A Practical View of the Prevailing Religious System of Professed Christians, in the Higher and Middle Classes in This Country, Contrasted with Real Christianity* (London: T. Cadell and W. Davies, 1797), 434. See also 436. For more on the identification of women with morality and spirituality, see Anthony Fletcher, "Beyond the Church: Women's Spiritual Experience at Home and in the Community 1600-1900," in *Gender and Christian Religion*, ed. Robert N. Swanson (Woodbridge, Suffolk, UK: Boydell Press, 1998), 187-203; F. Knight, "'Male and Female He Created Them': Men, Women and the Question of Gender," in *Religion in Victorian Britain*, Vol. 5, ed. John Wolffe (Manchester: Manchester University Press, 1997), 23-57; and Jane Rendall, *The Origins of Modern Feminism: Women in Britain, France and the United States, 1780-1860* (London: Macmillan, 1985), 73-107. Throughout the period in question, Nonconformist women outnumbered men in chapel attendance. See Clive D. Field, "Adam and Eve: Gender in the English Free Church Constituency," *The Journal of Ecclesiastical History* 44, 1 (January 1993): 63-79.

12   See Nancy A. Hardesty, *Women Called to Witness: Evangelical Feminism in the Nineteenth Century*, 2nd ed. (Knoxville, TN: University of Tennessee Press,

1999), 53. As Hardesty notes, evangelicals in the nineteenth century were steeped in scripture.

13 The average working-class child received between four and five years of formal schooling during the 1830s and 1840s. See Walter L. Arnstein, *Britain Yesterday and Today: 1830 to the Present*, 7th ed. (Toronto, ON: D.C. Heath and Co., 1996), 56-57.

14 Catherine Mumford's reading tastes mirrored the typical interests of early Victorian ministers. Ieuan Ellis discusses the clergy's reading habits in his essay "The Intellectual Challenge to 'Official Religion,'" in Thomas, ed., *The British*, 48-71.

15 See Joan N. Burstyn, *Victorian Education and the Ideal of Womanhood* (New Brunswick, NJ: Rutgers University Press, 1984), 70-83.

16 See Henry D. Rack, *Reasonable Enthusiast: John Wesley and the Rise of Methodism* (Philadelphia: Trinity Press International, 1989), 107-36; and Bebbington, *Evangelicalism in Modern Britain*, 36-40.

17 Catherine Booth, *Life and Death* (1883; reprint, Atlanta, GA: The Salvation Army, 1986), 124. See also 72-78, 119.

18 Catherine Booth, *Papers on Godliness* (1881; reprint, London: International Headquarters of The Salvation Army, 1890), 4-6; Catherine Booth, *Popular Christianity* (1887; reprint, London: The Salvation Army Book Department, n.d.), 33.

19 Booth Papers, British Library, Add. Mss. 64806, diary entry for November 28, 1847.

20 Booth, *Papers on Godliness*, 93-94; Catherine Booth, *Aggressive Christianity* (1880; reprint, Toronto, ON: William Briggs, 1883), 128-31.

21 Cited in St. John Ervine, *God's Soldier: General William Booth*, Vol. 1 (1934; reprint, New York: Macmillan, 1935), 78. A good introduction to the life and thought of Charles Finney is provided by Charles Hambrick-Stowe, *Charles G. Finney and the Spirit of American Evangelicalism* (Grand Rapids, MI: Eerdmans, 1996). For the popularity of Finney's *Lectures on Revivals of Religion* in Britain, see 156.

22 I am indebted to the numerous scholars who have explored how Finney's ideas had an impact on women's involvement in public church ministry. See, in particular, Nancy A. Hardesty, *Your Daughters Shall Prophesy: Revivalism and Feminism in the Age of Finney* (Brooklyn, NY: Carlson, 1991); Janette Hassey, *No Time for Silence: Evangelical Women in Public Ministry around the Turn of the Century* (Grand Rapids, MI: Zondervan, 1986); and Lucille Sider Dayton and Donald W. Dayton, "'Your Daughters Shall Prophesy': Feminism in the Holiness Movement," *Methodist History* 14 (January 1976): 67-92.

23 Charles Finney, *Lectures on Revivals of Religion* (1835; reprint, Cambridge, MA: Belknap Press, 1960), 138. See also 174-93, 259.

24 Ibid., 181. While Charles Finney was not the first to adopt "new measures," such as protracted meetings and mourners' benches, he did the most to promote this new kind of revivalism among respectable evangelicals. For a helpful

analysis of this issue, see Richard Carwardine, *Transatlantic Revivalism: Popular Evangelicalism in Britain and America, 1790-1865* (Westport, CT: Greenwood Press, 1978), 10-16.

25   [Catherine] Booth, "Our Commission," *All the World* 1, 6 (April 1885): 84. See also Booth, *Aggressive Christianity*, 51-66. Catherine encouraged her husband to adopt Finney's techniques. See Sears, "An Overview of the Thought of Catherine Booth," 141. The extent to which these views were incorporated into the early Salvation Army is apparent in *All about The Salvation Army* (London: S.W. Partridge and Co., 1882), 9-10.

26   See, for example, Catherine Booth, "An Address to the Society of Friends," in John D. Waldron, *The Quakers and the Salvationists* (Atlanta, GA: The Salvation Army Supplies, 1990), 51-52; and Catherine Booth, *The Salvation Army in Relation to the Church and State, and Other Addresses* (London: S.W. Partridge and Co., 1883), 74.

27   Roger Green is right to point out that, given her age at the time, Catherine Mumford could not possibly have comprehended the full substance of the temperance arguments. See Green, *Catherine Booth: A Biography*, 26.

28   See Rack, *Reasonable Enthusiast*, 238-42.

29   For more on the relationship between women and class meetings, see Paul Wesley Chilcote, *John Wesley and the Women Preachers of Early Methodism* (Metuchen, NJ: Scarecrow Press, 1991), 70-71; and Earl Kent Brown, *Women of Mr. Wesley's Methodism* (New York: Edwin Mellen Press, 1983), 42-50.

30   Stead, *Mrs. Booth of The Salvation Army*, 42.

31   Ibid.

32   This controversy is touched upon in Gerald Parsons, "From Dissenters to Free Churchmen: The Transitions of Victorian Nonconformity," in *Religion in Victorian Britain*, Vol. 1, ed. Gerald Parsons (Manchester: Manchester University Press, 1988), 82-85; and David Hempton, *Methodism and Politics in British Society 1750-1850* (Stanford, CA: Stanford University Press, 1984), 197-202. See also "The Recent Disciplinary Decisions of the Wesleyan Conference," *The Wesleyan Methodist Magazine* (October 1849): 1062-71; and Daniel Wise, ed., *Methodism in Earnest: Being the History of a Great Revival in Great Britain, in Which Twenty Thousand Souls Were Justified, and Ten Thousand Sanctified, in about Six Years, through the Instrumentality of Rev. James Caughey* (Boston, MA: Charles H. Peirce, 1850), 121-47, 232-52. Caughey was himself caught up in this controversy, as his revivalistic independence did not sit well with the English Wesleyan Methodist Conference.

33   See, in particular, Chilcote, *John Wesley and the Women Preachers of Early Methodism*, 117-240; David Shorney, "'Women May Preach but Men Must Govern': Gender Roles in the Growth and Development of the Bible Christian Denomination," in Swanson, ed., *Gender and Christian Religion*, 309-22; and Deborah M. Valenze, *Prophetic Sons and Daughters: Female Preaching and Popular Religion in Industrial England* (Princeton, NJ: Princeton University Press, 1985).

34 Booth Papers, British Library, Add. Mss. 64802, letter from Catherine to William, dated April 9, 1855. See also Harold Begbie, *The Life of General William Booth: The Founder of The Salvation Army*, Vol. 1 (New York: Macmillan, 1920), 248.

35 Cited in Booth-Tucker, *The Life of Catherine Booth*, Vol. 1, 123. It is unclear whether this article was ever published, since it cannot be found in any of the 1854 issues of *The Methodist New Connexion Magazine*. A careful examination of the 1853 and 1855 issues of this periodical yields the same result. Roger Green, too, has been unable to locate this article, but he continues to believe that it was published. See Green, *Catherine Booth: A Biography*, 303, note 52.

36 Cited in Werner, *The Primitive Methodist Connexion*, 143. See also Booth, "An Address to the Society of Friends," 43.

37 For more on the Palmers' revival campaign in the area, see Phoebe Palmer, *Four Years in the Old World* (Toronto, ON: Samuel Rose, 1866), 93-147; Robert Young et al., "Revival in Newcastle-Upon-Tyne," *The Wesleyan Methodist Magazine* (August 1860): 738-41; and Charles Edward White, *The Beauty of Holiness: Phoebe Palmer as Theologian, Revivalist, Feminist, and Humanitarian* (Grand Rapids, MI: Francis Asbury Press, 1986), 70-75.

38 Harold E. Raser argues that, while Phoebe Palmer never claimed to preach, she did in fact do so by redefining and expanding the word to include prophesying, testifying and exhorting. See Harold E. Raser, *Phoebe Palmer: Her Life and Thought* (Lewiston, NY: Edwin Mellen Press, 1987), 76-78. See also Phoebe Palmer, *Promise of the Father; or, A Neglected Speciality of the Last Days* (Boston, MA: Henry V. Degen, 1859), 329-38, where she conveys her biblical understanding of preaching.

39 Booth Papers, British Library, Add. Mss. 64805, letters from Catherine to her parents, dated September 16 and September 26, 1859.

40 See Booth-Tucker, *The Life of Catherine Booth*, Vol. 1, 243; and Palmer, *Four Years in the Old World*, 251-74.

41 Rees's pamphlet, entitled *Reasons for Not Co-operating in the Alleged "Sunderland Revivals,"* is examined in some detail by Walker, *Pulling the Devil's Kingdom Down*, 24-27.

42 Since no one has been able to find a copy of the 1859 original, the analysis that follows here is based on the second (1861) and third (1870) editions of the pamphlet. The second edition, *Female Teaching: Or, the Rev. A.A. Rees versus Mrs. Palmer, Being a Reply to a Pamphlet by the Above Gentleman on the Sunderland Revival* (London: G.J. Stevenson, 1861), was obviously still directed towards Rees. Nevertheless, it is apparent from an 1861 letter from Catherine to her parents that the pamphlet had been revised significantly for the second edition. In this letter she noted: "We have also the pamphlet on the go. I have finished the emendations.... There will be considerably more matter in it than the last one, principally quotations, and I think it is much improved." (Booth Papers, British Library, Add. Mss. 64805, letter from Catherine to her parents, dated October 18, 1861. See also Booth-Tucker, *The Life of Catherine Booth*, Vol. 1, 322). Pamela Walker appears to be unaware of this correspon-

dence, because she claims that the 1859 and 1861 editions were probably very similar. See Walker, *Pulling the Devil's Kingdom Down*, 254, note 95. The third edition of the pamphlet retained the central arguments of the 1861 edition, but also contained some changes, including a new title, *Female Ministry: Or, Woman's Right to Preach the Gospel* (1870; reprint, New York: The Salvation Army, 1975). This change reflected the fact that Catherine was no longer directing her arguments towards Rees, but was now aiming them more generally at all opponents of female preaching.

43   *Female Teaching*, 3; *Female Ministry*, 5.

44   *Female Teaching*, 23-25.

45   Palmer, *Promise of the Father*, 342. See also 15, 62-64, 316. Pamela Walker and Roger Green are mistaken when they seem to imply that Phoebe Palmer did not appeal to a woman's natural suitability for public ministry. See Walker, *Pulling the Devil's Kingdom Down*, 29-30; and Green, *Catherine Booth: A Biography*, 126. Notwithstanding the fact that Catherine's argument for natural suitability was more explicit and sophisticated than Phoebe Palmer's, and was placed explicitly within the context of rights, it is probable that Catherine's own reasoning owed something to her in this area. Catherine made extensive use of *Promise of the Father* elsewhere in *Female Teaching*, and she even offered to send a copy of Phoebe Palmer's book to the Reverend Stacey, the editor of *The Wesleyan Times*, in March 1861. In one letter to Stacey, Catherine stressed that Phoebe Palmer's book "contains much valuable matter on the subject of female agency in the Church." See Booth Papers, British Library, Add. Mss. 64806, letter from Catherine to the Rev. Stacey, dated March 19, 1861, as well as her correspondence to Stacey dated March 21, 1861. Although Phoebe Palmer stayed away from the language of rights, she could still put forward a forceful defence of women's public witness, which she equated with the scriptural notion of preaching. For Phoebe Palmer, to oppose female preaching was to oppose God. See Palmer, *Promise of the Father*, 329-38, 366. While not specifically addressing *Promise of the Father*, Chick Yuill is correct when he notes that students of Catherine Booth have often underestimated the impact that Phoebe Palmer had on her life and thought. See Chick Yuill, "Restoring the Image: Catherine Booth's Holiness Teaching," in Kew, ed., *Catherine Booth: Her Continuing Relevance*, 61. This argument was made several years earlier as well by John Kent, *Holding the Fort: Studies in Victorian Revivalism* (London: Epworth Press, 1978), 310-40. More recently, Norman Murdoch has underscored the debt that the Salvation Army owes to American revivalists like Phoebe Palmer, although he does not deal with *Promise of the Father*. See Norman H. Murdoch, *Origins of the Salvation Army* (Knoxville, TN: University of Tennessee Press, 1994), 1-39.

46   Catherine Booth's view of scripture as divinely inspired is clearly apparent in her book *Life and Death*, 32. See also her correspondence in Booth-Tucker, *The Life of Catherine Booth*, Vol. 2, 154.

47   *Female Teaching*, 31; *Female Ministry*, 19.

48 *Female Teaching*, 8, 30-31; *Female Ministry*, 19. See also Booth, *Life and Death*, 33. Janette Hassey has pointed out correctly that Catherine Booth's hermeneutical approach paralleled that of Phoebe Palmer in *Promise of the Father*. See Hassey, *No Time for Silence*, 99. Phoebe, like Catherine, wrote of the need to pay attention to contextual issues and compare scripture with scripture. See Palmer, *Promise of the Father*, 49, 161, 165, 227, 237, 326.

49 *Female Ministry*, 8; *Female Teaching*, 10. See also Palmer, *Promise of the Father*, 7.

50 *Female Teaching*, 12; *Female Ministry*, 9. Phoebe Palmer makes a similar argument in *Promise of the Father*, 47. This was a very common interpretation within Methodist and evangelical circles. William O'Bryan, the founder of the Bible Christians, defended female ministry in a similar manner. See Shorney, "'Women may preach…,'" 318. See also Hugh Bourne's 1808 defence of women preachers, *Remarks on the Ministry of Women*, which is reproduced in its entirety in Walford, *Memoirs of the Life and Labours of the Late Venerable Hugh Bourne*, Vol. 1, 184-89. Pamela Walker draws attention to Bourne's pamphlet in *Pulling the Devil's Kingdom Down*, 29, 255, note 105. Antoinette Brown, the first woman to be ordained in America, interpreted this passage in like manner. She utilized some of the same reference texts that Catherine used to make her case, such as Henry George Liddell's and Robert Scott's *Greek-English Lexicon*. See Antoinette L. Brown, "Exegesis of 1 Corinthians, xiv., 34, 35; and 1 Timothy, ii., 11, 12," *The Oberlin Quarterly Review* (January 1849): 358-73, esp. 361-69. Walker refers briefly to Brown's article in *Pulling the Devil's Kingdom Down*, 255, note 104. Catherine Booth was especially indebted to the Methodist biblical commentator Adam Clarke, whose exegesis she relied upon and quoted from extensively in *Female Teaching* and *Female Ministry*. Clarke's case for female ministry in the church is especially apparent in his comments on 1 Corinthians 14:34-35. See Adam Clarke, *The Holy Bible, Containing the Old and New Testament: Including the Marginal Readings and Parallel Texts, with a Commentary and Critical Notes*, Vol. 6 (1800; reprint, London: Ward, Lock and Co., n.d.). This edition is not paginated. Walker also notes the obvious influence of Clarke on Catherine Booth. See Walker, *Pulling the Devil's Kingdom Down*, 29, 255, note 104.

51 *Female Teaching*, 16-17; *Female Ministry*, 12-13.

52 *Female Teaching*, 21. Here, Catherine based her reasoning on Luke 1:35.

53 Ibid., 17-19, 25. See also *Female Ministry*, 14-17. This argument was made by Hugh Bourne as well in *Remarks on the Ministry of Women*. See Walford, *Memoirs of the Life and Labours of the Late Venerable Hugh Bourne*, Vol. 1, 186-87.

54 *Female Ministry*, 10. See also *Female Teaching*, 8, 15-16, 19; and *Female Ministry*, 16. The ramifications of Acts 2:17-21 for female ministry were undoubtedly something that Catherine Booth learned from Phoebe Palmer's *Promise of the Father*. The central thesis of this book was that the bestowal of the Holy Spirit upon women gave them the authority and obligation to testify publicly in the church. See *Promise of the Father*, 68, 87, 171-72, 231, 246, 320, 324, 338, 358, 366.

It should be recalled as well that Phoebe Palmer also equated prophesying with preaching. See *Promise of the Father*, 34-36, 43, 329-30. Referring to Acts 2, Primitive Methodists also argued that prophesying and preaching were one and the same thing. See Walford, *Memoirs of the Life and Labours of the Late Venerable Hugh Bourne*, Vol. 1, 185-86; and "On the Rise of Female Preachers in the Connexion which Originated in Cornwall," *The Primitive Methodist Magazine* (July 1821): 161-62.

55 *Female Ministry*, 17. See also *Female Teaching*, 21.

56 *Female Ministry*, 14.

57 Ibid., 17. Catherine placed great importance on the women mentioned in Paul's epistles, arguing that they shared prominent preaching and teaching functions with the men, even that of apostle.

58 *Female Teaching*, 30. See also 26-29; and *Female Ministry*, 17-19.

59 Cited in Walford, *Memoirs of the Life and Labours of the Late Venerable Hugh Bourne*, Vol. 1, 189. For William O'Bryan's very similar convictions in this area, see Shorney, "'Women may preach…,'" 317.

60 *Female Teaching*, 32; *Female Ministry*, 20.

61 Pamela Walker makes only passing reference to this point. See Walker, *Pulling the Devil's Kingdom Down*, 32.

62 Cited in Bramwell-Booth, *Catherine Booth*, 112.

63 Booth Papers, British Library, Add. Mss. 64804, letter from Catherine to her mother, dated December 23, 1857. See also Bramwell-Booth, *Catherine Booth*, 176. Pamela Walker's citation of this letter does not include any reference to Catherine Booth's lingering doubts about her potential for public ministry. See Walker, *Pulling the Devil's Kingdom Down*, 33. Self-doubt was also evident in a letter that Catherine had written to William years earlier, wherein she confessed: "I have often restrained thought for want of confidence in myself." See Booth Papers, British Library, Add. Mss. 64799, letter from Catherine to William, dated March 6, 1853.

64 Booth Papers, British Library, Add. Mss. 64805, letter from Catherine to her mother, dated September 26, 1859. See also Bramwell-Booth, *Catherine Booth*, 180-81.

65 Booth, *Aggressive Christianity*, 128.

66 Ibid. See also Booth, *Papers on Godliness*, 94.

67 Booth, *Aggressive Christianity*, 128-29.

68 Roger Green has done an admirable job of showing how much Catherine Booth contributed to the life and expression of the Christian Mission and Salvation Army. See Green, *Catherine Booth: A Biography*, esp. 151-298.

69 For a sampling of the many positive references to Catherine Booth by her Victorian peers, see Frances Power Cobbe, "The Last Revival," *The Contemporary Review* 42 (1882): 184-85; Mrs. Charles Garnett, "A Visit to the Training Home of The Salvation Army," *Sunday Magazine* (1884): 638; Leopold Katscher, "Some Aspects of The Salvation Army," *The National Review* 5 (1885): 77; Donald Fraser, "The Salvation Army," *The Presbyterian Review* 7 (April 1886): 261; "Memorial

Notices," *The Manchester Guardian* (October 6, 1890): 8; "General and Mrs. Booth of the Salvation Army," *The Christian* (October 17, 1890): 19-21; Josephine Butler, "Catherine Booth," *The Contemporary Review* 58 (November 1890): 639-54; Arnold White, "The Truth about The Salvation Army," *The Fortnightly Review* 58 (July 1892): 124; Charles A. Briggs, "The Salvation Army," *The North American Review* 159 (December 1894): 697-710; and the various memorial tributes paid to Catherine Booth by outsiders, in Bramwell Booth, *On the Banks of the River; Being a Brief History of the Last Days of Mrs. General Booth* (London: International Headquarters of The Salvation Army, 1900), 122-41.

70 Booth, *Aggressive Christianity*, 132.

71 Green, *Catherine Booth: A Biography*, 190.

72 When Catherine Booth referred to the origins of the Salvation Army, she often failed to mention the fact that her ministry and personal contacts had been the catalysts for her husband's work in the East of London. See Booth, "An Address to the Society of Friends," 46-47; and Booth, *The Salvation Army in Relation to the Church and State, and Other Addresses*, 67-69. Had Catherine Booth been more explicit about her contributions to the organization, there would have been less debate among later Salvationists about her influence upon the early Salvation Army.

73 Murdoch, *Origins of the Salvation Army*, 37-38.

74 Cited in Bramwell-Booth, *Catherine Booth*, 94.

75 [Catherine] Booth, "Compel Them to Come In," *The East London Evangelist* (March 1869): 84. This article reappeared in Catherine Booth, *Papers on Practical Religion* (1879; reprint, London: International Headquarters of The Salvation Army, 1884), 88-94.

76 Booth, *Papers on Godliness*, 66.

77 For more on these issues, see Ellen Jordan, *The Women's Movement and Women's Employment in Nineteenth-Century Britain* (London: Routledge, 1999), esp. 23-151; Linda Wilson, "'She Succeeds with Cloudless Brow ...': How Active Was the Spirituality of Nonconformist Women in the Home during the Period 1825-75?" in Swanson, ed., *Gender and Christian Religion*, 347-59; Anna Clark, *The Struggle for the Breeches: Gender and the Making of the British Working Class* (Berkeley, CA: University of California Press, 1995), esp. 1-118, 248-63; Joanna Bourke, *Working-Class Cultures in Britain, 1890-1960: Gender, Class and Ethnicity* (London: Routledge, 1994), 62-129; Leonore Davidoff and Catherine Hall, *Family Fortunes: Men and Women of the English Middle Class, 1780-1850* (Chicago: University of Chicago Press, 1987), 107-92, 319-451; and Jane Lewis, *Women in England, 1870-1950: Sexual Divisions and Social Change* (Bloomington, IN: Indiana University Press, 1984), 75-92.

78 Booth Papers, British Library, Add. Mss. 64799, letter from Catherine to William, dated December 27, 1852. See also Bramwell-Booth, *Catherine Booth*, 87.

79 See Booth Papers, British Library, Add. Mss. 64799, letter from Catherine to William, dated January 1, 1853; and Bramwell-Booth, *Catherine Booth*, 89.

80 Booth Papers, British Library, Add. Mss. 64799, letter from Catherine to William, dated January 1, 1853.

81 Cited in Begbie, *The Life of General William Booth*, Vol. 1, 246, 248. Part of this quotation survives in the Booth Papers, British Library, Add. Mss. 64802, incomplete letter from Catherine to William, dated April 9, 1855. The substance of this argument also appeared in an epistle that Catherine Mumford wrote to her Congregationalist minister, the Reverend David Thomas. See Booth Papers, British Library, Add. Mss. 64806, letter from Catherine to Rev. Thomas, dated 1855. This correspondence is also in the Catherine Booth Papers (women file) at the Salvation Army International Heritage Centre, London. See also Booth-Tucker, *The Life of Catherine Booth*, Vol. 1, 85-86. There is considerable debate about the actual date of this letter, because Booth-Tucker places it in the year 1853. Roger Green follows Booth-Tucker here, suggesting that Catherine was mistaken about the date of the letter. See Green, *Catherine Booth: A Biography*, 307, note 2. Pamela Walker, however, argues that the context surrounding this letter points to 1855 being the correct date. See Walker, *Pulling the Devil's Kingdom Down*, 251-52, note 50. Gordon Taylor, the archivist at the Salvation Army International Heritage Centre, also believes, like Walker, that there is no reason to question the date on this letter. He has verified that the date referred to in this correspondence—Sunday April 22—was in fact a Sunday in 1855. See his remarks in the Catherine Booth Papers, women file.

82 *Female Teaching*, 30.

83 Catherine Booth, "Courtship by Principle," in *The Highway of Our God: Selections from the Army Mother's Writings* (London: Salvationist Publishing and Supplies, 1954), 76.

84 For more on male headship in evangelical circles, see Davidoff and Hall, *Family Fortunes*, 107-14.

85 Booth Papers, British Library, Add. Mss. 64799, letter from Catherine to William, dated January 1, 1853. See also Bramwell-Booth, *Catherine Booth*, 89.

86 Cited in Booth-Tucker, *The Life of Catherine Booth*, Vol. 1, 220.

87 Booth, *Papers on Practical Religion*, 3.

88 William Stead's memorial tribute to Catherine Booth underscored her dying wish to promote the maternal role in Britain. See William T. Stead, "The Late Mrs. Booth," *The War Cry* (October 11, 1890): 8.

89 Booth, *Popular Christianity*, 181-82.

90 Ibid., 179. See also 177-78.

91 J.G., "Mothers' Meetings," *The Revival* (June 28, 1866): 357.

92 "Mother!" *The Christian Mission Magazine* (February 1875): 33.

93 Mary C. Billups, "Our Mothers' Meetings," *The East London Evangelist* (June 1869): 142-43. See also "A Letter to the Members of the Poplar Mothers' Meeting," *The East London Evangelist* (November 1868): 25; R. Wilson, "A Mothers' Meeting," *The Christian Mission Magazine* (March 1870): 47; "Our Mothers' Meeting,"

The Christian Mission Magazine (September 1874): 255; and Emma M.E. Stride, "Mothers' Meeting," *The Christian Mission Magazine* (February 1877): 50-51.

94 For more on the Mothers' Union, see Sean Gill, *Women and the Church of England: From the Eighteenth Century to the Present* (London: SPCK, 1994), 90-111; and Owen Chadwick, *The Victorian Church*, Part II (London: Adam and Charles Black, 1970), 192-93.

95 Cited in Bramwell-Booth, *Catherine Booth*, 190. See also 197; and Booth-Tucker, *The Life of Catherine Booth*, Vol. 1, 215.

96 See, for instance, Booth-Tucker, *The Life of Catherine Booth*, Vol. 1, 195, 256, 379; and Vol. 2, 105-06, 126.

97 The domestic assistance offered to Salvationist women is discussed in the next chapter, but it is worth noting that Army households were not economically well off. The financial hardships faced by Army officers are apparent in *All about The Salvation Army* (London: International Headquarters of The Salvation Army, 1888), 9; *The Why and Wherefore of The Salvation Army Regulations* (London: The Salvation Army, 1904), 57-58; and *Orders and Regulations for Field Officers of The Salvation Army* (London: The Salvation Army Book Department, 1917), 612-14. See also John Manson, *The Salvation Army and the Public: A Religious, Social, and Financial Study* (London: George Routledge and Sons, 1908), 137-53; and Alex M. Nicol, *General Booth and The Salvation Army* (London: Herbert and Daniel, 1910), 115.

98 The trend towards marriage in the Army was noted by William Booth, "The May Meeting Addresses: Summary of the Year's History," *The War Cry* (May 12, 1888): 10. Speaking of this period, biographer St. John Ervine notes that the Salvation Army was intent on filling its ranks with families. See Ervine, *God's Soldier*, Vol. 1, 511. This development continued throughout the 1890s and the 1900s. See Glenn K. Horridge, *The Salvation Army: Origins and Early Days, 1865-1900* (Godalming, Surrey, UK: Ammonite Books, 1993), 80; and E. Rentoul Esler, "The Salvation Army as a Social Influence," *Good Words* 45 (1904): 397.

CHAPTER 6

1 [Florence] Booth, "To the Women-Officers of The Salvation Army: Where We May Excel," *The Field Officer* 21, 4 (April 1913): 122.

2 [Catherine] Higgins, "Woman's Place in The Salvation Army World," *The Officer* 23, 9 (September 1915): 598.

3 British average incomes doubled between 1867 and 1908, so fewer working-class women needed to supplement their husband's wages. This was increasingly true for the period after the First World War. See Joan Perkin, *Victorian Women* (London: John Murray, 1993), 194-96; and Elizabeth Roberts, *A Woman's Place: An Oral History of Working-Class Women 1890-1940* (Oxford: Blackwell, 1984), 203. For more on the experiences of women during this period, see

Leonore Davidoff, *Worlds Between: Historical Perspectives on Gender and Class* (New York: Routledge, 1995); Joanna Bourke, *Working-Class Cultures in Britain, 1890-1960: Gender, Class and Ethnicity* (London: Routledge, 1994); Anne-Marie Sohn, "Between the Wars in France and England," in *A History of Women in the West. Vol. 5: Toward a Cultural Identity in the Twentieth Century*, ed. François Thébaud (Cambridge, MA: The Belknap Press of Harvard University Press, 1994), 92-119; Ellen Ross, *Love and Toil: Motherhood in Outcast London, 1870-1918* (New York: Oxford University Press, 1993); Jose Harris, *Private Lives, Public Spirit: A Social History of Britain, 1870-1914* (Oxford: Oxford University Press, 1993); Deirdre Beddoe, *Back to Home and Duty: Women between the Wars, 1918-1939* (London: Pandora Press, 1989); Jane Lewis, *Women in England, 1870-1950: Sexual Divisions and Social Change* (Bloomington, IN: Indiana University Press, 1984); and Carol Dyhouse, *Girls Growing Up in Late Victorian and Edwardian England* (London: Routledge and Kegan Paul, 1981). For the connection between motherhood, eugenics and empire, see Julia Bush, *Edwardian Ladies and Imperial Power* (London: Leicester University Press, 2000); and George Robb, "Race Motherhood: Moral Eugenics *vs* Progressive Eugenics, 1880-1920," in *Maternal Instincts: Visions of Motherhood and Sexuality in Britain, 1875-1925*, ed. Claudia Nelson and Ann Sumner Holmes (London: Macmillan, 1997), 58-74.

4 Ensign Quarterman, "A 'Housekeeper' for God," *The War Cry* (January 18, 1902): 4. Further sentiments along these lines are expressed in: "What a Man Can't Do," *The War Cry* (March 18, 1899): 4; "Home Duties," *The War Cry* (March 24, 1900): 4; "Mrs. Ensign [Louisa] Platts, Watford," *The War Cry* (May 5, 1900): 4; "Mother's Prayer," *The War Cry* (October 18, 1902): 4; [Jane] Kitching, "Pillars of the Home," *The War Cry* (October 15, 1921): 9; Mrs. Brigadier Stevens, "Home Building," *The War Cry* (January 14, 1922): 10; [Nellie] Swinfen, "The Joys of Motherhood," *The War Cry* (April 22, 1922): 9; Margaret Fitzgerald, "The Army's Call to Women," *The War Cry* (July 8, 1922): 9; "What Can a Woman Do to Continue the Great Salvation Siege?" *The War Cry* (December 10, 1927): 5; and [Catherine] Higgins, "God-Magnifying Motherhood," *The War Cry* (April 27, 1929): 5. See also "For Practical People," *The War Cry* (November 25, 1911): 11.

5 For more on the identification of women with morality, religion and the home, see Anthony Fletcher, "Beyond the Church: Women's Spiritual Experience at Home and in the Community 1600-1900," in *Gender and Christian Religion*, ed. Robert N. Swanson (Woodbridge, Suffolk, UK: Boydell Press, 1998), 187-203; and F. Knight, "'Male and Female He Created Them': Men, Women and the Question of Gender," in *Religion in Victorian Britain*, Vol. 5, ed. John Wolffe (Manchester: Manchester University Press, 1997), 23-57.

6 There remains no book-length biography of Florence Booth, but her serialized life story appeared in the 1930s in the British weekly *The Sunday Circle*. The first part of this series ran from January 21 to April 8, 1933, while the final portions of her life story were published between October 26, 1935 and February 15, 1936. For the first installment, see [Florence] Booth, "Chapters from My Life Story," *The Sunday Circle* (January 21, 1933): 50-51. Other sources for

her life include Bramwell Booth, *These Fifty Years* (London: Cassell, 1929), 89-94; Catherine Bramwell-Booth, *Bramwell Booth* (London: Rich and Cowan, 1933), 147-73; and Olwen Davies, *Florence the Home-Maker* (London: Salvationist Publishing and Supplies, 1962).

7   Florence Booth, *Mothers and the Empire, and Other Addresses* (London: The Salvation Army Book Department, 1914), 3.

8   Ibid., 10-11.

9   Florence Booth's rationale for establishing this body is discussed in "Inauguration of a Home League," *The War Cry* (February 9, 1907): 8. See also "A New League," *The Field Officer* 15, 2 (February 1907): 43-44.

10   See Ross, *Love and Toil*, 195-221.

11   For more on the Mothers' Union, see Sean Gill, *Women and the Church of England: From the Eighteenth Century to the Present* (London: SPCK, 1994), 90-111; and Brian Heeney, *The Women's Movement in the Church of England 1850-1930* (Oxford: Clarendon Press, 1988), 43-45.

12   See "Improving Home-Life: Work of the Women's League," *The War Cry* (July 2, 1910): 3. For the similarity of aims between the Home League and the earlier mothers' meetings, see Mary C. Billups, "Our Mothers' Meetings," *The East London Evangelist* (June 1869): 142-43; and *Orders and Regulations for The Home League* (London: Salvationist Publishing and Supplies, 1925), esp. 3, 10. See also William Burrows, *Heart of the Family: A History of the Home League in the British Territory* (London: National Headquarters of The Salvation Army, 1989), 9-31. I am grateful to Burrows for indicating the connection between mothers' meetings and the Home League.

13   "Home Beautiful!" *The War Cry* (March 17, 1917): 4. Similar successes are recorded in "Of National Importance," *The War Cry* (March 5, 1927): 5.

14   [Florence] Thomas, "The Ideal Housewife," *The Officer* 24, 11 (November 1916): 761-63.

15   [Jessie] Moffat, "Husbands and Wives in Unison," *The Officer* 27, 4 (October 1918): 326. See also [Phillis] Winterburn, "The Influence of a Christian Home," *The Officer* 30, 6 (June 1920): 607-609.

16   [Maggie?] Russell, "The Importance of a Mother's Life," *The Officer* 28, 1 (January 1919): 65. See also [Jean] Graver, "The Ideal Officer's Wife," *The Officer* 51, 1 (July 1930): 47.

17   Russell, "The Importance of a Mother's Life," 65-66.

18   Booth, *Mothers and the Empire*, 18. See also [Florence] Booth, "A Letter to Mothers," *The Officer* 25, 4 (April-May 1917): 229-30.

19   J[ane] W[ellman], "My Trials and Triumphs as a Wife and Mother on the Field," *The Field Officer* 18, 1 (January 1910): 19.

20   Booth, *Mothers and the Empire*, 17.

21   Florence Booth, quoted in "Mrs. Booth at Leeds Addresses a Mass Meeting for Women," *The War Cry* (October 14, 1905): 11. See also [Florence] Booth, "Salvation Family Life," *The War Cry* (July 20, 1895): 3.

22   [Beatrice] Wallis, "The Essentials of a Happy Home," *The Officer* 24, 9 (September 1916): 613-14.

23 Ibid., 613.

24 [Annie] Cheadle, "Patience versus Hastiness in the Home," *The Officer* 25, 1 (January 1917): 44. See also [Annie] Cheadle, "Patience in the Home," *The War Cry* (April 14, 1923): 13, which was essentially a condensed version of her 1917 article.

25 "The Mother and the Meetings," *The Officer* 5, 4 (April 1897): 126.

26 "Our Women Warriors. Mrs. Staff-Captain [Agnes] Lucas," *The War Cry* (December 14, 1895): 3.

27 "Women-Warriors," *The War Cry* (July 25, 1896): 6. While features and books on married female officers in the Salvation Army tended to spend a great deal of time describing their accomplishments while single, they devoted much less space to women's public activities after marriage. See, for example, "Women-Warriors," *The War Cry* (August 29, 1896): 3; "Women-Warriors," *The War Cry* (October 3, 1896): 6; Mildred Duff, *Three Coronations* (London: The Salvation Army Book Department, 1903); Ruth Tracy, *Marianne Pawson: "The Zulu Queen"* (London: Salvationist Publishing and Supplies, 1944); Edith Topley, *No Coward Soul* (London: Salvationist Publishing and Supplies, 1948); and Merle Hamilton, *Redhead on Fire* (London: Salvationist Publishing and Supplies, 1955).

28 "Mother's Most Precious Gift," *The Officer* 34, 6 (June 1922): 473-74.

29 A woman's right to equal opportunities with men in the public life of the Salvation Army was reiterated incessantly in the organization's earliest manuals. See William Booth, *Orders and Regulations for The Salvation Army* (London: The Salvation Army Headquarters, 1878), iii; William Booth, *Orders and Regulations for Field Officers of The Salvation Army* (London: International Headquarters of The Salvation Army, 1886), iv; William Booth, *Orders and Regulations for Staff Officers of The Salvation Army in the United Kingdom* (London: International Headquarters of The Salvation Army, 1895), 16-17; and William Booth, *Orders and Regulations for the Social Officers of The Salvation Army* (London: International Headquarters of The Salvation Army, 1898), 39-41. Further references to this right after 1900 include William Booth, *Orders and Regulations for Staff Officers of The Salvation Army* (London: International Headquarters of The Salvation Army, 1904), 8-9; Bramwell Booth, *Orders and Regulations for Officers of the Men's Social Work of The Salvation Army* (London: The Salvation Army Book Department, 1915), 21-22; *Orders and Regulations for Field Officers of The Salvation Army* (London: The Salvation Army Book Department, 1917), 309-10; Bramwell Booth, *Orders and Regulations for Territorial Commanders and Chief Secretaries of The Salvation Army* (London: International Headquarters of The Salvation Army, 1920), 100; and *Orders and Regulations for Officers of The Salvation Army* (London: International Headquarters of The Salvation Army, 1925), 51-52.

30 It is worth noting that almost all domestic work throughout this period was done manually. Electrical appliances did not become readily available in Britain until the early 1930s, and they were confined largely to the middle and upper classes. See Eric Hopkins, *The Rise and Decline of the English Working Classes 1918-1990: A Social History* (London: Weidenfeld and Nicolson, 1991),

24. For more on domestic life in this period, see Bourke, *Working-Class Cultures in Britain, 1890-1960*, 62-63; Davidoff, *Worlds Between*, 1-17, 73-102; and Roberts, *A Woman's Place*, 22-23, 131. On the need for clean clothes and houses in the Salvation Army, see William Booth, *Orders and Regulations for Field Officers of The Salvation Army* (London: Headquarters of The Salvation Army, 1901), 202; and *Orders and Regulations for Field Officers of The Salvation Army* (1917), 208.

31 [Emma] Booth-Tucker, "To Our Married Women Officers," *The Officer* 1, 2 (February 1893): 39.

32 In addition to the examples cited here, see brief references to a female officer's household chores in "A Woman's Work," *The War Cry* (March 18, 1899): 4; W[ellman], "My Trials and Triumphs as a Wife and Mother on the Field," 17-21; [Beatrice] Wallis, "Qualifications for Marriage," *The War Cry* (March 11, 1922): 9; and Winterburn, "The Influence of a Christian Home," 607.

33 [Marianne] Railton, "Honourable Service," *The War Cry* (April 7, 1900): 4.

34 M[arianne] Railton, "'Cheer Up!': For Our F.O.'s Wives," *The Field Officer* 8, 11 (November 1900): 404.

35 Ibid., 405.

36 "Healthy Homes and Children," *The War Cry* (February 13, 1904): 12.

37 Wallis, "The Essentials of a Happy Home," 612-13.

38 "A Good Housekeeper," *The War Cry* (July 15, 1922): 9.

39 See, for example, "A Woman Who Did Nothing," *The War Cry* (November 17, 1900): 4; "Women's Unseen Burdens," *The War Cry* (January 23, 1904): 12; "Don't Despise Your Work," *The War Cry* (April 2, 1904): 12; and Phebe Bird, "An Ideal Woman," *The Officer* 46, 1 (January 1928): 71-72.

40 Prospective salaries were spelled out in section 53 of the Salvation Army's application form for candidates for officership. Section 54 went on to stress that candidates for officership had no guarantee of a salary. John Manson reproduces this application form in its entirety in his *The Salvation Army and the Public: A Religious, Social, and Financial Study* (London: George Routledge and Sons, 1908), 185-89. See also *Orders and Regulations for Field Officers of The Salvation Army* (1917), 612-15, 623. When a salary was available, it was modest. For example, a married captain with young children could expect no more than twenty to thirty-five shillings a week between the 1880s and the 1920s, which was only an average subsistence wage for the period. For an indication of Army salaries, see Leopold Katscher, "Some Aspects of The Salvation Army," *The National Review* 5 (1885): 73; Francis Peek, "The Salvationists," *The Contemporary Review* 49 (January 1886): 57; *The Why and Wherefore of The Salvation Army Regulations* (London: The Salvation Army, 1904), 57-58; Manson, *The Salvation Army and the Public*, 187; and *Orders and Regulations for Corps Officers of The Salvation Army* (London: International Headquarters of The Salvation Army, 1925), 318-19. For an indication of wages in general at this time, see Carol Dyhouse, *Feminism and the Family in England 1880-1939* (Oxford: Basil Blackwell, 1989), 100; Perkin, *Victorian Women*, 191; and Hopkins, *The Rise and Decline of the English Working Classes 1918-1990*, 20-21. That officers some-

times received less than their allotted salaries is evident from *The Why and Wherefore of The Salvation Army Regulations*, 57-58. See also the ex-officer testimonials in Manson, *The Salvation Army and the Public*, 191-96. The less than stable income of an officer in the field is also noted by Alex M. Nicol, *General Booth and The Salvation Army* (London: Herbert and Daniel, 1910), 115.

41 "The Wife of a Salvation Army Officer," in *The Salvation Army Year Book: 1924* (London: Salvationist Publishing and Supplies, 1924), 23.

42 See [Maud] Beckett, "Officer-Wives and Mothers in Council: Economy of Kinds," *The Officer* 42, 2 (February 1926): 96; "Mother and Warrior: A Sketch of the Career of Adjutant Mrs. Narraway," *The Field Officer* 10, 11 (November 1902): 510; E.H., "Officer-Wives and Mothers in Council: The Claims of the Children and the Claims of the Corps," *The Officer* 42, 3 (March 1926): 188 ; [Minnie] McVeigh, "A Married Woman's Opportunities: As a Wife and Mother on the Field," *The Officer* 22, 1 (January 1914): 40; and "A Woman's Work," 4. For the odd exceptions to this rule, see "Mrs. Adjutant [Polly] Brogdale," *The War Cry* (October 17, 1903): 11; and "One of God's Good Women," *The War Cry* (October 1, 1904): 11. See also Laura E. Lauer, "Women in British Nonconformity, circa 1880-1920, with Special Reference to the Society of Friends, Baptist Union and Salvation Army" (Ph.D. thesis, University of Oxford, 1998), 286-93.

43 See Frederick Booth-Tucker, *The Consul: A Sketch of Emma Booth-Tucker* (New York: The Salvation Army Publishing Department, 1903), 127; and [Minnie L.] Carpenter, *Miriam Booth: A Sketch* (London: Salvationist Publishing and Supplies, 1920), 15-16. Miriam Booth was a daughter of Florence and Bramwell Booth.

44 "Married Women-Warriors. Mrs. Major [Mary] Aspinall," *The War Cry* (November 17, 1894): 13. For more on the life of Mary Aspinall, see the sketch of her husband's life in [Minnie L.] Carpenter, *Three Great Hearts* (London: Salvationist Publishing and Supplies, 1928), 181-219.

45 "Mother and Warrior: A Sketch of the Career of Adjutant Mrs. Narraway," 509-10; and "Women Who Succeed: Their Secrets," *The War Cry* (June 25, 1898): 11.

46 "Mother and Warrior: A Sketch of the Career of Adjutant Mrs. Narraway," 510.

47 Booth, *Orders and Regulations for Field Officers of The Salvation Army* (1886), 56. For more on the assumption that work within the home was the responsibility of women, see Booth, *Orders and Regulations for Staff Officers of The Salvation Army* (1904), 9; and Bramwell Booth, *Orders and Regulations for Territorial Commanders and Chief Secretaries of The Salvation Army*, 100.

48 Betty Pagaway, "The Home and The Army," *The War Cry* (May 13, 1899): 4.

49 Hay Tee, "Home or Platform?" *The War Cry* (November 10, 1900): 4.

50 [Emma] Booth-Tucker, "Woman's Part in the War. Your Place and Mine," *The War Cry* (February 4, 1893): 9. The substance of this article is expanded upon in [Emma] Booth-Tucker, *Heart Messages* (London: Salvationist Publishing and Supplies, 1926), 20-29. This book was a collection of Emma's writings, compiled after her tragic death in a railway accident in the United States in 1903.

51 Booth-Tucker, "Woman's Part in the War," 9.

52 "Officers Who Succeed," *The War Cry* (July 9, 1898): 11.

53 "Married Women-Warriors," *The War Cry* (April 13, 1895): 13.

54 Ibid. Another exceptional officer who pursued a very active ministry was Sarah Dowdle, but, as a *War Cry* correspondent noted, she possessed this freedom because she did not have any children. See "Mrs. Com. [Sarah] Dowdle," *The War Cry* (June 25, 1898): 3. For more on Sarah Dowdle, see the biography of her husband by George Scott Railton, *Commissioner Dowdle: The Saved Railway Guard* (London: The Salvation Army Book Department, 1901).

55 "A Mother's Sphere," *The War Cry* (October 3, 1903): 4.

56 "Always on Duty," *The War Cry* (March 12, 1904): 12.

57 N. Brookes, "Mrs. Colonel [Kate] Hodder on 'Woman's Rights,'" *The War Cry* (June 3, 1899): 4. For similar thinking in the wider Army world, see Maud Ballington Booth, *Beneath Two Flags: A Study in Mercy and Help Methods*, 4th ed. (Cincinnati: Cranston and Curts, 1894), 255; and [Shizu] Sashida, "A Call to Arms to the Women Officers in Japan," *The Officer* 30, 4 (April 1920): 386.

58 Ruth Tracy, "The Salvation Army and the Emancipation of Women," in *The Salvation Army Year Book: 1928* (London: Salvationist Publishing and Supplies, 1928), 17. This kind of reasoning can be found as well in "Married Women-Warriors. Mrs. Major [Mary] Aspinall," 13.

59 [Elsie] Shaw, "Staff Wives and That 'Settling-Down' Spirit," *The Staff Review* 9, 4 (November 1929): 419.

60 E.H., "Officer-Wives and Mothers in Council," 188. See also Graver, "The Ideal Officer's Wife," 47.

61 "An Officer's Wife," *The Field Officer* 17, 5 (May 1909): 190. Florence Booth also implied that this was a problem. See [Florence] Booth, *Wanted—An Elite* (London: Salvationist Publishing and Supplies, 1928), 42-43. While not suggesting that women should neglect their work in the home, she believed that they should be "helpmeets" to their spouses by witnessing in public.

62 "An Officer's Wife," 190-91.

63 Mrs. Wilmer, "My Trials and Triumphs as a Wife and Mother on the Field," *The Field Officer* 18, 3 (March 1910): 109. See also [Florence] Thomas, "We Officer Wives and Mothers," *The Officer* 25, 10 (November 1917): 665.

64 W[ellman], "My Trials and Triumphs as a Wife and Mother on the Field," 17. See also "The Bond of Service and Fellowship," *The Officer* 25, 6 (July 1917): 395.

65 "The Man and His Province," *The War Cry* (September 24, 1898): 4. For further references to a woman's domestic burdens, see "Women Warriors and the '100,000,'" *The War Cry* (February 1, 1902): 4; and "Mrs. Lieut.-Colonel [Martha] Jeffries," *The War Cry* (November 29, 1902): 4.

66 Thomas, "We Officer Wives and Mothers," 666.

67 "Married Women-Warriors. Mrs. Ensign Cloud," *The War Cry* (February 9, 1895): 4.

68 Fitzgerald, "The Army's Call to Women," 9.

69 Higgins, "Woman's Place in The Salvation Army World," 599.

70 [Marie] Gauntlett, "Are Some Women Officers Abandoning Their Dearly-Bought Privileges?" *The Officer* 25, 11 (December 1917): 755.

71 Beckett, "Officer-Wives and Mothers in Council," 97.

72 "Unemployed Staff Wives," *The Staff Review* 1 (1922): 111. The reality of this situation was strikingly apparent in [Minnie L.] Carpenter, *Commissioner Henry Howard* (London: Salvationist Publishing and Supplies, 1926), 24; and Arch R. Wiggins, *T.H.K.: Theodore Hopkins Kitching, A Biography* (London: Salvationist Publishing and Supplies, 1956), 30, 50-51. The burdens of domestic life clearly fell upon the wives of Howard and Kitching.

73 The one exception was William Booth, *Orders and Regulations for Soldiers of The Salvation Army* (1890; reprint, London: International Headquarters of The Salvation Army, 1927), 81. This manual urged the male soldier (lay member) to help his wife with the household chores whenever possible. Such an exhortation, however, never found its way into any *Orders and Regulations* for Salvation Army officers (clergy).

74 See Booth, *Orders and Regulations for Field Officers of The Salvation Army* (1901), 17-23.

75 "Our Women Warriors: Helps Upward, Part II," *The Field Officer* 11, 2 (February 1903): 51.

76 "Our Women Warriors: Room at the Top!, Part I, " *The Field Officer* 11, 1 (January 1903): 7-8.

77 Dyhouse, *Girls Growing Up in Late Victorian and Edwardian England, 26-28.*

78 [Florence] Booth, "The Officer and His Duties towards Women," *The Field Officer* 14, 8 (August 1906): 287.

79 [Florence] Booth, "To the Women-Officers of The Salvation Army: Our Precious Heritage," *The Field Officer* 21, 3 (March 1913): 82. Years later, Florence briefly noted that she wanted to see female officers develop business skills. See [Florence] Booth, *Powers of Salvation Army Officers* (London: Salvationist Publishing and Supplies, 1923), 91.

80 [Florence] Booth, "Recollections of Mrs. General Booth," *All the World* 31, 10 (October 1910): 534-35; [Florence] Booth, "The Army Mother as I Knew Her," *The Staff Review* 9, 1 (January 1929): 24.

81 [Florence] Booth, "The Place and Power of Woman in The Salvation Army," *The Officer* 22, 8 (August 1914): 511.

82 Ibid., 510-11.

83 See, for example, [Marianne] Railton, "A Personal Remembrance of Our Army Mother," *All the World* 21, 10 (October 1900): 594-96; Booth, "Recollections of Mrs. General Booth," 534-36; and Evangeline Booth, *Woman* (New York: Fleming H. Revell, 1930), 25-27.

84 [Minnie L.] Carpenter, *Some Notable Officers of The Salvation Army* (1925; reprint, London: Salvationist Publishing and Supplies, 1927), 16.

85 "Mother's Most Precious Gift," 473-74; Russell, "The Importance of a Mother's Life," 65; and [Elsie] Shaw, "The Opportunity and Influence of a Staff Wife," *The Staff Review* 8, 4 (October 1928): 462.

86 For more on Salvation Army Rescue Homes and work with prostitutes, see Louise A. Jackson, "'Singing Birds as Well as Soap Suds': The Salvation Army's Work with Sexually Abused Girls in Edwardian England," *Gender and History* 12, 1 (2000): 107-26; Ann R. Higginbotham, "Respectable Sinners: Salvation Army Rescue Work with Unmarried Mothers, 1884-1914," in *Religion in the Lives of English Women, 1760-1930*, ed. Gail Malmgreen (Bloomington, IN: Indiana University Press, 1986), 216-33; Jenty Fairbank, *Booth's Boots: Social Service Beginnings in The Salvation Army* (London: International Headquarters of The Salvation Army, 1983), 27-40; Madge Unsworth, *Maiden Tribute: A Study in Voluntary Social Service* (London: Salvationist Publishing and Supplies, 1949), 1-83; Booth, *Orders and Regulations for the Social Officers of The Salvation Army*, 290-341; *Orders and Regulations for the Rescue Work* (London: The Salvation Army, 1892); [Florence] Booth, "Our Own Rescue Home," in *The Salvation War 1884. Under the Generalship of William Booth* (London: The Salvation Army Book Depot, 1884), 143-48; and "Rescue Work in East London," *The War Cry* (September 3, 1884):4.

87 *Orders and Regulations for the Rescue Work*, 15.

88 Davidoff, *Worlds Between*, 55.

89 For a brief overview of slum work, see Robert Sandall, *The History of The Salvation Army*, Vol. 2 (1950; reprint, New York: The Salvation Army, 1979), 96-98; and Robert Sandall, *The History of The Salvation Army*, Vol. 3 (1955; reprint, New York: The Salvation Army, 1979), 20-24, 159-64. A popular account of Salvation Army slum work in the late 1920s is provided by Hugh Redwood, *God in the Slums* (1930; reprint, London: Hodder and Stoughton, 1964). Two excellent sources for Salvation Army slum work in the United States are Diane Winston, *Red-Hot and Righteous: The Urban Religion of The Salvation Army* (Cambridge, MA: Harvard University Press, 1999), esp. 53-95; and Maud Ballington Booth, "Salvation Army Work in the Slums," *Scribner's Magazine* 17 (January 1895): 102-14.

90 See Margaret Troutt, *The General Was a Lady: The Story of Evangeline Booth* (Nashville, TN: A.J. Holman Company, 1980), 41-42, 68. It is worth pointing out that Eva Booth did not go by the name "Evangeline" during her early days in Britain. Her name at birth was Eveline, and during her youth she was called Eva or, less commonly, Evangelyn. See Troutt, *The General Was a Lady*, 118.

91 For more on these trends, see Gerald Parsons, "Social Control to Social Gospel: Victorian Christian Social Attitudes," in *Religion in Victorian Britain*, Vol. 2, ed. Gerald Parsons (Manchester: Manchester University Press, 1988), 39-62; F.K. Prochaska, *Women and Philanthropy in Nineteenth-Century England* (Oxford: Clarendon Press, 1980), 123-29; and Owen Chadwick, *The Victorian Church*, Part II (London: Adam and Charles Black, 1970), 271-85.

92 See, for example, "Our Year's Retrospect," *The War Cry* (January 5, 1889): 9; William Booth, "With 27th Birthday Greetings," *The War Cry* (August 6, 1892): 12; and "Ministering Angels," *The War Cry* (May 13, 1905): 3.

93 Booth, *Orders and Regulations for Field Officers of The Salvation Army* (1886), 207.

94   Booth, *Orders and Regulations for the Social Officers of The Salvation Army,* 433. See also B[lanche] B. Cox, "Cellar, Gutter and Garret; or, the Training Home at Work in 'Outcast London,'" *The War Cry* (December 13, 1884):4; "Staff-Captain Blanche B. Cox," *The War Cry* (July 30, 1887): 3; "The London Slums," *The War Cry* (August 20, 1887): 4; [James] Cooke, "Slum Babies," *All the World* 4, 9 (September 1888): 302-04; "Immediate Extension of Slum Work," *The War Cry* (January 21, 1899): 1; "Sins and Sorrows of the Slums," *The War Cry* (July 4, 1903): 6; George Scott Railton, *Forward against Misery: Being an Illustrated Review of Part of the Social Operations of The Salvation Army* (London: International Headquarters of The Salvation Army, 1913), 43-46; *Views and Interviews: Records of Some Phases of Salvation Army Social Work, 1920-21* (London: International Headquarters of The Salvation Army, 1921), 55-63; "Glimpses of Army Slum Service," in *The Salvation Army Year Book: 1926* (London: Salvationist Publishing and Supplies, 1926), 10-11; and Redwood, *God in the Slums,* 12-15.

95   *The Salvation Army Year Book for 1906* (London: The Salvation Army Book Department, 1906), 67; "Glimpses of Army Slum Service," 10.

96   Booth, "With 27th Birthday Greetings," 12.

97   See "Four Years of Slum Life," *The War Cry* (October 19, 1895): 4; Margaret Allen, *Kingdom-Makers in Shelter, Street, and Slum* (London: The Salvation Army Book Department, 1902), 69-89; "The Army's Ministering Women," *The War Cry* (May 8, 1920): 1; "Glimpses of Army Slum Service," 11; and Cyril J. Barnes, *The Rising Sun: The Story of Matilda Hatcher* (London: Salvationist Publishing and Supplies, 1955), 7-20.

98   Emily Turner, "Caring for Slum Babies," in *Aspects of Social Work in The Salvation Army: Papers Read at the International Social Council, London, Conducted by The Founder, 1911* (London: The Salvation Army Book Department, 1917), 214.

99   "Unemployed Staff Wives," 111.

100 Ibid.

101 H. Rider Haggard, *Regeneration: Being an Account of the Social Work of The Salvation Army in Great Britain* (London: Longmans, Green and Co., 1910), 89. Frederick MacKenzie, another outsider who frequently wrote on the Salvation Army, was also quick to note how women trained for full-time service in the organization were taught to sacrifice all personal ambitions. See F.A. MacKenzie, *Waste Humanity: Being a Review of Part of the Social Operations of The Salvation Army in Great Britain* (London: International Headquarters of The Salvation Army, [1909]), 57.

102 For more on the Victorian notion of sexual difference, see Ellen Jordan, *The Women's Movement and Women's Employment in Nineteenth-Century Britain* (London: Routledge, 1999), 1-106; Perkin, *Victorian Women,* 1-3, 29, 38, 73; Joan N. Burstyn, *Victorian Education and the Ideal of Womanhood* (New Brunswick, NJ: Rutgers University Press, 1984), 99-102, 129-30; and Dyhouse, *Girls Growing Up in Late Victorian and Edwardian England,* 143-44, 152-53.

103 V[itty] F. Ward, "What Has The Salvation Army Done for Woman?" *All the World* 21, 9 (September 1900): 508.

104 Ibid.

105 Booth, *Mothers and the Empire*, 55.

106 See Norman Vance, *The Sinews of the Spirit: The Ideal of Christian Manliness in Victorian Literature and Religious Thought* (Cambridge: Cambridge University Press, 1985), 13-27.

107 Booth, "The Officer and His Duties towards Women," 286.

108 [Clara] Case, "The Leadership of Women," *The Staff Review* 3, 10 (April 1924): 161. Case spent many years in the mission field in India. For an account of her life, see A. Rendle Short and S. Carvosso Gauntlett, *Clara Case—Nurani: Lover of India* (London: Salvationist Publishing and Supplies, 1946).

109 [Agnes] Povlsen, "Are Equal Standards for Men and Women Officers Maintained?" *The Staff Review* 10, 4 (October 1930): 350.

110 Beckett, "Officer-Wives and Mothers in Council," 97.

111 W[ellman], "My Trials and Triumphs as a Wife and Mother on the Field," 17.

112 Wilmer, "My Trials and Triumphs as a Wife and Mother on the Field," 109.

113 Graver, "The Ideal Officer's Wife," 48. This theme is also apparent in [Emma] Millner, "Women's Influence in the Men's Social Work," *The Officer* 47, 4 (October 1928): 323.

114 McVeigh, "A Married Woman's Opportunities," 39.

115 Shaw, "Staff Wives and That 'Settling-Down' Spirit," 420. See also [Minnie L.] Carpenter, *Commissioner John Lawley* (London: Salvationist Publishing and Supplies, 1924), 95; "'I Expect Him to Do Well!'" *The War Cry* (November 15, 1930): 5; and Alfred J. Gilliard, *Sussex Yeoman: The Story of Charles Rich* (London: Salvationist Publishing and Supplies, 1956), 27-28.

116 William Booth, *Orders and Regulations for Field Officers of The Salvation Army* (London: Headquarters of The Salvation Army, 1891), 127-28. See also the 1917 edition of this manual, 69.

117 Booth, *Beneath Two Flags*, 256.

118 Railton, "'Cheer Up!': For Our F.O.'s Wives," 404-405.

119 Matilda Hatcher, "Women Who Work for Men Who Weep," *All the World* 44, 4 (October- December 1924): 201-202.

120 Ibid., 201-203. See also "Men's Social Officers' Wives," *The War Cry* (February 14, 1925): 9; and [Edith] Holbrook, "Women's Work in the Men's Social," *The Officer* 47, 2 (August 1928): 137-41.

121 Booth, "To the Women-Officers of The Salvation Army: Where We May Excel," 124.

122 See "Home League Secretaries Meet Mrs. Booth in Council," *The War Cry* (April 27, 1912): 11; and *Orders and Regulations for The Home League* (1925), 4-5. This continues to be reflected in more recent times. See, for example, *Orders and Regulations for Corps Officers of The Salvation Army* (London: International Headquarters of The Salvation Army, 1988), 195.

123 See *The Congress of Nations 1914: Souvenir and Guide* (London: International Headquarters of The Salvation Army, 1914), 118; *Orders and Regulations for The*

Home League (London: The Salvation Army Book Department, 1916), 3; and *Orders and Regulations for The Home League* (1925), 4-5. This practice continues into the present. See *Orders and Regulations for The Home League* (London: International Headquarters of The Salvation Army, 1986), 6-7.

124 Higgins, "Woman's Place in The Salvation Army World," 601.

125 "Of National Importance," 5.

126 Higgins, "Woman's Place in The Salvation Army World," 601.

127 See "An Honour to Be Pelted," *The War Cry* (May 21, 1904): 12; and the 1917 edition of *Orders and Regulations for Field Officers of The Salvation Army*, 414.

128 Florence Booth believed that all women had a natural capacity for dealing with the young. See her comments in "To the Women-Officers of The Salvation Army: Where We May Excel," 123.

129 "Woman's Work in America: A Talk with Consul Booth-Tucker," *All the World* 21, 3 (March 1900): 193.

130 Graver, "The Ideal Officer's Wife," 48. Women's involvement with young people's work in the corps is also evident in "The Bond of Service and Fellowship," 396; and "A Woman's Work," 4.

131 Booth, "The Place and Power of Woman in The Salvation Army," 510.

132 McVeigh, "A Married Woman's Opportunities," 39. See also Graver, "The Ideal Officer's Wife," 47; and Evangeline Booth, *Woman*, 15.

133 Shaw, "The Opportunity and Influence of a Staff Wife," 463. A woman's role in counselling is also noted in "A Plucky Wife," *The War Cry* (December 21, 1901): 11; Higgins, "Woman's Place in The Salvation Army World," 599; and "A Day in My Life," *The War Cry* (December 7, 1929): 5.

134 [Florence] Booth, "To the Women-Officers of The Salvation Army: Our Responsibility towards Our Own Sex," *The Field Officer* 21, 5 (May 1913): 163.

135 The top administrative positions being considered here are as follows: the General, the Chief of the Staff (second-in-command worldwide), national, special and territorial commanders (in charge of a country, a part of a country or several countries), special, joint and chief secretaries (second-in-command at national and territorial levels), officers commanding (responsible for Army work in areas smaller than territories), general secretaries (second-in-command to territorial commanders, officers commanding and sub-commanders), the leaders of sub-territories, the leaders and territorial secretaries of the Department of the West (USA), the leaders and chief secretaries of the British Men's and Women's Social Work Departments, and the leaders and chief assistants of the British training institutions. Vacant positions, while never very common, are not included in this tabulation. It should be noted as well that comprehensive international statistics prior to 1906, when the first yearbook was issued, are unavailable.

136 Approximately 70 percent of female officers were married by 1930. See "Woman's Position in The Army," in *The Salvation Army Year Book: 1930* (London: Salvationist Publishing and Supplies, 1930), 14. When the Salvation Army began, the vast majority of its women were single and young. See Glenn K. Horridge, *The*

Salvation Army: Origins and Early Days, 1865-1900 (Godalming, Surrey, UK: Ammonite Books, 1993), 80.

137 These and other international statistics can be found in *The Salvation Army Year Book for 1906, 22*; and *The Salvation Army Year Book for 1918* (London: The Salvation Army Book Department, 1918), 26.

138 Those associated with the Women's Social Work Department were over-whelmingly single women. Recruiters for this area of ministry generally did not accept women over the age of twenty-eight. See Alice Swain, "Candidates and the Social Work," in *Social Problems in Solution: Papers Read at the International Social Council 1921* (London: International Headquarters of The Salvation Army, 1923), 264. See also Allen, *Kingdom-Makers in Shelter, Street, and Slum*; *The Salvation Army Year Book for 1914* (London: The Salvation Army Book Department, 1914), 46-47; Mary Frances Billington, "Sisterhood of Service," *All the World* 44, 4 (October-December 1924): 195-200, 240; *The Salvation Army Year Book: 1926*, 46-47; and "Woman's Position in The Army," in *The Salvation Army Year Book: 1930*, 14.

139 The Salvation Army's third General, Edward J. Higgins, did not take office until 1929.

140 See Abner Sumner, *The New Papacy: Behind the Scenes in The Salvation Army* (Toronto, ON: Albert Britnell, 1889), 13-14; Brian Lunn, *Salvation Dynasty* (London: William Hodge and Co., 1936), 232-36, 246; F.A. MacKenzie, *The Clash of the Cymbals: The Secret Revolt in the Salvation Army* (New York: Brentano's, 1929), 61-64, 177; and Troutt, *The General Was a Lady*, 63. One early critic of the Salvation Army envisioned a succession of Booth "popes." See *Pope Booth: The Salvation Army A.D. 1950* (London: W. Lucas, [1890]), esp. 7, 12-16.

141 Although she was a provincial commander, Eva Booth had a higher rank than those in charge of the other provincial commands. See "Results of Self-Denial Week, 1895," *The War Cry* (October 26, 1895): 7; and Troutt, *The General Was a Lady*, 63. For references to Minnie Reid, see "Lieut.-Col. Reid: A Woman Provincial Commander," *The War Cry* (August 26, 1905): 5; and Arch Wiggins, *The History of The Salvation Army*, Vol. 5 (1968; reprint, New York: The Salvation Army, 1979), 178-79. Minnie Reid married Frederick Booth-Tucker, whose wife, Emma, had died in a railway accident in 1903. Reid's background is covered briefly in F.A. MacKenzie, *Booth-Tucker: Sadhu and Saint* (London: Hodder and Stoughton, 1930), 193-200; and Harry Williams, *Booth-Tucker: William Booth's First Gentleman* (London: Hodder and Stoughton, 1980), 172-76.

142 The divisional pages of early yearbooks did not always list the first names of divisional officers or divisional commanders, but I was able to verify gender by cross-checking last names with British corps indexes and relevant "Who's Who" sections of yearbooks. Reliable divisional statistics for the earliest years of the organization are not easy to come by, and the Salvation Army lost a great deal of valuable information during the Second World War, when its International Headquarters in London was bombed. Occasionally, however, *The War Cry* gave the names of those in charge of divisions. I found no other references to

female divisional officers between 1880 and 1906 in the pages of *The War Cry* or elsewhere. The Salvation Army was always quick to promote interesting developments in the field, as shown in the few announcements on female divisional officers cited in this chapter. In all likelihood, any further promotions in this area would have been cited by the Army's press or recorded in the organization's official history. Three things should be noted about table 6.3: (1) the 1906 yearbook claimed a total of thirty-seven divisions, but only listed thirty-six divisional commands; (2) the 1918 and 1930 yearbooks each listed one vacant divisional command, so they were not calculated into the total number of divisions for these years; and (3) the Iceland and Faroe Isles Division, which came under the British Territory in 1930, was not included in the statistics for this year.

143   See "Women Warriors," *The War Cry* (November 3, 1894): 5; and Carpenter, *Commissioner John Lawley*, 96. See also 91-104.

144   Except for a brief interval in 1923, Florence Booth held the post of territorial commander from March 1919 to March 1925. See "Mrs. Booth—The New British Commissioner," *The War Cry* (March 22, 1919): 5; and "The British Field: Change of Commissioners," *The War Cry* (February 28, 1925): 6. The first two female divisional commanders were appointed in 1919. See "The British Commissioner and Leaders of Home Field Forces," *The War Cry* (December 20, 1919): 12. One of these women was Annie Trounce, a widow, but she was no longer a divisional commander by 1922. See *The Salvation Army Year Book for 1920* (London: Salvationist Publishing and Supplies, 1920), 42.

145   *Outlines of Salvation Army History* (1927; reprint, London: Salvationist Publishing and Supplies, 1928), 30. A similar message was conveyed in "The Army and Woman," in *The Salvation Army Year Book for 1910* (London: The Salvation Army Book Department, 1910), 55-56; "The Position of Woman in The Salvation Army," in *Some Aspects of The Woman's Movement*, ed. Zoë Fairfield (London: SCM Press, 1915), 229-31; "Women and The Army," in *The Salvation Army Year Book for 1917* (London: The Salvation Army Book Department, 1917), 17; *The Salvation Army: Its Principles and Government* (London: The Salvation Army, 1920), 5; and "Woman's Position in The Army," in *The Salvation Army Year Book: 1930*, 13-14.

146   "Way for the Women!" *The War Cry* (November 11, 1899): 4.

147   See Mary MacFarlane, "Are Equal Standards for Men and Women Officers Maintained?" *The Staff Review* 10, 4 (October 1930): 339-44; and under the same heading in this issue, Povlsen, 347-52, and Johanna van de Werken, 352-53. I was unable to find any official response to these concerns in *The Staff Review*, which ceased publication in late 1931. It is interesting to note that an influential article appearing in the Salvation Army's 1960 yearbook mistakenly attributed MacFarlane's comments to Edward Higgins, thereby leaving the impression that early Army leaders frankly discussed the issue of sexual inequality in the ranks. In reality, Higgins never made an official response to these criticisms. See C[atherine] B[aird], "Enlightened Men," in *The Salvation Army Year Book:*

1960 (London: Salvationist Publishing and Supplies, 1960), 30-33. This article was reprinted in *Another Harvest of the Years: An Anthology of Salvation Army Year Book Articles (1957-1975)* (London: Salvationist Publishing and Supplies, 1975), 28-34.

❖

EPILOGUE

1   See Elaine Kaye, "A Turning-Point in the Ministry of Women: The Ordination of the First Woman to the Christian Ministry in England in September 1917," in *Women in the Church*, ed. W.J. Sheils and Diana Wood (Oxford: Basil Blackwell, 1990), 505-12; and Hugh McLeod, *Religion and Society in England, 1850-1914* (London: Macmillan, *1996)*, 161-68. For some indication of the long struggle towards female equality and ministry in the Anglican fold, see Brian Heeney, *The Women's Movement in the Church of England 1850-1930* (Oxford: Clarendon Press, 1988); and Sean Gill, *Women and the Church of England: From the Eighteenth Century to the Present* (London: SPCK, 1994), 206-59.

2   [Florence] Booth, "To the Women-Officers of The Salvation Army: Our Precious Heritage," *The Field Officer* 21, 3 (March 1913): 82.

3   It is interesting to note that the Salvation Army's latest doctrinal manual devotes a very small paragraph to one area of feminist concern, the maleness of God the Father. While rejecting the equation of God the Father with maleness, and allowing for maternal traits within the deity, this text remains very cautious on this subject. Moreover, sin remains essentially a matter of self-will and self-ishness within this theological handbook. See David Guy et al., *Salvation Story: Salvationist Handbook of Doctrine* (London: International Headquarters of The Salvation Army, 1998), 26, 61-62. This being said, however, a growing number of Army men and women are becoming disillusioned with the positions given to women in the organization. Aware of women's advances in other churches and the broader society, they contend that the Salvation Army's principle of equality has been less than commendable in practice. While praising female opportunities to preach in the Army, they point to women's relative absence from leadership and their relegation to numerous stereotypical roles. Criticism of this nature has been confined largely to internal publications, especially the Salvation Army's journal *The Officer*. See, for example, "A Woman's Place," *The Officer* 35, 7 (July 1984): 291; "Changing Roles," *The Officer* 35, 7 (July 1984): 295-96; Arthur Thompson, "The Ministry of Women," *The Officer* 35, 10 (October 1984): 459-61; Georgina Pinches, "The Place of Women," *The Officer* 36, 1 (January 1985): 18-20; Gladys R. Ford, "Changing Roles," *The Officer* 36, 2 (February 1985): 81-82; Hilda Cox, "Married Women's Officer-Role within The Salvation Army," *The Officer* 41, 9 (September 1990): 408-12, 415; Margaret Hay, "Married Women-Officers," *The Officer* 42, 2 (February 1991): 70-71; M[iriam] F[rederiksen], "Where Are the Women?" *The Officer* 42, 9 (September 1991):

385-86; John Coutts, "Neither Male nor Female ..." *The Salvationist* 386 (August 7, 1993): 5; and Donna Ames, "Changing Women's Roles: The Challenges of Implementing Equality," *The Officer* 47, 11 (November 1996): 511-14.

4   This commission did not receive extensive coverage within the organization in the early to mid-1990s, but it was referred to occasionally in *The Officer*. See, for example, "A Personal Insight into the High Council: The General Talks to *The Officer*," *The Officer* 44, 3 (March 1993): 105-106; and Ames, "Changing Women's Roles," 511-14. I tried to obtain the minutes from this commission, but my request was turned down by the General's office. For more on this body, and the recommendations it made, see Henry Gariepy, *Mobilized for God: The History of The Salvation Army Volume Eight 1977-1994* (Atlanta, GA: The Salvation Army USA Southern Territory, 2000), 317-19.

5   Gariepy, *Mobilized for God*, 318.

6   Minute 1A/20, issued on July 7, 1995 by the Salvation Army International Headquarters, London, England.

7   Minute 1A/15, issued on May 1, 1995 by the Salvation Army International Headquarters, London, England.

8   See *The Salvation Army Year Book 2001* (London: International Headquarters of The Salvation Army, 2000). I am grateful to the various International Secretaries at the Salvation Army's International Headquarters in London for verifying the gender of certain individuals in this yearbook.

9   John Coutts, *The Salvationists* (Oxford: Mowbrays, 1977), 30.

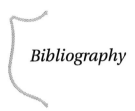

Bibliography

✤ **Primary Sources**

UNPUBLISHED MATERIAL

Some of the sources listed below are marked with an asterisk to indicate that they were consulted, but failed to yield anything related to the subject of gender and equality. For many of the men and women mentioned in the preceding chapters, there are no surviving files. Unfortunately, the Salvation Army lost a good deal of its records when its International Headquarters was bombed during the Second World War.

Booth Papers, British Library, London
British Corps Indexes, The Salvation Army International Heritage Centre, London
Catherine Booth Papers, The Salvation Army International Heritage Centre, London
Christian Mission Minutes, The Salvation Army George Scott Railton Heritage Centre, Toronto
Correspondence between William and Bramwell Booth, 1893-1912, The Salvation Army International Heritage Centre, London*
Personality files on Margaret Allen, Ballington (Maud Ballington) Booth, Bramwell Booth, Eva Booth, Florence Booth, William Booth, Lucy Booth-Hellberg, Frederick (Emma/Minnie) Booth-Tucker, Minnie Carpenter, Clara Case, Mildred Duff, Sidney (Marie) Gauntlett, Matilda Hatcher, James Hay, Edward (Catherine) Higgins, Henry (Kate) Hodder, Theodore (Jane) Kitching, John (Harriet) Lawley, Alex M. Nicol, George Scott (Marianne) Railton, Caroline Reynolds, Ruth Tracy, and Isaac Unsworth. These files are housed at The Salvation Army International Heritage Centre,

London. Information on the women listed in parentheses can be found in the files on their husbands.*

The Salvation Army Foundation Deed (1878) and Supplemental Deed of Constitution (1904), The Salvation Army George Scott Railton Heritage Centre, Toronto

BOOKS AND PAMPHLETS

A School of the Prophets: A Sketch of Training Home Life. London: The Salvation Army Book Department, 1901.

Allen, Margaret. *Kingdom-Makers in Shelter, Street, and Slum*. London: The Salvation Army Book Department, 1902.

All about The Salvation Army. London: S.W. Partridge and Co., 1882.

All about The Salvation Army. London: International Headquarters of The Salvation Army, 1888.

Aspects of Social Work in The Salvation Army: Papers Read at the International Social Council, London, Conducted by the Founder, 1911. London: The Salvation Army Book Department, 1917.

Barnes, Cyril J. *The Rising Sun: The Story of Matilda Hatcher*. London: Salvationist Publishing and Supplies, 1955.

Begbie, Harold. *The Life of General William Booth: The Founder of The Salvation Army*. 2 vols. New York: Macmillan, 1920.

Booth, Bramwell. *On the Banks of the River; Being a Brief History of the Last Days of Mrs. General Booth*. London: International Headquarters of The Salvation Army, 1900.

———. *Our Master. Thoughts for Salvationists about Their Lord*. 1908; reprint, London: Salvationist Publishing and Supplies, n.d.

———. *Servants of All: A Brief Review of the Call, Character, and Labours of Officers of The Salvation Army*. 4th ed. London: The Salvation Army Book Department, 1914.

———. *Orders and Regulations for Officers of the Men's Social Work of The Salvation Army*. London: The Salvation Army Book Department, 1915.

———. *Orders and Regulations for Territorial Commanders and Chief Secretaries of the Salvation Army*. London: International Headquarters of The Salvation Army, 1920.

———. *Echoes and Memories*. 1925; reprint, London: Hodder and Stoughton, 1977.

———. *These Fifty Years*. London: Cassell, 1929.

Booth, Catherine. *Female Teaching: Or, the Rev. A.A. Rees versus Mrs. Palmer, Being a Reply to a Pamphlet by the Above Gentleman on the Sunderland Revival*. 2nd ed. London: G.J. Stevenson, 1861.

———. *Female Ministry: Or, Woman's Right to Preach the Gospel.* 3rd ed. 1870; reprint, New York: The Salvation Army, 1975.

———. *Papers on Practical Religion.* 1879; reprint, London: International Headquarters of The Salvation Army, 1884.

———. *Aggressive Christianity.* 1880; reprint, Toronto, ON: William Briggs, 1883.

———. *Papers on Godliness.* 1881; reprint, London: International Headquarters of The Salvation Army, 1890.

———. *Life and Death.* 1883; reprint, Atlanta, GA: The Salvation Army, 1986.

———. *The Salvation Army in Relation to the Church and State, and Other Addresses.* London: S.W. Partridge and Co., 1883.

———. *The Holy Ghost, An Address.* Toronto, ON: The Salvation Army, [1885?].

———. *Popular Christianity.* 1887; reprint, London: The Salvation Army Book Department, n.d.

———. *The Highway of Our God: Selections from the Army Mother's Writings.* London: Salvationist Publishing and Supplies, 1954.

Booth, Evangeline. *Woman.* New York: Fleming H. Revell, 1930.

Booth, Florence. *Mothers and the Empire, and Other Addresses.* London: The Salvation Army Book Department, 1914.

———. *Powers of Salvation Army Officers.* London: Salvationist Publishing and Supplies, 1923.

———. *Friendship with Jesus.* London: Salvationist Publishing and Supplies, 1924.

———. *Likeness to God.* London: Salvationist Publishing and Supplies, 1925.

———. *Wanted—An Elite.* London: Salvationist Publishing and Supplies, 1928.

Booth, Maud Ballington. *Beneath Two Flags: A Study in Mercy and Help Methods.* 4th ed. Cincinnati: Cranston and Curts, 1894.

———. *A Rector's Daughter in Victorian England: Memories of Childhood and Girlhood.* Metairie, LA: Volunteers of America, 1994.

Booth, William. *Orders and Regulations for The Salvation Army.* London: The Salvation Army Headquarters, 1878.

———. *The Doctrines and Discipline of The Salvation Army.* London: The Salvation Army Headquarters, 1881.

———. *Orders and Regulations for Field Officers of The Salvation Army.* London: International Headquarters of The Salvation Army, 1886.

———. *In Darkest England and the Way Out.* 1890; reprint, Atlanta, GA: The Salvation Army, 1984.

———. *Orders and Regulations for Soldiers of The Salvation Army.* 1890; reprint, London: International Headquarters of The Salvation Army, 1927.

———. *Orders and Regulations for Field Officers of The Salvation Army.* London: The Salvation Army Headquarters, 1891.

————. *The Doctrines of The Salvation Army, Prepared for the Training Homes.* Toronto, ON: The Salvation Army, 1892.

————. *Orders and Regulations for Staff Officers of The Salvation Army in the United Kingdom.* London: International Headquarters of The Salvation Army, 1895.

————. *Orders and Regulations for the Social Officers of The Salvation Army.* London: International Headquarters of The Salvation Army, 1898.

————. *Orders and Regulations for Territorial Commissioners and Chief Secretaries of The Salvation Army.* London: International Headquarters of The Salvation Army, 1899.

————. *Orders and Regulations for Field Officers of The Salvation Army.* London: Headquarters of The Salvation Army, 1901.

————. *Religion for Every Day.* London: The Salvation Army Book Department, 1902.

————. *Orders and Regulations for Staff Officers of The Salvation Army.* London: International Headquarters of The Salvation Army, 1904.

————. *Orders and Regulations for Field Officers of The Salvation Army.* London: The Salvation Army Publishing Department, 1908.

————. *The Founder's Messages to Soldiers during Years 1907-8.* London: The Salvation Army Book Department, 1921.

————. *A Letter from the General to the Officers of The Salvation Army throughout the World on the Occasion of His Eightieth Birthday.* London: The Salvation Army, 1909.

Booth-Tucker, Emma. *The Cross Our Comfort: Being Selections from the Writings of Consul Emma Booth-Tucker.* London: The Salvation Army Book Department, 1907.

————. *Heart Messages.* London: Salvationist Publishing and Supplies, 1926.

Booth-Tucker, Frederick. *The Life of Catherine Booth: The Mother of The Salvation Army.* 2 vols. London: International Headquarters of The Salvation Army, 1892.

————. *The Consul: A Sketch of Emma Booth-Tucker.* New York: The Salvation Army Publishing Department, 1903.

Bourne, F.W. *The Bible Christians: Their Origin and History* (1815-1900). London: Bible Christian Book Room, 1905.

Bourne, Hugh. *History of The Primitive Methodists. Giving an Account of Their Rise and Progress Up to the Year 1823.* Bemersley Near Tunstall, UK: Primitive Methodist Connexion, 1835.

Bramwell-Booth, Catherine. *Bramwell Booth.* London: Rich and Cowan, 1933.

————. *Catherine Booth: The Story of Her Loves.* London: Hodder and Stoughton, 1970.

Carpenter, Minnie L. *Miriam Booth: A Sketch.* London: Salvationist Publishing and Supplies, 1920.

––––––. *The Angel Adjutant of "Broken Earthenware": Life Sketch of Staff-Captain Kate Lee.* 1921; reprint, London: Salvationist Publishing and Supplies, 1928.

––––––. *Commissioner John Lawley.* London: Salvationist Publishing and Supplies, 1924.

––––––. *Some Notable Officers of The Salvation Army.* 1925; reprint, London: Salvationist Publishing and Supplies, 1927.

––––––. *Commissioner Henry Howard.* London: Salvationist Publishing and Supplies, 1926.

––––––. *Three Great Hearts.* London: Salvationist Publishing and Supplies, 1928.

––––––. *Women of the Flag.* London: Salvationist Publishing and Supplies, 1945.

Clarke, Adam. *The Holy Bible, Containing the Old and New Testament: Including the Marginal Readings and Parallel Texts, with a Commentary and Critical Notes.* Vol. 6. 1800; reprint, London: Ward, Lock and Co., n.d.

Coutts, Frederick. *Portrait of a Salvationist.* London: Salvationist Publishing and Supplies, 1955.

Douglas, Eileen, and Mildred Duff. *Commissioner Railton.* London: Salvationist Publishing and Supplies, 1920.

Douglas, Eileen. *Elizabeth Swift Brengle.* 1922; reprint, Atlanta, GA: The Salvation Army Supplies, 1990.

Duff, Mildred. *Catherine Booth: A Sketch.* 1901; reprint, London: The Salvation Army Book Department, 1914.

––––––. *Three Coronations.* London: The Salvation Army Book Department, 1903.

Ervine, St. John. *God's Soldier: General William Booth.* 2 vols. 1934; reprint, New York: Macmillan, 1935.

Finney, Charles. *Lectures on Revivals of Religion.* 1835; reprint, Cambridge, MA: Belknap Press, 1960.

Gilliard, Alfred J. *Sussex Yeoman: The Story of Charles Rich.* London: Salvationist Publishing and Supplies, 1956.

Haggard, H. Rider. *Regeneration: Being an Account of the Social Work of The Salvation Army in Great Britain.* London: Longmans, Green and Co., 1910.

Hamilton, Merle. *Redhead on Fire.* London: Salvationist Publishing and Supplies, 1955.

Handbook of Salvation Army Doctrine. London: International Headquarters of The Salvation Army, 1923.

Hay, James. *The Fiery Cross: An Appeal to Salvationists and Others*. Auckland, NZ: Whitcombe and Tombs, 1929.

Hope, Noel. *Mildred Duff: A Surrendered Life*. London: Salvationist Publishing and Supplies, 1933.

Howard, T. Henry. *Standards of Life and Service*. London: The Salvation Army Book Department, 1909.

MacKenzie, F.A. *Waste Humanity: Being a Review of Part of the Social Operations of The Salvation Army in Great Britain*. London: International Headquarters of The Salvation Army, [1909].

———. *The Clash of the Cymbals: The Secret Revolt in the Salvation Army*. New York: Brentano's, 1929.

———. *Booth-Tucker: Sadhu and Saint*. London: Hodder and Stoughton, 1930.

Manson, John. *The Salvation Army and the Public: A Religious, Social, and Financial Study*. London: George Routledge and Sons, 1908.

Mearns, Andrew. *The Bitter Cry of Outcast London*. Edited with an Introduction by Anthony S. Wohl. 1883; reprint, Leicester, UK: Leicester University Press, 1970.

Mill, John Stuart. *The Subjection of Women*. 1869; reprint, Mineola, NY: Dover Publications, 1997.

More, Hannah. *The Works of Hannah More*. Vol. 2. New York: Harper and Brothers, 1835.

Nicol, Alex M. *General Booth and The Salvation Army*. London: Herbert and Daniel, 1910.

Orders and Regulations for Corps Officers of The Salvation Army. London: International Headquarters of The Salvation Army, 1925.

Orders and Regulations for Corps Officers of The Salvation Army. London: International Headquarters of The Salvation Army, 1988.

Orders and Regulations for Field Officers of The Salvation Army. London: The Salvation Army Book Department, 1917.

Orders and Regulations for Officers of The Salvation Army. London: International Headquarters of The Salvation Army, 1925.

Orders and Regulations for Officers of The Salvation Army. London: International Headquarters of The Salvation Army, 1936.

Orders and Regulations for Officers of The Salvation Army. London: International Headquarters of The Salvation Army, 1946.

Orders and Regulations for the Home League. London: The Salvation Army Book Department, 1916.

Orders and Regulations for the Home League. London: Salvationist Publishing and Supplies, 1925.

Orders and Regulations for the Home League. London: International Headquarters of The Salvation Army, 1986.

Orders and Regulations for the Rescue Work. London: The Salvation Army, 1892.

Outlines of Salvation Army History. 1927; reprint, London: Salvationist Publishing and Supplies, 1928.

Palmer, Phoebe. *Faith and Its Effects; Or, Fragments from My Portfolio.* 1848; reprint, Toronto, ON: G.R. Sanderson, 1856.

———. *Promise of the Father; or, a Neglected Speciality of the Last Days.* Boston, MA: Henry V. Degen, 1859.

———. *Four Years in the Old World.* Toronto, ON: Samuel Rose, 1866.

Pope Booth: The Salvation Army A.D. 1950. London: W. Lucas, [1890].

Railton, George Scott. *Twenty-One Years' Salvation Army.* 1886; reprint, London: International Headquarters of The Salvation Army, 1891.

———. *Heathen England: Being a Description of the Utterly Godless Condition of the Vast Majority of the English Nation, and of the Establishment, Growth, System, and Success of an Army for its Salvation, Consisting of Working People under the Generalship of William Booth.* 5th ed. London: International Headquarters of The Salvation Army, 1889.

———. *Commissioner Dowdle: The Saved Railway Guard.* London: The Salvation Army Book Department, 1901.

———. *The Authoritative Life of General William Booth: Founder of The Salvation Army.* London: Hodder and Stoughton, 1912.

———. *Forward against Misery: Being an Illustrated Review of Part of the Social Operations of The Salvation Army.* London: International Headquarters of The Salvation Army, 1913.

Redwood, Hugh. *God in the Slums.* 1930; reprint, London: Hodder and Stoughton, 1964.

Short, A. Rendle, and S. Carvosso Gauntlett. *Clara Case—Nurani: Lover of India.* London: Salvationist Publishing and Supplies, 1946.

Smiles, Samuel. *Self-Help.* 1859; reprint, London: John Murray, 1958.

Social Problems in Solution: Papers Read at the International Social Council 1921. London: International Headquarters of The Salvation Army, 1923.

Stanton, Elizabeth Cady. *The Woman's Bible.* 1898; reprint, Amherst, NY: Prometheus Books, 1999.

Stead, William T. *General Booth: A Biographical Sketch.* 1891; reprint, Oakville, ON: Triumph Press, n.d.

———. *Mrs. Booth of the Salvation Army.* 1900; reprint, Oakville, ON: Triumph Press, 1979.

Sumner, Abner. *The New Papacy: Behind the Scenes in The Salvation Army.* Toronto, ON: Albert Britnell, 1889.

The Advance of The Salvation Army: 1880. London: The Salvation Army Headquarters, 1880.

The Advance of The Salvation Army: 1886. London: International Headquarters of The Salvation Army, 1886.

The Congress of Nations 1914: Souvenir and Guide. London: International Headquarters of The Salvation Army, 1914.

The Present Position of The Salvation Army. London: International Headquarters of The Salvation Army, 1888.

The Salvation Army: Its Principles and Government. London: The Salvation Army, 1920.

The Salvation War 1884. Under the Generalship of William Booth. London: The Salvation Army Book Depot, 1884.

The Training of Salvation Army Officers: Glimpses of the Work at the International Training Garrison, London. London: The Salvation Army, 1927.

The Why and Wherefore of The Salvation Army Regulations. London: The Salvation Army, 1904.

The Why and Wherefore of Salvation Army Orders and Regulations. London: Salvationist Publishing and Supplies, 1924.

The Works of John Wesley. Vol. 12. Grand Rapids, MI: Zondervan, 1958.

Topley, Edith. *No Coward Soul.* London: Salvationist Publishing and Supplies, 1948.

Tracy, Ruth. *Marianne Pawson: "The Zulu Queen."* London: Salvationist Publishing and Supplies, 1944.

Unsworth, Madge. *Maiden Tribute: A Study in Voluntary Social Service.* London: Salvationist Publishing and Supplies, 1949.

Venn, Henry. *The Complete Duty of Man: Or, A System of Doctrinal and Practical Christianity.* 1763; reprint, London: The Religious Tract Society, 1799.

Views and Interviews: Records of Some Phases of Salvation Army Social Work, 1920-21. London: International Headquarters of The Salvation Army, 1921.

Waldron, John D., ed. *G.S.R.: Selections from Published and Unpublished Writings of George Scott Railton.* Oakville, ON: Triumph Press, 1981.

———. ed. *Women in the Salvation Army.* Oakville, ON: Triumph Press, 1983.

———. *The Quakers and the Salvationists.* Atlanta, GA: The Salvation Army Supplies, 1990.

Walford, John. *Memoirs of the Life and Labours of the Late Venerable Hugh Bourne.* 2 vols. 1856; reprint, Totton, UK: Berith Publications, 1999.

Wallis, Humphrey. *The Happy Warrior: The Life-Story of Commissioner Elijah Cadman.* London: Salvationist Publishing and Supplies, 1928.

Wiggins, Arch R. *T.H.K.: Theodore Hopkins Kitching, A Biography.* London: Salvationist Publishing and Supplies, 1956.

Wilberforce, William. *A Practical View of the Prevailing Religious System of Professed Christians, in the Higher and Middle Classes in This Country, Contrasted with Real Christianity.* London: T. Cadell and W. Davies, 1797.

Wilson, Andrew. *The Salvation Army: Its Government, Principles, and Practices.* Toronto, ON: James Bain and Son, 1884.

Wise, Daniel, ed. *Methodism in Earnest: Being the History of a Great Revival in Great Britain, in Which Twenty Thousand Souls Were Justified, and Ten Thousand Sanctified in about Six Years, through the Instrumentality of Rev. James Caughey.* Boston, MA: Charles H. Peirce, 1850.

PERIODICALS

All the World, 1884-
The Christian Mission Magazine, 1870-1878
The Contemporary Review
The Deliverer, 1889-
The East London Evangelist, 1868-1869
The Methodist New Connexion Magazine
The Officer, 1893- (Called *The Field Officer* between January 1900 and June 1913)
The Revival (Name changed to *The Christian* in 1870)
The Salvation Army Year Book, 1906-
The Salvationist, 1879
The Staff Review, 1922-1931
The War Cry, 1879-
The Wesleyan Methodist Magazine

ARTICLES

B[arker], J[ames]. "Should Married Women with Families Go Out to Work?" *The Social Gazette* 344 (January 27, 1900): 1, 3.

Barker, William. "The Women-Preachers of Early Methodism." *The Primitive Methodist Quarterly Review* 20 (April 1898): 268-83.

Booth, Bramwell. "The Salvation Army." In *Modern Evangelistic Movements,* edited by Two University Men, 21-35. London: Thomson and Cowan, 1924.

Booth, Florence. "Chapters from My Life Story." *The Sunday Circle* (January 21, 1933): 50-51.

Booth, Maud Ballington. "Salvation Army Work in the Slums." *Scribner's Magazine* 17 (January 1895): 102-14.

Booth, William. "Work in Which I Am Interested." *The Quiver* (September 1897): 963-71.

Briggs, Charles A. "The Salvation Army." *The North American Review* 159 (December 1894): 697-710.

Brown, Antoinette L. "Exegesis of 1 Corinthians, xiv., 34, 35; and 1 Timothy, ii., 11, 12." *The Oberlin Quarterly Review* (January 1849): 358-73.

Chichester, C. Raleigh. "The Salvation Army." *The Month* 44, 214 (April 1882): 467-83.

Esler, E. Rentoul. "The Salvation Army as a Social Influence." *Good Words* 45 (1904): 393-98.

Fraser, Donald. "The Salvation Army." *The Presbyterian Review* 7 (April 1886): 257-69.

Garnett, Mrs. Charles. "With The Salvation Army." *Good Words* (1883): 246-51.

———. "A Visit to the Training Home of The Salvation Army." *Sunday Magazine* (1884): 638-44.

"Irregular Religious Agencies." *The Nonconformist* (April 10, 1867): 289-90.

Katscher, Leopold. "Some Aspects of The Salvation Army." *The National Review* 5 (1885): 71-93.

Lewis. M.A. "The Salvation Army." *Macmillan's Magazine* 46 (September 1882): 403-16.

Manson, John. "The Salvation Army: A Review." *The Monthly Review* 17 (November 1904): 56-81.

Marshall, A.F. "The Salvation Army." *The Catholic World* 51 (September 1890): 738-46.

Murray, Andrew. "The Salvation Army." *The Catholic Presbyterian* 9, 50 (February 1883): 81-91.

"On the Rise of Female Preachers in the Connexion which Originated in Cornwall," *The Primitive Methodist Magazine* (July 1821):161-67.

"On the War-Path." *All the Year Round* (January 3, 1891): 12-17.

Stork, C.A. "The Salvation Army: Its Methods and Lessons." *The Lutheran Quarterly* 12 (October 1882): 548-70.

"The Position of Woman in The Salvation Army." In *Some Aspects of the Woman's Movement*, edited by Zoë Fairfield, 229-31. London: SCM Press, 1915.

"The Salvation Army." *The Church Quarterly Review* 14, 27 (April-July 1882): 107-34.

"The Salvation Army." *The Saturday Review* (October 6, 1883): 431-32.

Thomas, Constance E. "The Home Life of General Booth." *Sunday Magazine* 34 (November 1904-October 1905): 224-31.

White, Arnold. "The Truth about The Salvation Army." *The Fortnightly Review* 58 (July 1892): 111-24.

❖ Secondary Sources

BOOKS AND ARTICLES

Alexander, Sally. *Becoming a Woman and Other Essays in Nineteenth and Twentieth Century Feminist History*. London: Virago Press, 1994.

Anderson, Amanda. *Tainted Souls and Painted Faces: The Rhetoric of Fallenness in Victorian Culture*. Ithaca, NY: Cornell University Press, 1993.

Anderson, Olive. "Women Preachers in Mid-Victorian Britain: Some Reflections on Feminism, Popular Religion and Social Change." *The Historical Journal* 13 (1969): 467-84.

———. "The Growth of Christian Militarism in Mid-Victorian Britain." *The English Historical Review* 86, 338 (January 1971): 64-72.

Another Harvest of the Years: An Anthology of Salvation Army Year Book Articles (1957-1975). London: Salvationist Publishing and Supplies, 1975.

Arnstein, Walter L. *Britain Yesterday and Today: 1830 to the Present*. 7th ed. Toronto, ON: D.C. Heath and Co., 1996.

Bailey, Peter. *Popular Culture and Performance in the Victorian City*. Cambridge: Cambridge University Press, 1998.

Bailey, Victor. "Salvation Army Riots, The 'Skeleton Army' and Legal Authority in the Provincial Town." In *Social Control in Nineteenth-Century Britain*, edited by A.P. Donajgrodzki, 231-42. Totowa, NJ: Rowman and Littlefield, 1977.

Banks, Olive. *Faces of Feminism: A Study of Feminism as a Social Movement*. Oxford: Martin Robertson, 1981.

Barnes, Cyril J. *God's Army*. Berkhamsted, Herts, UK: Lion Publishing, 1978.

Bebbington, David W. *Evangelicalism in Modern Britain: A History from the 1730s to the 1980s*. 1989; reprint, Grand Rapids, MI: Baker Book House, 1992.

———. *Holiness in Nineteenth-Century England*. Carlisle, UK: Paternoster Press, 2000.

Beckson, Karl. *London in the 1890s: A Cultural History*. New York: W.W. Norton and Co., 1992.

Beddoe, Deirdre. *Back to Home and Duty: Women between the Wars, 1918-1939*. London: Pandora Press, 1989.

Bennett, Judith M. "Feminism and History." *Gender and History* 1, 3 (Autumn 1989): 251-72.

Benson, John. *The Working Class in Britain, 1850-1939*. London: Longman, 1989.

Berger, Peter L. *Invitation to Sociology: A Humanistic Perspective*. Garden City, NY: Anchor Books, 1963.

Berger, Peter L., and Thomas Luckmann. *The Social Construction of Reality: A Treatise in the Sociology of Knowledge.* 1966; reprint, Garden City, NY: Doubleday, 1989.

Bourke, Joanna. *Working-Class Cultures in Britain, 1890-1960: Gender, Class and Ethnicity.* London: Routledge, 1994.

Bowle, John. *The English Experience: A Survey of English History from Early to Modern Times.* New York: G.P. Putnam's Sons, 1971.

Bradley, Ian. *The Call to Seriousness: The Evangelical Impact on the Victorians.* New York: Macmillan, 1976.

Brantlinger, Patrick. *Rule of Darkness: British Literature and Imperialism, 1830-1914.* Ithaca, NY: Cornell University Press, 1988.

Brown, Callum. *Religion and Society in Scotland since 1707.* Edinburgh: Edinburgh University Press, 1997.

Brown, Earl Kent. *Women of Mr. Wesley's Methodism.* New York: Edwin Mellen Press, 1983.

Brown, Kenneth D. *A Social History of the Nonconformist Ministry in England and Wales, 1800-1930.* Oxford: Clarendon Press, 1988.

Burrows, William. *Heart of the Family: A History of the Home League in the British Territory.* London: National Headquarters of The Salvation Army, 1989.

Burstyn, Joan N. *Victorian Education and the Ideal of Womanhood.* New Brunswick, NJ: Rutgers University Press, 1984.

Bush, Julia. *Edwardian Ladies and Imperial Power.* London: Leicester University Press, 2000.

Caine, Barbara. *Victorian Feminists.* Oxford: Oxford University Press, 1993.

Carr, Anne E. *Transforming Grace: Christian Tradition and Women's Experience.* San Francisco: HarperCollins, 1988.

Carr, Anne E., and Mary Stewart Van Leeuwen, eds. *Religion, Feminism, and the Family.* Louisville, KY: Westminster John Knox Press, 1996.

Carwardine, Richard. *Transatlantic Revivalism: Popular Evangelicalism in Britain and America, 1790-1865.* Westport, CT: Greenwood Press, 1978.

Chadwick, Owen. *The Victorian Church,* Part II. London: Adam and Charles Black, 1970.

Chilcote, Paul Wesley. *John Wesley and the Women Preachers of Early Methodism.* Metuchen, NJ: Scarecrow Press, 1991.

Church, Leslie. *More about the Early Methodist People.* London: Epworth Press, 1949.

Clark, Anna. *The Struggle for the Breeches: Gender and the Making of the British Working Class.* Berkeley, CA: University of California Press, 1995.

Clark, Elizabeth A. "Women, Gender, and the Study of Christian History." *Church History* 70, 3 (September 2001): 395-426.

Clark, G. Kitson. *The Making of Victorian England.* New York: Atheneum, 1967.

Clarke, Douglas. "Female Ministry in The Salvation Army." *The Expository Times* 95, 8 (May 1984): 232-35.

Cobb, John. *Grace and Responsibility: A Wesleyan Theology for Today.* Nashville, TN: Abingdon Press, 1995.

Collier, Richard. *The General Next to God: The Story of William Booth and The Salvation Army.* 1965; reprint, London: Fontana Collins, 1983.

Cook, Chris. *The Longman Companion to Britain in the Nineteenth Century 1815-1914.* London: Longman, 1999.

Coutts, Frederick. *The History of The Salvation Army: The Better Fight.* Vol. 6. 1973; reprint, New York: The Salvation Army, 1979.

———. *No Discharge in This War: A One Volume History of The Salvation Army.* London: Hodder and Stoughton, 1974.

———. *Bread for My Neighbour: The Social Influence of William Booth.* 1978; reprint, London: Hodder and Stoughton, 1982.

Coutts, John. *The Salvationists.* Oxford: Mowbrays, 1977.

Cox, Jeffrey. *The English Churches in a Secular Society: Lambeth, 1870-1930.* Oxford: Oxford University Press, 1982.

Crompton, Rosemary, and Michael Mann, eds. *Gender and Stratification.* Cambridge, MA: Polity Press, 1986.

Daly, Mary. *The Church and the Second Sex.* 1968; reprint, Boston, MA: Beacon Press, 1985.

———. *Beyond God the Father: Toward a Philosophy of Women's Liberation.* Boston, MA: Beacon Press, 1973.

Davidoff, Leonore. *Worlds Between: Historical Perspectives on Gender and Class.* New York: Routledge, 1995.

Davidoff, Leonore, and Catherine Hall. *Family Fortunes: Men and Women of the English Middle Class, 1780-1850.* Chicago: University of Chicago Press, 1987.

Davies, Olwen. *Florence the Home-Maker.* London: Salvationist Publishing and Supplies, 1962.

Dayton, Donald W. *Discovering an Evangelical Heritage.* 1976; reprint, Peabody, MA: Hendrickson Publishers, 1994.

Dayton, Lucille Sider, and Donald W. Dayton. "Women as Preachers: Evangelical Precedents." *Christianity Today* 19 (May 23, 1975): 4-7.

———. "'Your Daughters Shall Prophesy': Feminism in the Holiness Movement." *Methodist History* 14 (January 1976): 67-92.

Dieter, Melvin E., et al. *Five Views on Sanctification.* Grand Rapids, MI: Zondervan, 1987.

Dyhouse, Carol. *Girls Growing Up in Late Victorian and Edwardian England.* London: Routledge and Kegan Paul, 1981.

————. *Feminism and the Family in England 1880-1939.* Oxford: Basil Blackwell, 1989.

Ehrenreich, Barbara, and Deirdre English. *For Her Own Good: 150 Years of the Experts' Advice to Women.* Garden City, NY: Anchor Press, 1978.

English, John C. "'Dear Sister': John Wesley and the Women of Early Methodism." *Methodist History* 33, 1 (October 1994): 26-33.

Entwistle, Dorothy. "'Hope, Colour and Comradeship': Loyalty and Opportunism in Early Twentieth-Century Church Attendance among the Working Class in North-West England." *The Journal of Religious History* 25, 1 (February 2001): 20-38.

Eriksson, Anne-Louise. *The Meaning of Gender in Theology: Problems and Possibilities.* Uppsala, Sweden: Uppsala University Press, 1995.

Fairbank, Jenty. *Booth's Boots: The Beginnings of Salvation Army Social Work.* London: International Headquarters of The Salvation Army, 1983.

Fellows, Lawrence. *A Gentle War: The Story of The Salvation Army.* New York: Macmillan, 1979.

Field, Clive D. "Adam and Eve: Gender in the English Free Church Constituency." *The Journal of Ecclesiastical History* 44, 1 (January 1993): 63-79.

Fisher, Trevor. *Scandal: The Sexual Politics of Late Victorian Britain.* Cornwall, UK: Alan Sutton, 1995.

France, R.T., and Alister E. McGrath, eds. *Evangelical Anglicans: Their Role and Influence in the Church Today.* London: SPCK, 1993.

Gariepy, Henry. *Christianity in Action: The Salvation Army in the U.S.A. Today.* Wheaton, IL: Victor Books, 1990.

————. *Mobilized for God: The History of The Salvation Army Volume Eight 1977-1994.* Atlanta, GA: The Salvation Army USA Southern Territory, 2000.

Geertz, Clifford. "Religion as a Cultural System." In *Anthropological Approaches to the Study of Religion,* ed. Michael Banton, 1-46. London: Tavistock Publications, 1966.

Gill, Sean. *Women and the Church of England: From the Eighteenth Century to the Present.* London: SPCK, 1994.

Gilley, Sheridan, and W.J. Sheils, eds. *A History of Religion in Britain: Practice and Belief from Pre-Roman Times to the Present.* Oxford: Blackwell, 1994.

Goldstein, Valerie Saiving. "The Human Situation: A Feminine View." *The Journal of Religion* 40 (1960): 100-12.

Graham, Elaine L. *Making the Difference: Gender, Personhood and Theology.* Minneapolis, MN: Fortress Press, 1996.

Green, Anna, and Kathleen Troup. *The Houses of History: A Critical Reader in Twentieth-Century History and Theory.* Washington Square, NY: New York University Press, 1999.

Green, Roger J. *War on Two Fronts: The Redemptive Theology of William Booth.* Atlanta, GA: The Salvation Army, 1989.

——. "Settled Views: Catherine Booth and Female Ministry." *Methodist History* 31, 3 (April 1993): 131-47.

——. *Catherine Booth: A Biography of the Cofounder of The Salvation Army.* Grand Rapids, MI: Baker Books, 1996.

Grugel, Lee. *Society and Religion during the Age of Industrialization: Christianity in Victorian England.* Lanham, MD: University Press of America, 1979.

Gunn, Simon. *The Public Culture of the Victorian Middle Class: Ritual and Authority and the English Industrial City, 1840-1914.* Manchester: Manchester University Press, 2000.

Guy, David, et al. *Salvation Story: Salvationist Handbook of Doctrine.* London: International Headquarters of The Salvation Army, 1998.

Hambrick-Stowe, Charles. *Charles G. Finney and the Spirit of American Evangelicalism.* Grand Rapids, MI: Eerdmans, 1996.

Hardesty, Nancy A. *Your Daughters Shall Prophesy: Revivalism and Feminism in the Age of Finney.* Brooklyn, NY: Carlson, 1991.

——. *Women Called to Witness: Evangelical Feminism in the Nineteenth Century.* 2nd ed. Knoxville, TN: University of Tennessee Press, 1999.

Harris, Jose. *Private Lives, Public Spirit: A Social History of Britain, 1870-1914.* Oxford: Oxford University Press, 1993.

Harris, William G. *Storm Pilot: The Story of the Life and Leadership of General Edward J. Higgins.* London: Salvationist Publishing and Supplies, 1981.

Harrison, J.F.C. *Late Victorian Britain 1875-1901.* London: Fontana Press, 1990.

Hassey, Janette. *No Time for Silence: Evangelical Women in Public Ministry around the Turn of the Century.* Grand Rapids, MI: Zondervan, 1986.

Hattersley, Roy. *Blood and Fire: William and Catherine Booth and Their Salvation Army.* New York: Doubleday, 2000.

Hawkesworth, M.E. *Beyond Oppression: Feminist Theory and Political Strategy.* New York: Continuum, 1990.

Heeney, Brian. *The Women's Movement in the Church of England 1850-1930.* Oxford: Clarendon Press, 1988.

Helmstadter, Richard J., and Bernard Lightman, eds. *Victorian Faith in Crisis: Essays on Continuity and Change in Nineteenth-Century Religious Belief.* London: Macmillan, 1990.

Helsinger, Elizabeth K., et al. *The Woman Question: Society and Literature in Britain and America, 1837-1883.* Vol. 2. London: Garland, 1983.

Hempton, David. *Methodism and Politics in British Society 1750-1850.* Stanford, CA: Stanford University Press, 1984.

——. *Religion and Political Culture in Britain and Ireland: From the Glorious Revolution to the Decline of Empire.* Cambridge: Cambridge University Press, 1996.

Higginbotham, Ann R. "Respectable Sinners: Salvation Army Rescue Work with Unmarried Mothers, 1884-1914." In *Religion in the Lives of English*

Women, 1760-1930, edited by Gail Malmgreen, 216-33. Bloomington, IN: Indiana University Press, 1986.

Hilton, Boyd. *The Age of Atonement: The Influence of Evangelicalism on Social and Economic Thought, 1795-1865*. Oxford: Clarendon Press, 1988.

Hogan, Anne, and Andrew Bradstock, eds. *Women of Faith in Victorian Culture: Reassessing the Angel in the House*. London: Macmillan, 1998.

Hopkins, Eric. *The Rise and Decline of the English Working Classes 1918-1990: A Social History*. London: Weidenfeld and Nicolson, 1991.

Horridge, Glenn K. "William Booth's Officers." *Christian History* 9, 2 (1990): 14-17.

———. *The Salvation Army: Origins and Early Days, 1865-1900*. Godalming, Surrey, UK: Ammonite Books, 1993.

Hunt, E.K. *Property and Prophets: The Evolution of Economic Institutions and Ideologies*. 5th ed. New York: Harper and Row, 1986.

Inglis, K.S. *Churches and the Working Classes in Victorian England*. Toronto, ON: University of Toronto Press, 1963.

Isherwood, Lisa and Dorothea McEwan, eds. *An A to Z of Feminist Theology*. Sheffield, UK: Sheffield Academic Press, 1996.

Isherwood, Lisa and Dorothea McEwan. *Introducing Feminist Theology*. 2nd ed. Sheffield, UK: Sheffield Academic Press, 2001.

Jackson, Louise A. "'Singing Birds as Well as Soap Suds': The Salvation Army's Work with Sexually Abused Girls in Edwardian England." *Gender and History* 12, 1 (2000): 107-26.

Johnson, Dale A., ed. *Women in English Religion, 1700-1925*. Lewiston, NY: Edwin Mellen Press, 1983.

Johnson, Elizabeth A. *She Who Is: The Mystery of God in Feminist Theological Discourse*. New York: Crossroad, 1992.

Jordan, Ellen. *The Women's Movement and Women's Employment in Nineteenth-Century Britain*. London: Routledge, 1999.

Juster, Susan. *Disorderly Women: Sexual Politics and Evangelicalism in Revolutionary New England*. Ithaca, NY: Cornell University Press, 1994.

Kelly, Joan Gadol. "The Social Relation of the Sexes: Methodological Implications of Women's History." *SIGNS* 1, 4 (1976): 809-23.

Kent, John. *Holding the Fort: Studies in Victorian Revivalism*. London: Epworth Press, 1978.

Kent, Susan Kingsley. "The Politics of Sexual Difference: World War I and the Demise of British Feminism." *Journal of British Studies* 27, 3 (July 1988): 232-53.

Kew, Clifford W., ed. *Catherine Booth: Her Continuing Relevance*. London: International Headquarters of The Salvation Army, 1990.

King, Ursula, ed. *Religion and Gender*. Oxford: Blackwell, 1995.

LaCugna, Catherine Mowry, ed. *Freeing Theology: The Essentials of Theology in Feminist Perspective*. San Francisco: HarperCollins, 1993.

Larsson, Flora. *My Best Men Are Women*. London: Hodder and Stoughton, 1974.

Lauer, Laura E. "Soul-Saving Partnerships and Pacifist Soldiers: The Ideal of Masculinity in the Salvation Army." In *Masculinity and Spirituality in Victorian Culture*, edited by Andrew Bradstock et al., 194-208. London: Macmillan, 2000.

Lerner, Gerda. "Placing Women in History: Definitions and Challenges." *Feminist Studies* 3, 1 (Fall 1975): 5-14.

———. *The Majority Finds Its Past*. New York: Oxford University Press, 1979.

———. *The Creation of Patriarchy*. New York: Oxford University Press, 1986.

———. *The Creation of Feminist Consciousness: From the Middle Ages to Eighteen-Seventy*. New York: Oxford University Press, 1993.

Levine, Philippa. *Victorian Feminism: 1850-1900*. London: Hutchinson, 1987.

Lewis, Donald M. *Lighten Their Darkness: The Evangelical Mission to Working-Class London, 1828-1860*. Westport, CT: Greenwood Press, 1986.

Lewis, Jane. *Women in England, 1870-1950: Sexual Divisions and Social Change*. Bloomington, IN: Indiana University Press, 1984.

Lips, Hilary M. *Sex and Gender: An Introduction*. 3rd ed. Mountain View, CA: Mayfield Publishing Company, 1997.

Livingston, James C. *Modern Christian Thought: From the Enlightenment to Vatican II*. New York: Macmillan, 1971.

Lunn, Brian. *Salvation Dynasty*. London: William Hodge and Co., 1936.

Marks, Lynne Sorrel. "The 'Hallelujah Lasses': Working-Class Women in the Salvation Army in English Canada, 1882-1892." In *Gender Conflicts: New Essays in Women's History*, edited by Franca Iacovetta and Mariana Valverde, 67-117. Toronto, ON: University of Toronto Press, 1992.

Marsden, George. *Understanding Fundamentalism and Evangelicalism*. Grand Rapids, MI: Eerdmans, 1991.

McCaughey, Betty, ed. *William and Catherine, with Love*. Oakville, ON: Triumph Press, 1989.

McFadden, Margaret. "The Ironies of Pentecost: Phoebe Palmer, World Evangelism, and Female Networks." *Methodist History* 31, 2 (January 1993): 63-75.

McGuire, Meredith B. *Religion: The Social Context*. 4th ed. Belmont, CA: Wadsworth, 1997.

McKinley, Edward H. *Marching to Glory: The History of The Salvation Army in the United States, 1880-1992*. 2nd ed. Grand Rapids, MI: Eerdmans, 1995.

McLeod, Hugh. *Religion and the Working Class in Nineteenth-Century Britain*. London: Macmillan, 1984.

————. *Religion and Irreligion in Victorian England: How Secular Was the Working Class?* Bangor, UK: Headstart History, 1993.

————. *Religion and Society in England, 1850-1914.* London: Macmillan, 1996.

————. *Religion and the People of Western Europe 1789-1989.* Oxford: Oxford University Press, 1997.

Metcalf, Joan. *God Used a Woman: Catherine Booth.* London: Challenge Books, 1967.

Mews, Stuart. "The General and the Bishops: Alternative Responses to Dechristianisation." In *Later Victorian Britain, 1867-1900,* edited by T.R. Gourvish and Alan O'Day, 209-28. New York: St. Martin's Press, 1988.

Mitchell, Sally. *Daily Life in Victorian England.* Westport, CT: Greenwood Press, 1996.

Moyles, R.G. *A Bibliography of Salvation Army Literature in English 1865-1987.* Lewiston, NY: Edwin Mellen Press, 1988.

————. *The Salvation Army and the Public: Historical and Descriptive Essays.* Edmonton, AB: AGM Publications, 2000.

Mueller, J.J. *What Are They Saying about Theological Method?* New York: Paulist Press, 1984.

Murdoch, Norman H. "Female Ministry in the Thought and Work of Catherine Booth." *Church History* 53, 3 (September 1984): 348-62.

————. "Evangelical Sources of Salvation Army Doctrine." *The Evangelical Quarterly* 59 (July 1987): 235-44.

————. "The Army Mother." *Christian History* 9, 2 (1990): 5-9.

————. *Origins of the Salvation Army.* Knoxville, TN: University of Tennessee Press, 1994.

Nelson, Claudia, and Ann Sumner Holmes, eds. *Maternal Instincts: Visions of Motherhood and Sexuality in Britain, 1875-1925.* London: Macmillan, 1997.

Noll, Mark A., David W. Bebbington, and George A. Rawlyk, eds. *Evangelicalism: Comparative Studies of Popular Protestantism in North America, the British Isles, and Beyond, 1700-1990.* Oxford: Oxford University Press, 1994.

Ortner, Sherry B. "Is Female to Male as Nature Is to Culture?" In *Women, Culture and Society,* edited by Michelle Z. Rosaldo and Louise Lamphere, 67-87. Stanford, CA: Stanford University Press, 1974.

Parkin, Christine. "Pioneer in Female Ministry." *Christian History* 9, 2 (1990): 10-13.

Parr, Joy. "Gender History and Historical Practice." *The Canadian Historical Review* 76, 3 (September 1995): 354-76.

Parsons, Gerald, ed. *Religion in Victorian Britain.* Vols. 1-2. Manchester: Manchester University Press, 1988.

Paz, D.G., ed. *Nineteenth-Century English Religious Traditions: Retrospect and Prospect.* Westport, CT: Greenwood Press, 1995.

Perkin, Joan. *Victorian Women.* London: John Murray, 1993.

Prochaska, F.K. *Women and Philanthropy in Nineteenth-Century England.* Oxford: Clarendon Press, 1980.

Pyke, Richard. *The Early Bible Christians.* London: Epworth Press, 1941.

Rack, Henry D. *Reasonable Enthusiast: John Wesley and the Rise of Methodism.* Philadelphia: Trinity Press International, 1989.

Randle, John. *Understanding Britain: A History of the British People and Their Culture.* Oxford: Basil Blackwell, 1981.

Raser, Harold E. *Phoebe Palmer: Her Life and Thought.* Lewiston, NY: Edwin Mellen Press, 1987.

Rawlyk, George A., and Mark A. Noll, eds. *Amazing Grace: Evangelicalism in Australia, Britain, Canada, and the United States.* Grand Rapids, MI: Baker Books, 1993.

Rendall, Jane. *The Origins of Modern Feminism: Women in Britain, France and the United States, 1780-1860.* London: Macmillan, 1985.

Rhemick, John R. *A New People of God: A Study in Salvationism.* Des Plaines, IL: The Salvation Army, 1993.

Rightmire, R. David. *Sacraments and the Salvation Army: Pneumatological Foundations.* Metuchen, NJ: Scarecrow Press, 1990.

Roberts, Elizabeth. *A Woman's Place: An Oral History of Working-Class Women 1890-1940.* Oxford: Blackwell, 1984.

———. *Women's Work 1840-1940.* London: Macmillan, 1988.

Rosman, Doreen M. *Evangelicals and Culture.* London: Croom Helm, 1984.

Ross, Ellen. *Love and Toil: Motherhood in Outcast London, 1870-1918.* New York: Oxford University Press, 1993.

Rubin, Gayle. "The Traffic in Women: Notes on the 'Political Economy' of Sex." In *Toward an Anthropology of Women*, edited by Rayna Reiter, 157-210. New York: Monthly Review Press, 1975.

Rubinstein, W.D. *Britain's Century: A Political and Social History 1815-1905.* London: Arnold, 1998.

Ruether, Rosemary Radford. *Sexism and God-Talk: Toward a Feminist Theology.* Boston, MA: Beacon Press, 1983.

Ruether, Rosemary Radford, and Rosemary S. Keller, eds. *Women and Religion in America. Volume 3: 1900-1968.* San Francisco: Harper and Row, 1986.

Sandall, Robert. *The History of The Salvation Army.* Vol. 1. 1947; reprint, New York: The Salvation Army, 1979.

———. *The History of The Salvation Army.* Vol. 2. 1950; reprint, New York: The Salvation Army, 1979.

————. *The History of The Salvation Army.* Vol. 3. 1955; reprint, New York: The Salvation Army, 1979.

Scanzoni, Letha, and Nancy Hardesty. *All We're Meant to Be: A Biblical Approach to Women's Liberation.* 1974; reprint, Waco, TX: Word Books, 1976.

Schlossberg, Herbert. *The Silent Revolution and the Making of Victorian England.* Columbus, OH: Ohio State University Press, 2000.

Schwarzkopf, Jutta. *Women in the Chartist Movement.* London: Macmillan, 1991.

Scott, Joan W. "Gender: A Useful Category of Historical Analysis." *American Historical Review* 91, 5 (December 1986): 1053-75.

Sheils, W.J., and Diana Wood, eds. *Women in the Church.* Oxford: Basil Blackwell, 1990.

Shiman, Lilian Lewis. *Women and Leadership in Nineteenth-Century England.* New York: St. Martin's Press, 1992.

Snell, K.D.M., and Paul S. Ell. *Rival Jerusalems: The Geography of Victorian Religion.* Cambridge: Cambridge University Press, 2000.

Sohn, Anne-Marie. "Between the Wars in France and England." In *A History of Women in the West. Volume Five: Toward a Cultural Identity in the Twentieth Century,* edited by François Thébaud, 92-119. Cambridge, MA: The Belknap Press of Harvard University Press, 1994.

Swanson, Robert N., ed. *Gender and Christian Religion.* Woodbridge, Suffolk, UK: Boydell Press, 1998.

Taiz, Lillian. *Hallelujah Lads and Lasses: Remaking the Salvation Army in America, 1880-1930.* Chapel Hill, NC: University of North Carolina Press, 2001.

Taylor, Barbara. *Eve and the New Jerusalem: Socialism and Feminism in the Nineteenth Century.* London: Virago, 1983.

Thomas, Terence, ed. *The British: Their Religious Beliefs and Practices 1800-1986.* London: Routledge, 1988.

Thompson, F.M.L. *The Rise of Respectable Society: A Social History of Victorian Britain, 1830-1900.* London: Fontana Press, 1988.

Troutt, Margaret. *The General Was a Lady: The Story of Evangeline Booth.* Nashville, TN: A.J. Holman Co., 1980.

Unger, Rhoda, and Mary Crawford. *Women and Gender: A Feminist Psychology.* New York: McGraw-Hill, 1992.

Valenze, Deborah M. *Prophetic Sons and Daughters: Female Preaching and Popular Religion in Industrial England.* Princeton, NJ: Princeton University Press, 1985.

Vance, Norman. *The Sinews of the Spirit: The Ideal of Christian Manliness in Victorian Literature and Religious Thought.* Cambridge: Cambridge University Press, 1985.

Vicinus, Martha, ed. *Suffer and Be Still: Women in the Victorian Age*. Bloomington, IN:Indiana University Press, 1972.

———. *A Widening Sphere: Changing Roles of Victorian Women*. Bloomington, IN: Indiana University Press, 1977.

Walker, Pamela J. "Proclaiming Women's Right to Preach." *The Harvard Divinity Bulletin* 23, 3-4 (1994): 20-23, 35.

———. "A Chaste and Fervid Eloquence: Catherine Booth and the Ministry of Women in the Salvation Army." In *Women Preachers and Prophets through Two Millennia of Christianity*, edited by Beverly Mayne Kienzle and Pamela J. Walker, 288-302. Berkeley, CA: University of California Press, 1998.

———. *Pulling the Devil's Kingdom Down: The Salvation Army in Victorian Britain*. Berkeley, CA: University of California Press, 2001.

Walkowitz, Judith R. *Prostitution and Victorian Society: Women, Class and the State*. Cambridge: Cambridge University Press, 1980.

Warne, Randi R. "Gender and the Study of Religion." *Method and Theory in the Study of Religion* 13, 2 (2001): 141-52.

Watson, Bernard. *A Hundred Years' War: The Salvation Army, 1865-1965*. London: Hodder and Stoughton, 1965.

———. *Soldier Saint: George Scott Railton*. 1970; reprint, New York: The Salvation Army, 1977.

Watts, Michael R. *The Dissenters*. Vol. 2. Oxford: Clarendon Press, 1995.

Welter, Barbara. *Dimity Convictions: The American Woman in the Nineteenth Century*. Athens, OH: Ohio University Press, 1976.

Werner, Julia Stewart. *The Primitive Methodist Connexion: Its Background and Early History*. Madison, WI: University of Wisconsin Press, 1984.

White, Charles Edward. *The Beauty of Holiness: Phoebe Palmer as Theologian, Revivalist, Feminist, and Humanitarian*. Grand Rapids, MI: Francis Asbury Press, 1986.

Wickes, Michael J.L. *The Westcountry Preachers: A New History of the Bible Christian Church (1815-1907)*. Bideford, Devon, UK: Jamaica Press, 1987.

Wiggins, Arch. *The History of The Salvation Army*. Vol. 4. 1964; reprint, New York: The Salvation Army, 1979.

———. *The History of The Salvation Army*. Vol. 5. 1968; reprint, New York: The Salvation Army, 1979.

Williams, Harry. *Booth-Tucker: William Booth's First Gentleman*. London: Hodder and Stoughton, 1980.

Williams, Sarah. *Religious Belief and Popular Culture in Southwark, c. 1880-1939*. Oxford: Oxford University Press, 1999.

Winston, Diane. *Red-Hot and Righteous: The Urban Religion of The Salvation Army*. Cambridge, MA: Harvard University Press, 1999.

Wolff, Janet, and John Seed, eds. *The Culture of Capital: Art, Power and the Nineteenth-Century Middle Class.* Manchester: Manchester University Press, 1988.

Wolffe, John. *God and Greater Britain: Religion and National Life in Britain and Ireland, 1843-1945.* London: Routledge, 1994.

———, ed. *Religion in Victorian Britain.* Vol. 5. Manchester: Manchester University Press, 1997.

Young, Pamela Dickey. *Feminist Theology/Christian Theology: In Search of Method.* Minneapolis, MN: Fortress Press, 1990.

UNPUBLISHED MATERIAL

Cuff, Dwight. "The Two Shall Become One: An Examination of the Impact of a One Flesh Theology on The Salvation Army Officer-Wife." Paper presented at the Catherine Booth Bible College [now known as the William and Catherine Booth College] Symposium, Winnipeg, MB, 1989. The Salvation Army George Scott Railton Heritage Centre, Toronto has a copy of this paper.

Eason, Andrew Mark. "Gender and Equality in God's Army: An Examination of Women's Public and Domestic Roles in the Salvation Army, British Origins to 1930." M.A. thesis, University of Windsor, Windsor, ON, 1998.

Lauer, Laura E. "Women in British Nonconformity, circa 1880-1920, with Special Reference to the Society of Friends, Baptist Union and Salvation Army." Ph.D. thesis, University of Oxford, 1998.

Minute 1A/15, issued on May 1, 1995 by the Salvation Army International Headquarters, London

Minute 1A/20, issued on July 7, 1995 by the Salvation Army International Headquarters, London

Sears, David J. "An Overview of the Thought of Catherine Booth." S.T.M. thesis, University of Winnipeg, 1995.

Walker, Pamela J. "Pulling the Devil's Kingdom Down: Gender and Popular Culture in the Salvation Army, 1865-1895." Ph.D. thesis, Rutgers University, 1992.

❖

Index

See also domestic service; evangelicalism; female ministry; motherhood; separate spheres; sexual difference
Salvation Army Year Book, The, 129
Salvation Story, 213n3
Sankey, Ira, 26
Scott, Joan, 4
Sears, David, 189n2
Self-Help (Smiles), 12
self-sacrifice. *See* motherhood; separate spheres; sexual difference; slum work; theology
separate spheres, 4, 14-15, 112; The Salvation Army and, 54-57, 59-61, 69, 71-82, 119-152, 155
Servants of All (Bramwell Booth), 81
settlements (slum), 138. *See also* slum work
sexual difference, 3-4, 17-18; The Salvation Army and, 39-40, 53-55, 58- 61, 69-72, 76-79, 104-105, 119, 136-46, 154-55. *See also* separate spheres
Shaw, Elsie, 132
Short, Jane, 174n33
sin. *See* theology; gender
sisterhoods, 22
Skeleton Armies, 48
slum work, 138-40, 148. *See also* settlements
Smiles, Samuel, 12
Smith, Barbara Leigh, 17
social control: Salvation Army, 48, 56, 88
Social Gazette, The (periodical), 73
stratification. *See* gender
sociology of knowledge, 163n11
Staff Review, The (periodical), 152
Stanton, Elizabeth Cady, 84
statistics: The Salvation Army, 6, 146-51, 157
Stead, William T., 100
suffrage (female), 63, 79, 140. *See also* women's movement
Sumner, Abner, 177n65
Sumner, Mary, 116,
Sunday schools, 22
Swinfen, Nellie, 200n4
T
Tables (statistical), 147, 149-50
Taiz, Lillian, 179n89

temperance, 99, 101, 108
theology, 7-9, 21-22, 48-49, 82-89; doctrine of sin, 8, 85-86, 155; God-language, 7-8, 84-85, 156; holiness doctrine, 8, 56, 86-89, 96-97, 156; male headship, 27-28, 58-61, 85, 89-90, 112-15, 143, 151, 155; within evangelicalism, 21-30
Thomas, Florence, 134
Thomas, Reverend David, 38
Thompson, Arthur, 213n3
Thursfield, G., 70
Tracy, Ruth, 205n58
Trounce, Annie, 212n144
Turner, Emily, 208n98
U
Unitarians, 153
urbanization, 13-14
V
van de Werken, Johanna, 212n147
Venn, Henry, 27
W
wages, 12, 14-15; and female preachers in Methodism, 24, 52, 89; in The Salvation Army, 52, 89, 129, 203-204n40
Walker, Pamela J., 179n89, 194n45
Wallis, Beatrice, 126
Wallis, Humphrey, 175n40
War Cry, The (periodical), 11, 74, 121, 124, 126-28, 132, 134, 148, 151
Ward, Vitty, 142
Watson, Bernard, 64
Wellman, Jane, 201n19
Wesley, John, 16, 65; and female ministry, 22-23; and holiness, 87, 97; influence on Catherine Booth, 96-97
Wesleyans. *See* Methodists; female ministry
Wilberforce, William, 95
Williams, Sarah, 168n35
Winterburn, Phillis, 201n15
Woman's Bible, The (Stanton), 84
women's movement, 17, 63. *See also* suffrage
Wordsworth, William, 18. *See also* romanticism
worldliness, 86, 95
Y
Yuill, Chick, 194n45

19. *Memory and Hope: Strands of Canadian Baptist History*
    Edited by David T. Priestley / 1996 / viii + 211 pp.
20. *The Concept of Equity in Calvin's Ethics**
    Guenther H. Haas / 1997 / xii + 205 pp.
    *Available in the United Kingdom and Europe from Paternoster Press.
21. *The Call of Conscience: French Protestant Responses to the Algerian War, 1954-1962*
    Geoffrey Adams / 1998 / xxii + 270 pp.
22. *Clinical Pastoral Supervision and the Theology of Charles Gerkin*
    Thomas St. James O'Connor / 1998 / x + 152 pp.
23. *Faith and Fiction: A Theological Critique of the Narrative Strategies of*
    Hugh MacLennan and Morley Callaghan
    Barbara Pell / 1998 / v + 141 pp.
24. *God and the Chip: Religion and the Culture of Technology*
    William A. Stahl / 1999 / vi + 186 pp.
25. *The Religious Dreamworld of Apuleius' Metamorphoses: Recovering a Forgotten*
    Hermeneutic
    James Gollnick / 1999 / xiv + 178 pp.
26. *Edward Schillebeeckx and Hans Frei: A Conversation on Method and Christology*
    Marguerite Abdul-Masih / 2001 / vi + 194 pp.
27. *Radical Difference: A Defence of Hendrik Kraemer's Theology of Religions*
    Tim S. Perry / 2001 / x + 170 pp.

Comparative Ethics Series /
Collection d'Éthique Comparée

1. *Muslim Ethics and Modernity: A Comparative Study of the Ethical Thought of*
   Sayyid Ahmad Khan and Mawlana Mawdudi
   Sheila McDonough / 1984 / x + 130 pp. / OUT OF PRINT
2. *Methodist Education in Peru: Social Gospel, Politics, and American Ideological and*
   Economic Penetration, 1888-1930
   Rosa del Carmen Bruno-Jofré / 1988 / xiv + 223 pp.
3. *Prophets, Pastors and Public Choices: Canadian Churches and the Mackenzie Valley*
   Pipeline Debate
   Roger Hutchinson / 1992 / xiv + 142 pp. / OUT OF PRINT
4. *In Good Faith: Canadian Churches Against Apartheid*
   Renate Pratt / 1997 / xii + 366 pp.
5. *Towards an Ethics of Community: Negotiations of Difference in a Pluralist Society*
   James H. Olthuis, editor / 2000 / x + 230 pp.
6. *Doing Ethics in a Pluralistic World: Essays in Honour of Roger C. Hutchinson*
   Phyllis J. Airhart, Marilyn J. Legge and Gary L. Redcliffe, editors / 2002 /
   viii + 264 pp.

Studies in Christianity and Judaism /
Études sur le christianisme et le judaïsme

1. *A Study in Anti-Gnostic Polemics: Irenaeus, Hippolytus, and Epiphanius*
   Gérard Vallée / 1981 / xii + 114 pp. / OUT OF PRINT
2. *Anti-Judaism in Early Christianity Vol. 1, Paul and the Gospels*
   Edited by Peter Richardson with David Granskou / 1986 / x + 232 pp.
   Vol. 2, *Separation and Polemic*
   Edited by Stephen G. Wilson / 1986 / xii + 185 pp.
3. *Society, the Sacred, and Scripture in Ancient Judaism: A Sociology of Knowledge*
   Jack N. Lightstone / 1988 / xiv + 126 pp.
4. *Law in Religious Communities in the Roman Period: The Debate Over* **Torah**
   and **Nomos** *in Post-Biblical Judaism and Early Christianity*
   Peter Richardson and Stephen Westerholm with A. I. Baumgarten, Michael Pettem
   and Cecilia Wassén / 1991 / x + 164 pp.

5. *Dangerous Food: 1 Corinthians 8-10 in Its Context*
   Peter D. Gooch / 1993 / xviii + 178 pp.
6. *The Rhetoric of the Babylonian Talmud, Its Social Meaning and Context*
   Jack N. Lightstone / 1994 / xiv + 317 pp.
7. *Whose Historical Jesus?*
   Edited by William E. Arnal and Michel Desjardins / 1997 / vi + 337 pp.
8. *Religious Rivalries and the Struggle for Success in Caesarea Maritima*
   Edited by Terence L. Donaldson / 2000 / xiv + 402 pp.
9. *Text and Artifact in the Religions of Mediterranean Antiquity*
   Edited by Stephen G. Wilson and Michel Desjardins / 2000 / xvi + 616 pp.
10. *Parables of War: Reading John's Jewish Apocalypse*
    by John W. Marshall / 2001 / viii + 262 pp.
11. *Mishnah and the Social Formation of the Early Rabbinic Guild:*
    A Socio-Rhetorical Approach
    by Jack N. Lightstone / 2002 / xii + 240 pp.
12. *The Social Setting of the Ministry as Reflected in the Writings of Hermas,*
    Clement and Ignatius
    Harry O. Maier / 1991, second impression 2002 / x + 234 pp.

The Study of Religion in Canada /
Sciences Religieuses au Canada

1. *Religious Studies in Alberta: A State-of-the-Art Review*
   Ronald W. Neufeldt / 1983 / xiv + 145 pp.
2. *Les sciences religieuses au Québec depuis 1972*
   Louis Rousseau et Michel Despland / 1988 / 158 p.
3. *Religious Studies in Ontario: A State-of-the-Art Review*
   Harold Remus, William Closson James and Daniel Fraikin / 1992 / xviii + 422 pp.
4. *Religious Studies in Manitoba and Saskatchewan: A State-of-the-Art Review*
   John M. Badertscher, Gordon Harland and Roland E. Miller / 1993 / vi + 166 pp.
5. *The Study of Religion in British Columbia: A State-of-the-Art Review*
   Brian J. Fraser / 1995 / x + 127 pp.
6. *Religious Studies in Atlantic Canada: A State-of-the-Art Review*
   Paul W. R. Bowlby with Tom Faulkner / 2001 / xii + 208 pp.

Studies in Women and Religion /
Études sur les femmes et la religion

1. *Femmes et religions**
   Sous la direction de Denise Veillette / 1995 / xviii + 466 p.
   *Only available from Les Presses de l'Université Laval
2. *The Work of Their Hands: Mennonite Women's Societies in Canada*
   Gloria Neufeld Redekop / 1996 / xvi + 172 pp.
3. *Profiles of Anabaptist Women: Sixteenth-Century Reforming Pioneers*
   Edited by C. Arnold Snyder and Linda A. Huebert Hecht / 1996 / xxii + 438 pp.
4. *Voices and Echoes: Canadian Women's Spirituality*
   Edited by Jo-Anne Elder and Colin O'Connell / 1997 / xxviii + 237 pp.
5. *Obedience, Suspicion and the Gospel of Mark: A Mennonite-Feminist Exploration*
   of Biblical Authority
   Lydia Neufeld Harder / 1998 / xiv + 168 pp.
6. *Clothed in Integrity: Weaving Just Cultural Relations and the Garment Industry*
   Barbara Paleczny / 2000 / xxxiv + 352 pp.
7. *Women in God's Army: Gender and Equality in the Early Salvation Army*
   Andrew Mark Eason / 2003 / xiv + 246 pp.

SR Supplements

Series discontinued

Available from:

Wilfrid Laurier University Press

Waterloo, Ontario, Canada N2L 3C5
Telephone: (519) 884-0710, ext. 6124
Fax: (519) 725-1399
E-mail: press@wlu.ca
World Wide Web: http://www.wlupress.wlu.ca

8555